Ireland and Europe in the Nineteenth Century

Ireland and Europe in the Nineteenth Century

EDITED BY

Leon Litvack and Colin Graham

FOUR COURTS PRESS

Set in 10 on 12.5 point Bembo for
FOUR COURTS PRESS LTD
7 Malpas Street, Dublin 8, Ireland
e-mail: info@four-courts-press.ie
and in North America
FOUR COURTS PRESS
c/o ISBS, 920 N.E. 58th Avenue, Suite 300, Portland, OR 97213.

A catalogue record for this title
is available from the British Library.

ISBN (10-digit) 1–85182–918–0
ISBN (13-digit) 978–1–85182–918–7

Printed in Great Britain
by MPG Books, Bodmin, Cornwall

Contents

List of illustrations

LUCY McDIARMID

Acknowledgments

The editors would like to thank the following for their assistance in bringing this project to completion: Ivan Ewart and Martyn Boyd, Queen's University Belfast; Nicholas Dunlop, Queen's University Belfast; Hugh Magennis, Queen's University Belfast; Gabriele Woolever, Dallas Museum of Art; Holly Frisbee, Philadelphia Museum of Art; Erin Schleigh, Museum of Fine Arts, Boston; Vivien Adams, National Gallery, London.

We also acknowledge the financial assistance provided for this project by the Publications Fund, Queen's University Belfast, and the Society for the Study of Nineteenth-Century Ireland (SSNCI).

Contributors

ASIER ALTUNA GARCIA DE SALAZAR was formerly a post-doctoral research fellow at the Centre for Irish Studies NUI Galway. Dr Altuna holds a PhD on the topic of 'Spain in Anglo-Irish Literature (1789–1850)' from the University of Deusto, Bilbao.

ARTHUR BROOMFIELD is a research student at Mary Immaculate College, University of Limerick, working on Maria Edgeworth's novels.

MARY BURKE was formerly NEH Keough Fellow at the University of Notre Dame, Indiana and is now assistant professor at the University of Connecticut. She is writing a book on the subject of the 'tinker' figure in Irish writing, and has published extensively on the subject of the depiction of travellers in Irish literature, including essays in *Études Irlandaises*, the *Australian Journal of Irish Studies*, *Travellers and their language*, *New voices in Irish criticism 3*, and *The Irish Revival reappraised*.

COLIN GRAHAM is a lecturer in English at NUI Maynooth. He is author of *Ideologies of epic: nation, empire and Victorian epic poetry* (1998) and *Deconstructing Ireland* (2001), and editor (with Richard Kirkland) of *Ireland and cultural theory* (1999) and (with Glenn Hooper) of *Irish and postcolonial writing* (2002). He has edited the poetry of Elizabeth Barrett Browning and Robert Browning and is currently co-editor of the *Irish Review*.

ANDREAS HÜTHER joined UL as a doctoral student in September 2000, having studied history at Mannheim, Durham, and Freiburg Universities. He was awarded the Scholarship in German of the Department of Languages & Cultural Studies for work on his thesis 'The Irish Celt: a nineteenth-century German construct?' He has compiled a bibliography of German publications in the field of Irish-German Studies for the *Yearbook of the Centre for Irish-German Studies*.

SIOBHÁN KILFEATHER is lecturer in nineteenth-century Irish writing at the Queen's University of Belfast. She was one of the editors of *The Field Day anthology of Irish writing, volumes 4 & 5: Irish women's writing and traditions* (2002) and has edited Maria Edgeworth's *Belinda* for Pickering and Chatto (2003). She is also author of *Dublin: a cultural and literary history* (2005).

JASON KING is a lecturer in the English Department at the National University of Ireland, Maynooth. He has published several articles on the nineteenth-century Irish novel, the Irish theatre, literature of the Irish diaspora, the Irish in Canada, the writing of Irish emigrants, and the representations of immigrants in Ireland.

LEON LITVACK is Reader in Victorian Studies at the Queen's University of Belfast. He is a past president of the Society for the Study of Nineteenth-Century Ireland, and editor of *Ireland in the nineteenth century: regional identity* (Four Courts, 2000). His publications are largely in the areas of nineteenth-century fiction (especially Dickens), art history, periodical culture, imperialism and post-colonialism.

PADDY LYONS works in the English Literature Department at the University of Glasgow, and is also visiting professor at the University of Warsaw. He has published largely in the fields of Restoration literature and literary theory, and is a translator of Louis Althusser.

PATRICK MAUME teaches in the Department of Politics at the Queen's University of Belfast. Among his many publications are *'Life that is exile': Daniel Corkery and the search for Irish Ireland* (1993) and *The long gestation: Irish nationalist life, 1891–1918* (1999).

LUCY McDIARMID is Carole and Gordon Segal Visiting Professor of Irish Literature at Northwestern University, Professor of English at Villanova University, and former president of the American Conference for Irish Studies. She has also taught in the English Department at Princeton. Her most recent book is *The Irish art of controversy* published by Cornell UP and Lilliput.

ALAN O'DAY is Fellow in Modern History, Greyfriars, University of Oxford. He has written and edited 30 volumes and published more than 40 articles. His works include *The English face of Irish nationalism* (1977), *Parnell and the first Home Rule episode* (1986), *Irish Home Rule, 1867–1921* (1998) and *Charles Stewart Parnell* (1998). His most recent volume, edited with D. George Boyce, is *The Ulster crisis, 1885–1921* (Palgrave-Macmillan, 2005).

GARY K. PEATLING is a joint University of Guelph/Institute of Ulster-Scots Studies Postdoctoral Fellow. He is author of *British opinion and Irish self-government, 1865–1925* (2001) and *The failure of the Northern Ireland peace process* (2004).

MARY S. PIERSE works in the Department of English, University College Cork, where she has taught courses on seventeenth- and eighteenth-century poetry, and late-nineteenth-century prose. A former Government of Ireland Scholar, she has also been IRCHSS Government of Ireland Post-Doctoral Fellow in the Humanities and the Social Sciences; her present research concerns Literary Impressionism in the writings of the Irish writer, George Moore (1852–1933).

MATTHEW POTTER holds the position of Co-ordinator of the Limerick City Council History Project and is based in the City Library. He is writing a book entitled *The changing faces of Limerick Corporation/City Council, 1197–2004.*

Introduction

COLIN GRAHAM AND LEON LITVACK

In the twenty-first century, when we are all Europeans now, 'our Europositivity is being put to the test'.[1] Europe as a cultural idea, and the European Union as a political entity, are so vast that they are beyond the sympathetic comprehension of many Europeans. Nations, by contrast, seem to offer a knowable and traditional sense of commonality. And yet Europe underwrites our rights, and our belief in rights, and still maintains a working model of relative peace, and even prosperity, within its boundaries. This mixture of trepidation at the sheer scale of Europe, along with a belief in its capacity to shed a universalist light on our local difficulties, is not new. It is a long-developing legacy stemming from the Enlightenment and the French Revolution, and it parallels the possibilities and disappointments which are characteristic of what Europe meant in nineteenth-century Ireland. Over the course of the nineteenth century in Ireland, Europe was many things (often simultaneously): a place of exotic or cosmopolitan attractions; an influence to be resisted; an extended classroom for the arts and politics; a theatre of war; a crucible of ideas. The essays collected in this volume are testament to the diverse ways in which the reality and the idea of Europe helped form Ireland and Irishness in the nineteenth century. The effects which Europe had on Ireland in the period range from the most broadly ideological (as in the development of the very idea of nationalism, outlined in Alan O'Day's essay), to the micro-histories of individual lives (as described in Patrick Maume's and Matthew Potter's contributions). In each instance, the reality of what Europe is, is washed in the colours of what Ireland might become.

European travellers criss-crossed nineteenth-century Ireland, always passing Irish people moving in the opposite direction. Paschal Grousset's *Ireland's disease: the English in Ireland* (1887), for example, brings Ireland and Europe together in a logical tactic of cultural politics, dismissing the troublesome 'English', who lie conceptually and geographical in the way. Not many years later (in 1893), Edith Somerville and Martin Ross were bemoaning 'a singularly detestable journey'[2] to London, as they headed off jauntily to experience the wine-growing industry of the Médoc at sometimes tipsy first hand. Rural France, for Somerville and Ross, was populated by individuals and types who existed in a world that was a twisted and erratic version of County Cork. London, and England more generally, lie annoyingly in-between, a 'headachy' obstacle to be negotiated before reaching the excitement of the 'Continent' and its half-recognized customs.

1 Jean Baudrillard, 'Holy Europe' in *New Left Review*, 33 (2005), 24.   2 E.Œ. Somerville and Martin Ross, *In the vine country* (London: Vintage, 2001), p. 14.

Such Continental travels, literal or imaginative, were occasions when Ireland was to be remembered from afar and thought of anew. Lucy McDiarmid's sparkling account of 'Irish men and French food' traces a gustatory line of Franco-Irish interchange from Tone to Wilde in which the Irish body consumes Europe, symbolically undertaking 'routes of exchange', as McDiarmid calls them. And throughout the nineteenth century Irish culture absorbed 'Europe' into its body politic in ways which liberated ideas and the forms which they took. Leon Litvack details the European shapes which emerge in a fresh examination of Maclise's painting, while Mary S. Pierse describes the to and fro of images and words which nestle in the intertexts of George Moore's writings. As these essays emphasize, we should never assume that European art and literature is merely an influence on Irish artists, because the dynamic involved in such influence is multi-layered and reciprocal. James Clarence Mangan's is a good case in point. His poems and 'translations' have their own idiosyncratic 'routes of exchange' with European poetry and history – his 'Song of the Albanian', for example, written in 1847, displaces anxiety about a 'Gaunt Famine' and allows for a melancholic celebration of the 'few heroic souls' which death leaves behind 'to wrest/Their birthright from the Turk!'[3] Europe's extremities here act as a conduit for Mangan's rage at the effects of the Famine in Ireland, as well as coming at a time when Young Ireland looked to the small nations of Europe as hints of what a different, freer Ireland might look like.

If Mangan's 'translations' from the German are sometimes versions of the German in the loosest of senses, then this only signifies the freedom and the intellectual space which such interaction was capable of producing. In this kind of literary arena, Irish writers found many modes of being European, while testing their own 'positivity'. So Siobhán Kilfeather makes a compelling case which suggests that the Banims shaped their fictional Ireland through their German reading, while Jason King reveals how Charles Lever is able to use a trope of the 'raparee' to configure Ireland as a transitory and unsettled European nation and Asier Altuna-García de Salazar's reading of Alicia Le Fanu's fiction is another example of such cross-Continental creativity. The literary conjunction of Ireland and Europe in the nineteenth century is not, then, all on the level of hopeful analogy or productive influence. The 'routes of exchange' bring anxiety as well as sustenance. So Arthur Broomfield, in his essay on Maria Edgeworth, suggests that Paris, and all that is associated with it, operates in a disruptive textual fashion, in which the logos at the centre of authoritative language is unsettled by a kind of linguistic and cultural untranslatability. Mary Burke's account of Synge's Parisian days reveals that a comparative European experience underlies the repetitively nomadic imagination of Synge's writing.

3 James Clarence Mangan, 'Song of the Albanian', in Jacques Chuto, Rudolf Patrick Holzapfel, Peter van de Kamp and Ellen Shannon-Mangan (eds), *Selected poems of James Clarence Mangan* (Dublin: Irish Academic Press, 2003), pp 272–4.

Entwined with the formal and aesthetic cross-Continental traffic which traverses Ireland Europe in the nineteenth century is an exchange of ideas which takes place at a textual and intellectual level. As Paddy Lyons shows, Ireland was capable of being used as a European test-case for new endeavours which were essentially about extending and controlling the intellectual franchise through reading. Gary K. Peatling and Andreas Hüther uncover German interests in Ireland which initially seem to be contained within Germany's sphere of cultural influence but which eventually and inevitably spill over into Ireland. One of the great debts which any academic writing on Ireland owes to Europe is the scholarly fascination with Ireland held for the French and German philologists of the nineteenth century. Ernest Renan's rapture at the 'nobility' of the Celtic races was based on a belief in their separateness ('Never has a human family lived more apart from the world, and been purer from all admixture').[4] The irony is that his interest and that of others like him was part of the complex matrix of dialogue and inter-change at all levels which took place between Ireland and Europe in the nineteenth century. Where Renan wishes to see a pure culture cut off from the ills of over-civilized Europe, he himself is taking part in disproving his own assumptions. And as the essays in this volume show, between Ireland and Europe there is not an 'impassable barrier against external influences';[5] instead there are tangled 'routes of exchange', many of them seen here for the first time, and all of them telling us more about Ireland's historical, and contemporary, Europeanness.

4 Ernest Renan, 'From "The poetry of the Celtic races"', in Mark Storey (ed.), *Poetry and Ireland since 1800: a source book* (London: Routledge, 1988), p. 55. **5** Renan, 'From "The poetry of the Celtic races"', p. 55.

Ireland and Europe:
theoretical perspectives[1]

ALAN O'DAY

The fidelity and fortitude with which the national ideal had been pursued would command admiration, even if the ideal itself where to be altogether abandoned, or if it were to be ultimately realised in a manner which showed that the methods by which its attainment had been sought were the cause of its long postponement. Whatever the future may have in store for the remnant of the Irish people at home, the continued pursuit of a separate national existence by a nation which is rapidly disappearing from the land of all its hopes, and the cherishing of these hopes, not only by those who stay but also by those who go, will stand as a monument to human constancy. (Sir Horace Plunkett)[2]

Nationalism is the most potent ideology in Europe since the eighteenth century.[3] It is an expression of the preoccupation with radical freedom in modernity and succeeds because of its ability to combine the political and cultural project of modernity with everyday life.[4] At the same time, nationalism influences notions of freedom and democracy. Once primarily identified with the ideals of emancipation and liberal ambitions of Risorgimento nationalism, it now has a largely negative perception, being associated with aggression, intolerance, violence and inhumanity.[5] In spite of the obvious relationship between nationalism and ethnicity in Ireland and Europe – especially its south-eastern and eastern regions – scholars of both areas have tended to treat the two regions in relative isolation. Theories of nationalism and ethnicity also have developed largely in separate compartments. In the 1980s and 90s, George Boyce and Tom Garvin made some telling connections; but until recently these have not been followed up.[6] Since Ireland and the United Kingdom joined the European

1 I wish to thank George Boyce for allowing me to use some jointly prepared material. Also, I am indebted to Liam Kennedy; Brian Walker; Neil Fleming; John Hutchinson; Institute of Irish Studies, Queen's University Belfast; Rothermere American Institute, University of Oxford and my aunt, Col. Helen E. O'Day.   2 Horace Plunkett, *Ireland in the new century* (Port Washington, NY, 1970), pp 1–2.   3 This argument draws upon Peter Alter, *Nationalism* (London, 1994), pp 1–38.   4 Gerard Delanty and Patrick O'Mahony, *Nationalism and social theory: modernity and the recalcitrance of the nation* (London, 2002) p. xv. 5 Umut Özkirimli offers a useful consideration of the evolution of concepts of nationalism (*Theories of nationalism: a critical introduction* [Basingstoke and London, 2000], pp 12–63). 6 D. George Boyce, *Nationalism in Ireland* (London, 1995); Tom Garvin, *The evolution of Irish*

Economic Community (now the EU), there has been a growing interest in discovering connections with the Continent, though the number of works specifically devoted to placing Ireland in a European dimension is small. Nineteenth-century Irish history remains essentially centred in the British Isles and anglophone culture. This essay takes a slightly different direction: rather than illustrating the linkages between Ireland and Europe, it underlines the connections through reference to theoretical constructs of nationalism and ethnicity. Most works on nationalism in particular, focus on Continental examples; but a handful, notably those by Jim Mac Laughlin, and Gerard Delanty and Patrick O'Mahony, have broken the mould, by advancing the integration of the Irish and European experiences.

To date there is no agreed definition of nationalism: it possesses no clear boundaries or common agenda linking the various manifestations. A useful description is that it is 'a semantic space, that expresses through manifold discourses the many kinds of projects, identities, interests and ideologies that make it up' constituting the 'recombination of ever-shifting modalities of thinking and feeling about society'.[7] Nationalist ideas coordinate common interests among élites, mobilise support from groups hitherto excluded from the political process, and legitimize the goals of the movement.[8] Irish nationalism is typical of this process. Nationalists everywhere had to locate and then persuade people whom they wish to mobilize that distinctions between themselves and the dominant state were fundamental and more important than any common bonds. Irish nationalism has three fundamental components – a historic territory, a population 'entitled' to live in the national territory, and an aspiration to establish a separate political state coterminous with the land and people. Within this framework four aspects of the attainment of its goals are stressed by Garvin: the origins of political culture; development of popular political organization; growth of public opinion; and the development of the machinery of a state.[9] Irish nationalism was least effective in devising a satisfactory definition of what constituted the 'Irish people'.[10] In spite of a language resplendent with the terminology of 'race', nationalists never developed a 'blood' definition of what being 'Irish' meant. Religion was a partial and incomplete, though important, substitute: it served the function held by the language issue in much of Europe, being the quintessential entitlement issue.[11] Language was a late incursion into the Irish case and never gained assent as a definition of who were the legitimate inheritors of the island. Still, this did not create the divisions of the peoples of Ireland. Separations were instead between Protestants and Catholics and within the two communities, with the first proving easily the most decisive. In Europe lateral divisions within the ethnic community were more typical and significant. Early attempts to include all creeds and classes in Ireland ultimately dissolved in a nationalism focused by the mid-1880s

nationalism (Dublin, 1981). **7** Delanty and O'Mahony, p. xv. **8** See John Breuilly's argument in John Hutchinson and Anthony D. Smith (eds), *Nationalism* (Oxford, 1994), pp 166–7. **9** Garvin, p. 6. **10** Quoted in D.H. Greene and D.H. Lawrence, *The matter with Ireland* (London, 1962), p. 294. **11** See David Horowitz's argument in John Hutchinson and Anthony D. Smith (eds), *Ethnicity* (Oxford, 1996), p. 288.

on uniting Catholics alone, perhaps because forging a common secular identity proved
discordant with Irish realities.[12]

   Anthony Smith points to five conditions necessary for entrenching national identity among a significant section of a putative nation's inhabitants: historic territory or
homeland; common myths and historic memories; a common, mass public culture;
common legal rights and duties for all members; and a common economy with territorial mobility for members.[13] Catholics only realized these conditions fully around
1867. Ironically, Ireland's Protestants most completely met the criteria in the eighteenth century. Smith's description is appropriate at the point when nationalism
reaches relative maturity; but other concepts are required to explain how and when
it arrived at this juncture, and to determine when nationalism achieved its completed
or 'post-mature' state. Miroslav Hroch, in *Social preconditions of national revival in Europe*
(1985) identifies the intelligentsia as the prime agents in the process of creating the
nation. Hroch constructs a threefold typology for national movements. In the initial
stage, intellectuals develop an interest in the antiquities of the territory. This corresponds to the establishment of the (Royal) Dublin Society and the (Royal) Irish
Academy in the eighteenth century. He notes that the purveyors of this culture lack
a political programme at the outset, and do not seek to mobilize the masses until a
further metamorphosis has taken place. In the second phase, the now numerically
expanding intelligentsia develop a political programme and seek to incorporate the
masses into their conception of the nation. Finally, his third stage is mass mobilization – that is, when a significant sector of the population is converted to, and pursues,
political aspirations. In the case of Ireland these stages certainly existed, though not
always in Hroch's sequence. His model highlights the core ingredient of leadership,
and indirectly offers a framework for understanding different forms of its manifestation during phases of nationalism. The intelligentsia, according to Hroch, are
superseded by moderate bourgeois leaders who in turn give way to politicians advo-
cating more radical national goals. Nationalist appeals did not meet with unqualified
acceptance, even from Catholics, who did not adopt them fully before the 1880s; the
full-scale success of ethnic nationalism was delayed until the twentieth century, and
even then never completed. As nationalist and ethnic nationalist appeals struck a
responsive chord with Catholics, nearly all Protestants took up an anti-nationalist
stance. John Hutchinson's explanation of blocked mobility – the rate of Catholic
advancement did not keep pace with escalating expectations – helps to resolve the
apparent contradiction in Hroch's scheme. He also demonstrates that this blockage
became acute at the beginning of the twentieth century, inflaming a younger generation of the intelligentsia which vented its frustration against both the established
state and the nationalists in control of patriotic organizations. This explanation affords
a useful modification of Hroch's phases, thus explaining why further increments of
cultural and literary nationalism bloom after mass mobilization as well as at the beginning of a national movement's unfolding, and become more assertive in its late form.

12 B.M. Walker, *Ulster politics: the formative years, 1868–86* (Belfast, 1989), pp 201–11.
13 Anthony D. Smith, *National identity* (London, 1991), p. 14.

Hroch shows the importance of a completed social structure for a political movement prioritizing political demands. He also suggests that until a late point in its
progression, autonomy (not independence) is the focus of national movements. His
emphasis upon the sequences and social composition accords with Ireland's experience and closes the loopholes between general theory and actual Irish experience.

Gellner muses on the question of what determined who did or did not subscribe
to nationalist doctrine. He suggests that nationalism arises among groups who feel
themselves disadvantaged during the upheaval of industrialisation; yet there are many
exceptions, including, in part, Ireland. Protestants and Catholics, and the west of the
country, entered the British industrial world at different rates of speed. Thomas
Hylland Eriksen broadly supports Gellner's view though suggesting that ethnicity is
constituted through social contact.[14] Ethnic identity, he maintains, becomes crucially
important the moment it is perceived as threatened. Michael Hechter and Margaret
Levi suggest that ethnic solidarity arises in regions developed as internal colonies
where there is a hierarchical cultural division of labour determining life's chances.[15]
Solidarity increases when members interact within the boundaries of their own
group. They distinguish between regional and ethnoregional movements: the first
couches claims solely in terms of material demands; the second bases its claim on
ethnic distinctiveness. These propositions are germane to Ireland. At early moments,
but most definitively during the Land War between 1879 and 1881, Catholics were
mobilized by a collectively held notion of the land for the people in opposition to
the 'alien' landowners – an idea imbued with the sense of 'native' dispossession.
Linkage of the land and national demands gave nationalism its dynamic after 1879
though, in part, at the cost of making nationalism primarily a Catholic rural movement. Ulster Protestants reached a similar stage of mobilisation during the crisis of
1912 to 1914, after which it became increasingly difficult to construct a political state
that appealed across the religious divide. Completion of the process of conversion to
an ethnic concept of the nation was the final step in the transition of popular aspirations from a western European, territorially centred expansionist ideology of a
dominant group to an central/eastern European nationalism based on ethnicity/
religion, in which grievances directed against the dominant state/culture were the
motivating ingredient.

As Hechter and Levi observe, when life-chances are seen as independent of
inclusion in a particular ethnic group, the subjective significance of membership
recedes or disappears. Their thesis helps to explain the very high degree of Catholic
mobilization over a long time in Ireland, and its much more attenuated echo among
the Irish diaspora. The concept of allegiance is vital to understanding why the
national political project failed to achieve unanimity; there were tensions between
peoples holding differing notions of the nation and the problem of dual allegiance.
Those holding distinctly different and frequently incompatible aspirations often used
the same or similar terminology, thus creating semantic confusion.

14 Thomas Hylland Eriksen, *Ethnicity and nationalism: anthropological perspectives* (London,
1993), pp 18, 76. **15** See Michael Hechter and Margaret Levi's argument in Hutchinson
and Smith (eds), *Nationalism*, pp 184–95.

In Ireland nationalism had four problems: how to define the 'nation'; how to define the ideological movement, 'nationalism'; how to explain the formation of the 'nation'; and how to foster the emergence of the nationalist movement.[16] Locating the beginnings of Irish nationalism is no simple matter. Three contrasting views – primordialist, modernist and ethnicist – have been advanced.[17] The primordial concept of the nation has two meanings. One is that nations have existed time out of mind, and thus are 'natural' and 'persistent'. This idea is open to the criticism that the nation is seen as a kind of perpetual, spiritual entity, disassociated from any social, political or economic change. But the more refined meaning is that given by Clifford Gertz, who argues that human beings classify themselves and others in accordance with primordial criteria; the family, the locality – one's own people (however defined) succour and protect us.[18] Thus people are prepared to sacrifice their lives for such support and protection. It is not a big step, therefore, for individuals to transfer such important allegiances – of kin, family, locality – to the nation and to the nation state. Thus, while class or economic interests threaten revolution, they rarely threaten the integrity of the state; but primordial attachments threaten partition, irredentism, and a redrawing of state boundaries. Hence the state needs to base itself on these primordial attachments (such as blood ties, language, race religion and custom) if it is to survive. Primordialism does not presuppose some eternal, fixed, unchanging ties, but rather emphasizes the importance of powers over our lives that are exercised by family, locality and one's own 'people' – that is, powers that make primordial attachments both powerful and enduring. Eoin Mac Neill articulates this position: as a cultural nationalist, he sees the past as a story of the nation embedded in human nature and a history revealed through an Irish way of life.[19] Marc Bloch and Hugh Seton-Watson espouse similar views, tracing the origin of nationalism back over centuries. Gellner dismisses such claims as accretions amounting to florid theories formulated by nationalists themselves. The influence of the primordialists has been eclipsed since 1945; for them a difference of kind exists between pre-modern 'patriotism' and the concept of the nation and nationalism, which is contingent upon industrialization, democracy, rationality and communal citizenship. Nationalism is portrayed as a response from traditional groups to the threat posed by the rush of modernity, bringing to their aid novel and non-traditional classes and strata. Benedict Anderson observes that ethnic communities are necessarily 'imagined' in the sense of linking groups of people together who have not had and can not anticipate having direct physical acquaintance with one another. This, he insists, only happens when modernization reaches the stage where communication allows disparate peoples to experience a common bond.[20] Ethnicists, such as Anthony Smith and John Anderson, accept the modernity of nationalism but locate its origins in the pre-

16 Anthony D. Smith, *Theories of nationalism* (London, 1971), p. 148. **17** This argument is based on John Hutchinson, *Modern nationalism* (London, 1994), pp 3–38. **18** See Clifford Geertz's argument in Hutchinson and Smith (eds), *Nationalism*, pp 31–4; and *Ethnicity*, 41–5. **19** See Eoin MacNeill, *Phases of Irish history* (Dublin, 1926). **20** Benedict Anderson, *Imagined communities; reflections on the origin and spread of nationalism* (London, 1991).

existing ethno-cultural community shaped by shared myths about origins, history, culture and ideas of space, that give members identity and purpose. Smith's term *ethnie* describes a process which is only a difference of degree rather than of kind between pre-modern societies and modern nations. For Eriksen 'ethnicity can be non-modern, nationalist must be identified with the modern age'. He also notes that ethnically-based political organisations, as well as mass movements based on ethnic identity, are recent and a consequence of the modernization process.[21]

Nationalism and the nation are related, but not identical, concepts. The term nationalism was first used by the German philosopher Johann Gottfried Herder in 1774 and did not enter the general vocabulary until the mid-nineteenth century. Nationalism displays a number of common components, typically including consciousness of the uniqueness or peculiarity of a group of people, particularly with respect to their ethnic, linguistic or religious homogeneity; stress upon shared social-cultural attitudes; a mutual historical past or sense of it; belief in a common mission; and a conception of who is the 'enemy', the counter-force seeking to deprive the 'nation' of its legitimate destiny. The collective grievances of, and the belief that, the country was a victim of British/English oppression were central propositions in Irish national cosmology and played a part in the anti-colonial rhetoric, if not invariably the practice, of popular politics.[22] In later national historiography the Great Famine of the 1840s assumed a special place in the construction of this idea of 'victimization', allowing for the diaspora to share perhaps even to be the standard-bearers for the collective sense of oppression. This obsession warrants Declan Kiberd's observation: 'if England had never existed, the Irish would have been rather lonely. Each nation badly need the other, for the purpose of defining itself'.[23] Much the same can be said of Ulster Unionism, which, in spite of its triumphalism, is based on a collective sense of 'virtual' victimization at the hands of an engrossing Catholicism, and a constant feeling of impending British betrayal. Nationalism is frequently associated with an even more recent term, 'ethnicity', which made its initial appearance in 1953; but nationalism differs by being broader and more inclusive. Whereas ethnicity applies to a specified group (whether it properly exists or not), nationalism can be a quality shared by a multiplicity of separate communities seeking a mutually desired end – that is, usually some degree of political autonomy. Ireland for the Irish is pregnant with contradictory meanings. To many it conveyed an ethnic message: either Ireland for the 'native', that is, Catholic Irish, or Ireland for the people who inhabited the country irrespective of origins. This, too, corresponds to Continental developments.

The term nation has two meanings. As applied in central and Eastern Europe it is a social group of people which as a consequence of historically evolved linguistic, cultural, religious or political relations, has become conscious of its coherence, polit-ical unity and particular interests. This exists irrespective of whether all or part of it becomes an autonomous nation-state; however, 'nations' of this type when they reach

---

21 Eriksen, pp 15, 79.   **22** Garvin perhaps assumes too blithely that rhetoric and practice are identical; see *Evolution of Irish nationalist politics*, p. 2.   **23** Declan Kiberd, *Inventing Ireland* (London, 1995), p. 2.

a stage of maturity, usually demand the right to political self-determination. In English usage, a nation refers to the political apparatus known as the nation or state, expressed conveniently as nation-state. When this nation comes into existence, it is assigned a superior and more universal significance than other bodies of joint social action such as class, confession, community or the family. Nationalists and nationalism are, respectively, people and the movement seeking substantial political autonomy and more usually to create the nation-state. This definition ignores other forms of nationalism, including the German and Italian types in the twentieth century, American expansionism in the nineteenth century, European imperialism overseas, along with others found in the Third or Emergent World since 1945.[24] A restricted definition allows a lens to be focused on the quests of ethnic, religious and national groups in Europe to distinguish themselves from, and seek autonomy or concessions from, dominant ruling states. After a long gestation in which alternative options were possibilities, Irish nationalism emerged in this context as a species of peripheral nationalism rather than the state-building nationalism of the English, French, Italian or German variety, which were multi-ethnic, multi-confessional and expansionist.[25] It had, Garvin points out, the cultural trait of communal solidarity, generating a conformist consensus based on pragmatism with the development of the militant, pragmatic, disciplined mass political party as the characteristic political institution.[26] Nationality in one context describes the legal status of a person or collective of people. It confers no rights, though it may impose obligations; citizenship defines members and non-members becoming coeval with nationality.[27]

Ethnicity, too, has a plethora of interpretations. A satisfactory working description for current purposes is that it comprises a named human population with myths of common ancestry, shared historical memories, one or more elements of common culture, a link with a homeland and a sense of solidarity among at least some of its members.[28] Abner Cohen injects a further ingredient, identifying ethnicity as 'a political phenomenon as traditional customs are used only as idioms, and as mechanisms for political alignment'.[29] David Horowitz supports political action as an essential element, and suggests that 'politics has a commanding position for determining group status ... the state become[s] the focal point for ethnic claims'.[30] Ethnicity is distinguished from nationalism in two senses: nationalism *per se* is not predicated on a 'common ancestry' but only on 'uniqueness' and it presupposes the ambition to obtain a significant measure of political autonomy, whereas ethnicity does suppose 'common ancestry' (socio-biology) not just occupation of a specific territory and may seek merely to attain recognition of a degree of distinctiveness

24 Delanty and O'Mahony distinguish ten types of nationalism: state patriotism, liberal nationalism, reconstructive nationalism, integral nationalism, irredentist nationalism, sucessionist nationalism, cultural nationalism, religious nationalism, transnationalism and new radical nationalism (*Nationalism and social theory*, p. 120). Other typologies can be found in Özkirimli, pp 12–63.   25 Michael Hechter, *Containing nationalism* (Oxford, 2000), pp 15–17.   26 Garvin, p. 7.   27 Delanty and O'Mahony, pp 9–10.   28 Hutchinson and Smith (eds), *Ethnicity*, p. 7.   29 Quoted in ibid., p. 84.   30 Horowitz, in ibid., p. 286.

rather than the erection of a state or sub-state. Ethnicity can restrict its demands to special rights for religious practice, language, education or a share of state offices rather than formal political autonomy. This formula felicitates incorporating the Irish Catholic diaspora into the ethnic community, while the Protestants in Ireland were left outside it. In orthodox Irish nationalist rhetoric two peoples or traditions existed in Ireland which, though separated by origins and religious affiliation, had a joint destiny in an Irish nation-state. However, mutual co-operation proved elusive, except for brief spells such as in the late eighteenth century. In nationalist rhetoric the divisions were deliberately fostered by Great Britain and therefore, as the century progressed, the British – or in common parlance, the English – connection had to be severed before Ireland (and innate Irishness) could flourish. On the ground, as Mac Laughlin demonstrates, the vast majority of nationalists viewed Irishness and Ulster Unionism in ethno-religious terms. However, the official nationalist view expressed in the Proclamation of an Irish Republic in 1916 ('The Irish Republic is entitled to, and hereby claims, the allegiance of every Irishman and Irishwoman'), was wedded to a territorial dogma.

Ireland possessed characteristics generally present among those European nationalities that developed successful national movements forming nation-states.[31] Progression from people to nation to state is seen as a natural, legitimate and inevitable course of history. This can be expressed as thresholds on the road to statehood: patriotic to national agitation; agitation to mass appeal; and mass appeal to success for the goals.[32] Nationalists demanded self-determination and statehood as a historic right, an ideal given voice by John Redmond: 'the national demand, in plain and popular language, is simply this, that the government of every purely Irish affair shall be controlled by the public opinion of Ireland, and by that alone. We demand this self-government as a right'.[33] As O.P. Rafferty points out, 'nations, like individuals, are not simply the product of material circumstances. Often those at the extremes of society can, perhaps even in spite of themselves, provide a more penetrating understanding of the forces that shape public consciousness than individuals engaged in more convention pursuits.'[34] Mac Laughlin expresses it slightly differently: 'nations were not just "imagined communities" each with its own distinctive styles of living and thinking. They were also the building blocks of modernity and the territorial expressions of national capitalism'.[35] In this situation, Delanty and O'Mahony suggest, the process of collective identity-formation creates a new perception of structural and resource configuration.[36] According to them, a further dimension arises when collectivities set the requirements of cultural identification above material resources as a motive for action.

31 See Hugh Seton-Watson's argument in Hutchinson and Smith (eds), *Nationalism*, p. 137. 32 Delanty and O'Mahony, p. 119. 33 R. Barry O'Brien (ed.), *Home rule speeches of John Redmond, MP* (London, 1910), pp 337–8. 34 Oliver P. Rafferty, *The church, the state and the Fenian threat, 1861–75* (Basingstoke, 1999), p. 157. 35 Jim Mac Laughlin, *Reimaging the nation-state: the contested terrains of nation-building* (London, 2001), p. 100. 36 Delanty and O'Mahony, pp 108–9.

Yet, over the long haul, Irish nationalists devoted far fewer words to questions of abstract rights, the primordial basis of the nation or the uniqueness of Irish culture; nevertheless this theme, with its language of 'historical wrongs', peppered their rhetoric. Emphasis upon 'wrongs' offered the widest common denominator, and provided a unifying principle capable of binding together peoples, including potentially a significant segment of Protestants. Its limitation was that such appeals were primarily materialistic – that is, they were based on concrete grievances. It was Daniel O'Connell who held out the temptation that if the British state met Catholic grievances fairly, his co-religionists would become loyal, contented subjects. Though, as Rafferty notes, while the Catholic Church's reformist proclivities augured a desire to place 'institutional Catholicism in much the same position, socially, as the established Church of Ireland', this ambition was superseded when Fenianism radicalized political thinking by pushing the goal of political autonomy to the forefront.[37] Aspiring, upwardly mobile Catholics, who found a niche in the British community by the late nineteenth century, discovered themselves straddling two worlds: that visualized by O'Connell and the Church, and an increasingly militant but by no means consistent nationalism, which lauded their achievements on the one hand, yet frequently labelled them dupes seduced by the plums of the dominant alien culture on the other. The problem reflected a dichotomy generally present in parallel movements: social and economic elevation necessitated penetration of the state bureaucracy; but this also meant that those who made the jump were often lost to the national cause. These 'Castle Catholics' came to occupy an uncertain portal in their native land. The language of 'wrongs' handed tempting alternative possibilities to the dominant and flexible British state which could, and did, respond with policies directed towards remedying grievances or at the very least to drive a wedge in the potential solidarity of the country's people. A section of Britain's leadership preferred to believe in O'Connell's recipe; Gladstone was its most articulate proponent, but it should not be overlooked that an earlier Conservative, Sir Robert Peel and then late in the century, Arthur Balfour, were anxious to promote the resolution of grievances. In Ireland itself, Horace Plunkett became the most prominent apostle of social and economic remedies as a means to undermine support for political nationalism, thereby rendering himself anathema to many of his own order.

The unfolding of nationalism in Ireland and elsewhere always took place against the backdrop of opposition of the dominant political community, which in the case of Great Britain had immense resources to mount the counter-attack. Imperial states had three strategies: assimilation, domination/segregation, and an ideology of multiculturalism; these were often pursued simultaneously. Indeed Great Britain resorted to all three, and the application of these moulded Irish national responses.[38] As was true for other national minorities in Europe, the Irish had three options: to express loyalty to the dominant state, to voice specific grievances demanding redress and to seek to break the bonds with the larger community. In spite of state counter-

37 Rafferty, pp xi, xiii.   **38** Eriksen, pp 123–4.

strategies, Irish nationalists over time proved remarkably capable of mobilizing and retaining the loyalty of most Catholics for the patriotic platform. Nationalists were able to override regional, economic, class and cultural distinctions despite concessions that granted the substance of their material claims. Delanty and O'Mahony suggest the need for 'consideration of the social context of nationalism as a movement of resistance to differentiation and to certain aspects of the modern form of integration. The social logic of the nationalist movement in Ireland was to call for a different kind of integration that in fact amounted to a certain kind of de-differentiation'.[39]

Elie Kedourie points out that a nation must have a past and, no less fundamentally, a future, the two being irrevocably linked. Possession of the past therefore is fundamental to all national movements; but establishing an 'approved' version is never uncontested, for inevitably there are other competing interpretations of the same history. Historical memory is vital to how the national mission is understood, both by the Irish and by outsiders. Irish nationalism scored an impressive success in dictating the historical agenda; but like the vast majority of similar movements across Europe, achievement of the full programme proved tantalisingly elusive, an agonising outcome finding expression in the derisory republican song:

> God save the southern part of Ireland
> Three quarters of a nation once again.[40]

Yet if nationalists were less than completely successful in their political struggle, they did much better in winning over posterity. Historians, politicians and popular consciousness subscribe to a version of the Irish past mainly fashioned by the hands of nationalists – a history that may contain elements of invention or be an imagined community[41] – but is no less pervasive for all that.

Unsurprisingly, 'history', for both nationalists and unionists, has a major place in contemporary discourse. Brian Walker's discussion of the use and abuse of history in Ireland today offers a perceptive account of these practices.[42] He notes that the constant reference to the past in Ireland merits close attention because it is so frequently used to explain '"unresolved" historical problems, which are part of a special deterministic history going back, in many unionists' views to the seventeenth century, or in many nationalists' views, to the twelfth century'.[43]

Herbert Butterfield points out that 'our knowledge of the past is seriously affected if we learn how that knowledge came into existence'.[44] He was not referring to Irish history at this juncture, but rather to the recent role of historians in the construction of the German past. His comment is of particular importance for an investigation of Irish nationalism, especially in the light of the controversy in the last two decades over 'revisionism'. New evidence, fresh perspectives, cross-fertilization

---

39 Delanty and O'Mahony, p. 80, n. 3. **40** See Boyce, p. 22. **41** Ibid., pp 15, 177–84. **42** Brian Walker, *Dancing to history's tune: history, myth and politics in Ireland* (Belfast, 1996), pp 37–74; Walker extends this theme in *Past and present: history, identity and politics in Ireland* (Belfast, 2000). **43** Ibid., p. 58. **44** *Man on his past* (New York, 1962), p. 26.

with other disciplines, changes in methodology and technology are the stuff of the historians' trade, and re-interpreting past events an inevitable outcome. In the Irish context, however, 'revisionism' has a more specific and often pejorative connotation: it has come to mean, in the words of one of its leading critics, Desmond Fennell:

> A retelling of Irish history which seeks to show that British rule of Ireland was not, as we have believed a bad thing, but a mixture of necessity, good intentions and bungling, and that Irish resistance to it was not as we have believed a good thing, but a mixture of wrong-headed idealism and unnecessary, often cruel violence. The underlying message is that in our relations with Britain on the Irish question the Irish have been very much at fault. This is the popular image of historical revisionism.[45]

While it is assuredly true that interpretations of Irish nationalism shifted during the past three decades with a greater tendency to take a cold-eyed appraisal of its claims, tactics and consistency, this has not undermined, but rather re-enforced its centrality, underlining Butterfield's observation that it is vital to establish how a particular view has come into existence, and how it has been perpetuated and modified.

History is part of literate culture, and thus a facet of modernization. Only when people could read and communicate efficiently did written history take on universal significance. Until this level was achieved, history was the product of a small cultural élite which drew upon the well of existing histories and myths. History had three crucial purposes: as an analytical tool, allowing nations to discover their existence, their innate personalities or souls which had been obscured earlier; to create solidarity; and point to the future, and to inspire a resurrected people.[46] From the mid-eighteenth century, history increasingly employed the techniques of science, thereby facilitating its legitimacy as a true reflection of the past. Emphasis upon historic legal systems (in Ireland's case, the Brehon laws) differentiated the national community from the dominant imperial state, and the Ordnance Survey maps were influential in creating a sense of physical place. History provided an ideological nucleus, presenting the past as a series of conflicts with the dominant society, also pointing to a 'golden age' that had once existed. This history reflected the social origin of the leaders and social affiliation of the people who were being addressed. Over time in Irish historical writing this spelt a shift from an élite patriot historiography, to a largely though not exclusively Catholic bourgeois posture and finally an emphasis on the suffering and dignity of the Catholic peasants. Historians were the generals leading the charge to national consciousness and, though initially they lacked an army, in time they created their own foot-soldiers.

45 'Against revisionism' in Ciaran Brady (ed), *Interpreting Irish history: the debate on historical revisionism* (Dublin, 1994), pp 184–5.   **46** Gerhard Brunn, 'Historical consciousness and historical myths', in Andreas Kappeler, Firket Adanir and Alan O'Day (eds), *The formation of national elites: comparative studies on governments and non-dominant ethnic groups in Europe, 1850–1940* (Aldershot and New York, 1992), vol. 6, pp 327–38.

No less important was the role of historic memory. Jack Magee observes that the Irish imbibe the past through largely sectarian mythologies acquired as part of their political or religious experience.[47] This, he points out, often came through popular legends and songs learned in the home. Many of these sentiments have ancient roots and in Catholic Ireland contempt for Protestantism was endemic, just as Protestant myths were its mirror image. A Swiss, Georges-Denis Zimmerman, provides a treasure-trove of political street ballads which give vent to this popular imagery.[48] Popular or folk 'history', like its written counterpart was, in part, a creation and had an ulterior purpose. Mac Laughlin suggests that as the chief cultural/political entrepreneurs, the clergy, with the aid of school teachers, invested the entire landscape with Catholic nationalist symbolism.[49] According to him, the priests were engaged in Christianizing places, and claiming them for nationalist rule; in this environment nationalism should be seen as 'a political ideology and social movement that literally developed out of the country's socio-economic and ethnic geography'.[50] Nationalism became a vehicle for the advancement and hegemony of an increasingly self-confident church and its secular allies: teachers, minor bureaucrats, well-off farmers and shopkeepers. Mac Laughlin contends:

> In ethnically divided nations, nationalists and national separatists also emphasised the dangers of cultural miscegenation and stressed the centrality of nation-building to the preservation and accumulation of individual aptitudes. This was particularly the case in early twentieth-century Ulster where nationalism, as in Irish nationalism and national separatism, and unionism as in Ulster unionism, reflected the political and economic concerns of regionally-based social blocs and contending ethnic collectivities.[51]

Historical memory was reinforced with a myriad of festivals, commemorations and the erection of monuments.[52] St Patrick's Day, for instance, took on the functions of a national celebration: a Catholic religious event and a nationalist political commemoration rolled into one.

Later history – or more properly historiography – is a further dimension. From Young Ireland pamphlets onward, there emerged a vigorous tradition of recounting Irish history as a nationalist allegory. By the 1880s writers such as Justin McCarthy, R. Barry O'Brien and T.P. O'Connor created a virtual sub-industry of popular nationalist history, though curiously these men belonged to an anglicized literary culture garrisoned in London. The success of Young Ireland and subsequent efforts

47 See Walker, *Dancing to history's tune*, p. 59.   **48** Georges-Denis Zimmermann, *Songs of Irish rebellion: political street ballads and rebel songs, 1780–1900* (Dublin, 1967).   **49** Jim Mac Laughlin, 'The politics of nation-building in post-famine Donegal' in William Nolan, Liam Ronayne and Mairead Dunlevy (eds), *Donegal, history and society: interdisciplinary essays on the history of an Irish county* (Dublin, 1995), pp 583–624.   **50** Ibid., pp 585–6.   **51** Ibid., p. 597.   **52** For a useful discussion of commemorations after 1920 see, Walker, *Past and present*, pp 78–100.

can be measured by Gladstone's public recognition of an Irish past filled with wrongs and grievances. In his introduction of the land bill in 1870 he insisted that 'old Irish ideas and customs were never supplanted except by the rude hand of violence and by laws written in the statute book, but never entering into the heart of the Irish people'.[53] Then in 1886 he treated the first home rule debates as a giant national tutorial on Irish history, in which the morality tale of English wrongs became the pre-eminent theme. Gladstone accepted the existence of two Irish peoples but believed that 'history' showed that the Protestants, relieved of the baleful influence of British intervention, would revert to their eighteenth-century patriotism. Grattan's Parliament then had 'the spark, at least, and the spirit of true patriotism'.[54] 'There was', he declared, 'a spirit there which, if free scope had been left to it, would in all probability have been enabled to work out a happy solution to every Irish problem and difficulty, and would have saved to the coming generation an infinity of controversy and trouble'. This verdict spared him the complicating problem of grappling with claims to distinct treatment of Protestants, particularly Ulster Protestants, and, above all, nonconformists.[55] More tellingly, this 'history' created a blockage for Protestants, a few of whom, if they might attempt to share it intellectually, were largely excluded in actuality.

With the creation of the Irish Free State and Northern Ireland, historians in both states busied themselves with outfitting them with suitable histories. This division into two 'historic' Irelands was not simply an intellectual genuflection to the existence of separate political statues but rooted in a now ethnically divided land where communal tension and violence was a reality. Yet overall a nationalist interpretation of history retains primacy in the face of sometimes stubborn counter-claims.

This short survey reveals the complexity of Irish identity, nationalism and ethnicity along with the continuing difficulty of explaining the same; however, it points to the need to integrate Ireland into conceptual models and to place them in wider European and possibly extra-European context. Ireland in Europe has many possible linkages; the one proposed here differs slightly from the usual, and is meant to suggest fresh and intriguing possibilities.

---

53 *Parliamentary debates*, Third Series, 199 (15 February 1870), cc. 378–9. **54** Ibid., 304 (8 April 1886), c. 1054. **55** D. George Boyce, 'In the front rank of the nation: Gladstone and the Unionists of Ireland, 1868–1893', in D. Bebbington and R. Swift (eds), *Gladstone centenary essays* (Liverpool, 2000), pp 184–201. For some reflections on the historiography of Gladstone's Irish reputation, see Alan O'Day, 'Gladstone and Irish nationalism: achievement and reputation' in ibid., pp 163–83.

Ireland and Europe in 1825:
situating the Banims

SIOBHÁN KILFEATHER

At that moment the lance of an Arab might have changed the destinies of the world.[1]

But regret for these changes is futile: there are ruins made by time which time will never repair.[2]

Why not 1824? Or 1829? 1825 was not after all an *annus mirabilis* – nor more than usual of an *annus horribilis* – for Ireland, in spite of Pastorini's prophecies.[3] No important literary work causes the date to resonate in the ways we associate with England in 1819. The publication of the first series of the Banim brothers' *Tales of the O'Hara family* is significant, but not of any obviously greater significance than the publication of Charles R. Maturin's *Melmoth the wanderer* in 1820 or Gerald Griffin's *The Collegians* in 1829. The reason for choosing to situate a discussion of the first series of *Tales by the O'Hara family* so precisely in Ireland in 1825 is to press for a particular attention to ways in which the emergent historical novel of the 1820s was preoccupied with the significance of dates and dating, with periodisation, and with the potentially different historical outcomes available at any particular moment in time. The first series of *Tales by the O'Hara family* might be read as a trilogy on the themes of identity and death. The supernatural figures strongly in these stories, and it is worth pausing to examine what this turn to the supernatural means.

1 Thomas Moore, quoting Edward Gibbon, in *Memoirs of Captain Rock, the celebrated Irish chieftain, with some account of his ancestors, written by himself* (London: Baldwin Cradock, 1824), p. 26. **2** Augustin Thierry, *History of the Conquest of England by the Normans; its causes and consequences, in England, Scotland, Ireland, and on the Continent*, translated from the seventh Paris edition by William Hazlitt (London: David Bogue, 1847), vol. 2, p. 51. **3** Signor Pastorini was the pseudonym of Charles Walmesley (1722–97), whose *General history of the Christian church* (1771) formed the basis for an outbreak of millenarianism in the 1820s. Walmesley's elaborate interpretation of the Apocalypse of St John seemed to promise the violent destruction of Protestantism in 1825. Pastorini's prophecies and other forms of millenarianism had been popular in the 1790s, in the period leading up to the rebellion. There were also reports of prophetic texts attributed to St Colum Cille in circulation among the Ribbonmen in the 1820s. Thomas Moore, touring Ireland in the summer of 1823, noticed the contribution made by these prophecies in forging solidarity amongst Catholics, for whom they offered alternative forms of knowledge and discourse to those emanating from official sources, including the Catholic Church.

The Irish readership of troubled Irish Protestants and protesting Irish Catholics campaigning for emancipation in the 1820s might well have felt that Ireland had been sidetracked over the Act of Union, and arbitrary power was grounded on occasional arbitrary contingencies. The lance of an Arab might have changed the destinies of the world. Rebellions, revolutions, wars might have had different outcomes. In the 1820s many Irish intellectuals were asking whether Ireland had the same relationship to modernity as other European countries and whether the Irish were experiencing historical time in similar ways to their European counterparts. This comparative impulse led Irish writers to engage with aspects of emerging French historiography, German folklore and romanticism, and Scottish historical fiction as useful analogues for interpreting the state of Ireland.

> 'An; doesn't Pastorini say it? Sure, when Twenty-five comes, we'll have our own agin, the right will overcome the might – the bottomless pit will be locked – ay, double bolted, if St. Pether gets the kays, for he's the very boy that will acommodate the heretics wid a warm corner; an' yit, faith, ther's many o' them that myself 'ud put in a good word for, afther all.'[4]

The growing influence of Daniel O'Connell and the strengthening campaign for Catholic Emancipation led government, church leaders, charitable institutions and foreign observers to speculate on the state of Ireland. Like Thomas Moore, though with a different inflection, William Carleton presents an Irish peasantry traumatized by the events of 1798 and the Act of Union, disaffected from official knowledge and from enlightenment scepticism, reliant on the promises held out by superstitions, prophecies and miracles. This strong sense of living at a particular historical juncture was crucial in the shaping of Irish romanticism. Claire Connolly insists on the distinctiveness of the period from the Act of Union to Catholic Emancipation as dating romanticism proper in Ireland:

> Hopes that the Act [of Union] might allow Catholics a greater share in public life were swiftly disappointed, and lingered as an open sore on the surface of the new body politic. The literary culture of Irish romanticism is thus strongly marked by a sense of grievance, generated by broken political promises and failed rebellion. The note of complaint, however, was heard alongside persistent calls to mould civil society in a more progressive shape.[5]

Sectarian strife seemed about to come to a head in 1825, following a couple of years of agrarian insurgency, prompting the British government to represent Ireland as in a state of particular crisis.

4 William Carleton, 'The poor scholar' in *Traits and stories of the Irish peasantry*, ed. Barbara Hayley (Gerrards Cross: Colin Smythe, 1990), vol. 2, p. 253.   **5** Claire Connolly, 'Irish Romanticism, 1800–1829', in Margaret Kelleher and Philip O'Leary (eds), *The Cambridge history of Irish literature* (Cambridge: Cambridge UP, forthcoming 2006).

1825: THE STATE OF THINGS

At this particular moment it seems that over the whole of Europe the old generations are expiring in the persons of their more august representatives; a solemn regeneration is taking place; the sacred heads of the masters of intellect and art are falling down on all sides. In Germany, Goethe, the last of his age, died, after seeing nearly all the poets born with him, or from him, pass away; a different era, an era of politics and social order is being inaugurated, and it is still seeking its men . . . May the continual disappearances, the mysterious blows which strike, as if by design, revered groups of geniuses in their zenith, the last chiefs of a movement that has done its work, have the force of religious warnings, bidding the new generation hasten and draw its ranks closer into the paths in which it is walking, and where soon it will be left to guide itself.[6]

Sainte-Beuve's proclamation of a changing of the guard amongst Europe's intellectual elite is linked to the death of Walter Scott. Scott was credited with inaugurating not only a new genre (the historical novel) but a new kind of historiography, exemplified in the work of Thierry, in which historical narrative was told as a set of stories and driven by close-up representations of character. For Thierry, the story of Ireland was crucial in a narrative of the history of imperialism, but for many Irish writers Scott's trajectory, with its focus on mourning and melancholy in the decline of 'Gaelic' culture, failed to do justice to the disjunctive experience of historical time in Ireland.[7]

There were several investigations into the state of Ireland published or undertaken in 1825. The Ordnance Survey began its project to map Ireland. There was a report of the Royal Commission established to investigate education in Ireland. The third and fourth reports from the Select Committee on the State of Ireland were published. Thomas Crofton Croker produced his influential *Fairy legends and traditions*

6 Charles Augustin Sainte-Beuve, 'Sir Walter Scott (1832)', in *Essays by Sainte-Beuve*, trans. Elizabeth Lee (London: Walter Scott, n.d.), pp 164–5. **7** These matters are treated at length in Katie Trumpener, *Bardic nationalism: the romantic novel and the British Empire* (Princeton: Princeton UP, 1997) and Joep Leerssen, *Remembrance and imagination: patterns in the historical and literary representation of Ireland in the nineteenth century* (Cork: Cork UP/Field Day, 1996). **8** See Gillian Doherty, *The Irish Ordnance Survey: history, culture and memory* (Dublin: Four Courts, 2004); *First report of the commissioners of education inquiry* (HMSO: 1825); *Second report from the select committee on the state of Ireland* (HMSO: 1825); *Third report from the select committee on the state of Ireland* (HMSO, 1825); Thomas Crofton Croker, *Fairy legends and traditions of the south of Ireland* (London: J. Murray, 1825–8); D. J. O'Donoghue, *Sir Walter Scott's tour in Ireland in 1825 now first fully described* (Glasgow: Gowans and Gray; Dublin: O'Donoghue and Co., 1905); Thomas Carlyle, *The life of Friedrich Schiller: comprehending an examination of his works* (London: Taylor and Hessey, 1825); Augustin Thierry, *Histoire de la conquête de l'Angleterre par les Normands de ses causes et de ses suites jusqu'a nos jours en Angleterre, en Ecosse, en Irlande, et sur le Continent* (Paris: Didot, pere et fils, 1825).

of the south of Ireland in 1825 and 1828. Meanwhile in Britain in 1825 Thomas Carlyle published his *Life of Schiller*, the first English biography of a major German writer, and in France Augustin Thierry brought out *Histoire de la conquête de l'Angleterre* (*History of the Conquest of England by the Normans, its causes, and its effects down to the present day, in England, Scotland, Ireland, and on the Continent*), which had an important influence on French and Irish attitudes to historiography.[8] Anna Doyle Wheeler and William Thompson published their *Appeal of one half the human race, women, against the pretensions of the other half, men, to retain them in political, and thence in civil and domestic slavery; in reply to a paragraph of Mr Mill's celebrated 'Argument on Government'*, although there is little in Wheeler and Thompson's pamphlet to signal their Irish origins, the impact of feminism on Irish cultural life was already beginning to be felt through the novels of Edgeworth and Owenson, and the activities of women in politics and philanthropy.[9]

In the summer of 1825 Sir Walter Scott came over to Ireland from Scotland for a holiday from 13 July to 17 August, visiting Belfast, Dublin, Limerick, Killarney, Kerry and Cork. Concurrent and perhaps coincidentally with the Ordnance Survey's project to map Ireland, 1825 saw a number of writers touring Ireland in search of material for books. I have already mentioned Crofton Croker's researches in the south of Ireland. Samuel Lover was travelling in the west, a journey which bore fruit in his *Legends and stories of Ireland* (1831). When Lover describes one native informant – an old boatman on Lough Corrib – as offering 'his "round, unvarnish'd tale"; and, by the way, in no very measured terms either, whenever his subject happened to touch upon the wrongs his country had sustained in her early wars against England' the nod is to Maria Edgeworth as well as to *Othello*.[10] As the first series of *Tales by the O'Hara family* was coming from the press John and Michael Banim began their researches on another book. In May 1825 John wrote to Michael from London: 'Your guess about Derry is right; and what you recommend is my own plan, long since chalked out. I will visit every necessary spot in the north and south.'[11] By the end of the month John was in the north and describing the 'uninterrupted interest' of his route from Belfast. When he returned to London he asked Michael to travel to the West, where Michael 'traced on the spot the localities connected with the last siege of Limerick'.[12] In the introductory letter to *The Boyne Water* (1826) the Banims write about the difficulties and at the same time the necessity of making some intervention into the living history of 'traditionary gossip and popular stories' and 'dispersing the mist' of prejudice.[13]

---

9 See Siobhán Kilfeather, 'Irish feminism', in Joe Cleary and Claire Connolly (eds), *The Cambridge companion to modern Irish culture* (Cambridge: Cambridge UP, 2005), pp 96–116. 10 Samuel Lover, *Legends and stories of Ireland* (London: Baldwin, Cradock, 1831; reprinted London: Richard Edward King, n.d.), p. 13. 11 Letter from John Banim to Michael Banim, quoted by Michael Banim in his preface to *The Boyne water: by the O'Hara family* (Dublin: James Duffy, 1865), p. iii. 12 Banim, *The Boyne water*, p. iv. 13 Banim, *The Boyne water*, pp xii–xiii.

IRISH LITERARY PRODUCTION

The Act of Union had seen the extension of the 1709 Copyright Act to Ireland and that extension effectively suppressed the Irish publishing industry over the first couple of decades of the nineteenth century. In 1825 there were no full-length novels published in Ireland (as far as I have been able to ascertain), but *British fiction, 1800–1829: a database of production, Circulation & Reception* lists seven novels published in London in 1825 with Irish authorship or content. Six of these were historical novels, and all were by men.[14] The 1820s saw a significant masculinization of novel writing in English.[15] Claire Connolly points out the tendency in literary histories to date the historical novel from this period and to discount the precedent of a number of historical novels by women in the first two decades of the nineteenth century, many of which addressed the recent events of the 1798 rebellion. In the late 1820s there was a revival of periodical publication in Ireland – though it was only in the 1830s that periodicals like the *Dublin University Magazine* and the *Dublin Penny Journal* began to occupy a certain cultural centrality. In the mid 1820s *The Rushlight*, the *Belfast Magazine and Literary Journal* and the *Literary and Mathematical Asylum* all had brief runs in Belfast. In Cork *Bolster's Quarterly Magazine* started in 1826 and the *Dublin and London Magazine* began publication in 1825. These periodicals produced a blend of articles of parochial interest with material that looked towards European enlightenment interest in science, folklore and historiography.

APOCALYPSE NOW

One political dimension to the millenarian influence on Irish aesthetics in the 1820s can be seen in the work of the artist, Francis Danby. Danby left Ireland in 1813 with James Arthur O'Connor and George Petrie, travelling to London where they failed to make the impact they desired. They started back to Ireland on foot but Danby stopped and settled in Bristol, where he produced landscapes and watercolours. In the late 1820s, following a domestic crisis, Danby moved on to Switzerland. During his time in Bristol two large paintings in oils, *The Upas, or Poison Tree, in the Island of Java* (1819) and *The Delivery of the Israelites* (1825) brought him some celebrity and led

---

14 John Banim and Michael Banim, *Tales, by the O'Hara family: containing 'Crohoore of the bill-hook', 'The Fetches', and 'John Doe'* (London: W. Simpkin and R. Marshall, 1825); Eyre Evans Crowe, *To-day in Ireland* (London: Charles Knight, 1825); Francis S. Higginson, *Manderville; or, the Hibernian chiliarch: a tale* (London: Thomas Dolby, 1825); Mac-Erin O'TARA [pseud.], *Thomas Fitz-Gerald the lord of Offaley: a romance of the sixteenth century* (London: A.K. Newman, 1825); James MacHenry, *The hearts of steel: an Irish historical tale of the last century.* (London: Wightman and Cramp, 1825); William Hamilton Maxwell, *O'Hara; or, 1798* (London: J. Andrews, 1825); John O'Driscol, *The Adventurers; or, Scenes in Ireland, in the reign of Elizabeth* (London: Longman, Hurst, Rees, Orme, Brown, and Green, 1825). 15 See Peter Garside, 'The English novel and the romantic era', in Peter Garside and Rainer Schöwerling (eds), *The English novel, 1770–1829: a bibliographic survey of prose fiction published in the British Isles, vol. II: 1800–1829* (Oxford: Oxford UP, 2000).

to his election as an associate of the Royal Academy. In 1828 Danby exhibited his *An Attempt to Illustrate the Opening of the Sixth Seal* at the British Institution, receiving from that body a prize of 200 guineas. The painting was purchased by William Beckford who encouraged Danby to work on further apocalyptic paintings. The central figures in *An Attempt to Illustrate the Opening of the Sixth Seal* are the collapsed tyrant and the newly emancipated slave shaking off his manacles. They are situated in a landscape strewn with corpses. For Danby the apocalypse is also a political revolution. By the early 1830s Beckford, himself a slave owner, had sold on the painting. For Beckford the apocalypse offered an occasion to imagine libertarianism, whereas Danby had taken it as an opportunity to represent liberation. Another scene strewn with corpses is that in *The Upas, or Poison Tree, in the Island of Java.* The legend of the upas tree, popularised by Erasmus Darwin in *The Loves of the Plants* (1789), was that the upas gave off a poisonous odour so intense that it killed all plant and animal life in its vicinity. The air in the vicinity of the upas was reputedly so dangerous that only prisoners already condemned to death could be persuaded to take a risk and gamble with the promise of freedom in return for making an attempt to harvest the tree's sap. In Danby's painting the landscape is that of the charnel house produced by many failed attempts. The upas tree is in allegorical opposition to the tree of liberty, which flourishes when it is watered by blood sacrifice. The upas tree is indifferent to the corpses at its feet. At one level the island of Java is the island of Ireland after 1798, scattered with the corpses of condemned criminals. The bleakness of Danby's vision is also part of a wider preoccupation in European romanticism, one that might be related both to the terror after the French revolution and to the influence (or, more accurately, effects) of Immanuel Kant on certain writers and artists.

MIRACLES

'Pastorini says that there will soon be a change, an' tis a good skame it'ill be to have him a sogarth when the fat livins will be walkin' back to their ould owners.'[16]

In his fictional *Memoirs of Captain Rock*, published in April 1824, Thomas Moore mischievously lists 'Pastorini's Prophecies, and the Miracles of Prince Hohenloe' amongst the works of 'Theology' as part of the 'course of study for ourselves' adopted by Catholics deprived of formal education.[17] Moore's list was confirmed the following year in Appendix 221 to the *First Report of the Commissioners of Education Inquiry* (1825): 'A List of books used in the various schools situated in the four following counties in Ireland; abstracted from the sworn Returns made to the Commissioners', those counties being Donegal, Kildare, Galway and Kerry. 'Pastorini's Prophecies' and 'Prince Hohenlohe's Prayer Book' both appear under 'Religious Works'.[18]

16 Carleton, 'The poor scholar', p. 261.   17 Thomas Moore, *Memoirs of Captain Rock,* p. 187.   18 This appendix is reprinted as an appendix to Antonia McManus, *The Irish hedge*

Alexander Leopold Franz Emmerich, prince of Hohenlohe-Valdenburg-Schillingsfurst (1794–1849) was a German Catholic priest and reputed miracle-worker. He was ordained in 1815, and in the following year he went to Rome, where he entered the society of the Fathers of the Sacred Heart. He acquired fame as a performer of miraculous cures. Pilgrims from various countries flocked to see him, and he also became noted for his distance-cures. On the tenth of every month he would pray for the sick and it became common for people seeking cures to perform novenas for the first nine days of a month and celebrate mass on the tenth. In 1821 Prince Hohenlohe moved to Vienna and then to Hungary, where he became canon at Grosswardein and in 1844 titular bishop of Sardica. He was particularly celebrated for his cures of nuns.

In 1823, Daniel Murray, newly appointed Roman Catholic Archbishop of Dublin, appeared to endorse the testimony of Mary Stuart, a nun in the Ranelagh Convent, that she had received a distance cure from Prince Hohenlohe.[19] These facts were sworn to before a Dublin magistrate. Of course sceptics were inclined to believe that a nervous illness was the product of depression and might rather easily be cured by attention and excitement. For many Catholics, however, the possibility of miraculous intervention in contemporary life offered an alternative to dominant enlightenment modes of scepticism and to the universalist politics which seemed to go hand in hand with the enlightenment. Miracles seemed to justify attachments to the local and particular. Murray's support was something of an anomaly. On the whole the Roman Catholic hierarchy distanced itself from miracles, prophecies, and in many cases from the Irish language and from local cultural expressions of faith. Niall Ó Ciosáin suggests that Pastorini's popularity was found suspect by the Catholic clergy because it was itself a tribute to the effectiveness of the policy of distributing Protestant bibles in the Irish language to Irish-speaking homes.[20] Pastorini's exercise in scriptural exegesis led ordinary Catholics to follow his argument in their own bibles. Thomas Moore, in *Memoirs of Captain Rock*, makes the case that the way in which the Catholic hierarchy set its face against bible reading – making a rejection of biblical readings in schools one of the key objections to the Society for Promoting the Education of the Poor in Ireland (from which the Church withdrew support after 1820) – drove hedgeschool teachers and other readers towards the more eccentric theology of Pastorini and Hohenlohe. Catholic witnesses before the parliamentary select committees on the state of Ireland were interrogated

school and its books, 1695–1831 (Dublin: Four Courts Press, 2004), pp 245–53. **19** Stuart had suffered with a nervous malady for four years. She learned that Prince Hohenlohe had designated 1 August as a day when all sufferers should pray solemnly for relief from their ills. Two priests and four nuns joined her in mass that day, and before the day was over she began to recover. Daniel Murray's pastoral, 'On the miraculous recovery of Sister Mary Stuart', appeared in the *Dublin Evening Post*, 19 August 1823. See Laurence M. Geary, 'Prince Hohenlohe, Signor Pastorini and miraculous healing in early nineteenth-century Ireland', in Elizabeth Malcolm and Greta Jones (eds), *Medicine, disease and the state in Ireland, 1650–1940* (Cork: Cork UP, 1999), pp 40–58. **20** Niall Ó Ciosáin, *Print and popular culture in Ireland, 1750–1850* (London: Palgrave Macmillan, 1997).

rigorously over prohecies and miracles – indeed a surprisingly high proportion of the evidence selected for publication in 1825 was on this theme. Most of these witnesses trod a line on which they at once argued that Roman Catholics were not as fool- ishly credulous as widely represented (Catholics did not believe in these miracles), and yet at the same time the witnesses suggested that the widespread circulation of miracle stories was a symptom of profound discontent (Catholics believed in these miracles because they had so little else to believe in):

> Can you state to the Committee, whether the prophecies that have circulated of Pastorini have produced any effect in the country with which you are acquainted? – The people laugh at them; nothing beyond that. The pastoral address of the Roman Catholic bishop of the diocese lately disabused them of any idea they might have had of their truth.

> What has been the opinion entertained with regard to the miracles in your country? – I think it has caused among the people a profound veneration for the Deity, to whom alone they attribute the working of miracles, not to men.
> They believe that those miracles have been performed? – There is a general belief, that, in certain cases, people have been restored.
> You believe that those miracles have been generally believed amongst the Roman Catholics in that part of Ireland? – They have.
> The miracles of Prince Hohenlohe? – They do not consider them the miracles of prince Hohenlohe or any man.[21]

One of Moore's strategies for countering propaganda about the credulity of Catholics is to talk about Protestant superstition – a tactic elaborated upon the following year by John Banim in *The Fetches*.[22]

SITUATING CROHOORE-NA-BILEOG/CROHOORE OF THE PAGES

> . . . short as was my absence from London, matters got into a pretty pickle with the printers before I came back. The labour of getting 'Crohoore'

21 *The evidence taken before the select committees of the Houses of Lords and Commons appointed in the sessions of 1824 and 1825, to inquire into the state of Ireland* (London: J. Murray, 1825), p. 4. 22 'That there was, in a conflict so long and so violent, the usual quantum of horrors, which bigotry on both sides is always sure to generate, cannot be denied; but how far those Depositions are worthy of belief, on which the heaviest charge of cruelty against the Catholics rest, may be judged from the following specimen of their rationality. It was deposed that the ghosts of the Protestants drowned by the rebels at Portadown Bridge were seen for a long time moving in various shapes upon the river, and Doctor Maxwell, bishop of Kilmore (one of the most credible, perhaps, of all deponents) enters into grave particulars about these ghosts in his depositions, and describes them as "sometimes having been seen, day and night, walking upon the river; sometimes brandishing their naked swords; sometimes singing psalms, and at other times shrieking in a most hideous and fearful manner." We see by this, too, that Protestant bishops can occasionally rival even Catholic ones in their deglutition of the miraculous': Thomas Moore, *Memoirs of Captain Rock*, pp 93–4.

through the ordeal has been hideous: almost every sheet of him came back to me three or four times. It is tremendous work to compel English types to shape themselves into Irish words. Happily he is now equipped for his début, as well as I can shape him.[23]

'Next, then, no books; no stewing of any kind; and, least of all, over the German fairy-tales – agreed also?'

'Also' repeated Tresham, 'though I scarcely know, Doctor Butler, what books you honour with that name.'[24]

The first series of *Tales by the O'Hara family* is a trilogy of novellas: *Crohoore of the bill-hook, The Fetches* and *John Doe.*[25] *Tales by the O'Hara family* comes out of the Scottish and Irish national tales pioneered by Maria Edgeworth, Sydney Owenson, John Galt and Walter Scott, by way of the framed novella cycle as developed in German by Weiland, Goethe, Hoffmann and Tieck, and inflected by the Grimm brothers' collection of folk and fairy tales.[26]

23 Patrick Joseph Murray, *The life of John Banim, the Irish novelist* (London: William Lay, 1857), pp 152–3; quoted in P.D. Garside, J.E. Belanger, and S.A. Ragaz, *British fiction, 1800–1829: a database of production, circulation & reception*, designer A.A. Mandal. Online internet 10 December 2004 <http://www.british-fiction.cf.ac.uk>. **24** Banim, 'The Fetches' in *Tales by the O'Hara family*, vol. 2, pp 269–70. **25** *Crohoore of the bill-hook* seems to have been written by Michael Banim, *The Fetches* by John Banim, and *John Doe* possibly by John Banim, although it may be a collaborative effort. Attribution to each brother of work by the Banims is unsettled; their decision to work collaboratively seems more interesting than the questions of individual authorship, particularly as it echoes the collaboration of the Grimm brothers, who so clearly influence aspects of the Banims. **26** The popularity of the German tale in the Anglophone world in the 1820s is indicated by a spate of translations: see *The devil's elixir. from the German of E.T.A. Hoffmann*, a translation of *Die elixiere des teufels* (Berlin, 1815–16) by Robert Pierce Gillies (Edinburgh: William Blackwood, and T. Cadell, London, 1824); Thomas Carlyle's translation, *German romance: specimens of its chief authors; with biographical and critical notices by the translator of Wilhelm Meister, and author of the Life of Schiller* appeared in London and Edinburgh in 1827; Friedrich Heinrich Karl, Baron de la Motte Fouqué (translator: Robert Pierce Gillies), *The magic ring: a romance* a translation of *Der Zauberring* (Edinburgh: Oliver & Boyd, 1825); *German stories: selected from the works of Hoffmann, de la Motte Fouqué, Pichler, Kruse, and others* (Edinburgh: William Blackwood, and T. Cadell, London, 1826). The Irish writer was working on his translation of Goethe's *Faust*, which appeared in installments between 1820 and 1835. The publication in 1823 of their fairy tales in an English translation by Edgar Taylor, with illustrations by George Cruickshank, is supposed to have influenced the Grimms to recast their collection less as a scholarly exercise and more as a book for family readership, and particularly for children. The Banims' publisher, Simpkin and Marshall, produced a number of translations from the German: Heinrich Zschokke, *The bravo of Venice: a romance*, translated from the German by M.G. Lewis (1818); Immanuel Kant, *Prolegomena to every future metaphysic, which can appear as a science* translated by John Richardson (1819); de la Motte Fouqué, *Undine, a romance translated from the German. By George Soane* (1818); de la Motte Fouqué, *Minstrel-Love; from the German of the author of Undine by George Soane* (1821); *Popular tales and romances of the*

Thomas Flanagan in 1959 observed that *Crohoore of the bill-hook* introduces 'a world for which neither the novels of Maria Edgeworth nor those of Lady Morgan have prepared us – the secret, strangely self-sufficient Gaelic world'.[27] This attention to Banim's privileged access to Catholic (and Gaelic) Ireland has tended to push critical writing on the Banims in the direction of attending to the brothers' realism and positioning them with Gerald Griffin and William Carleton as proto-Dickensian and proto-Victorian writers who are most modern when they describe the nuances of class conflict and least interesting when they deploy the tropes of the Gothic and the fantastic. For Flanagan it would seem that the O'Hara brothers, unlike Edgeworth's Thady Quirk or Owenson's Glorvina, are authentic native informants. It is their Catholicism more than anything else which seems to give them this authority. The Gaelic world of Crohoore is not, after all, self-sufficient, since the un-Gaelic law can and does intervene to collect tithes, and to arrest, prosecute and execute. Crohoore's intervention to save Pierce from the gallows depends on soliciting help from a Protestant member of the Irish parliament. But on the whole Flanagan is correct in identifying in the Banims some new narrative strategies for representing Irish character from within. These strategies are indebted to Edgeworth and Owenson; where they part company is that the Banims imagine the possibility of an Irish-speaking readership in a way that unbalances the translation acts characteristic of some of their precursors. Of course, Edgeworth and Owenson were interested in translation and thematized it in a number of ways – through unreliable narration, glossaries, antiquarian annotations, and references to the Irish as practiced translators. In the *Essay on Irish Bulls* (1802) Richard and Maria Edgeworth use trial scenes to demonstrate that translation in Ireland might well be a matter of life and death. One way of reading *Crohoore of the Bill-Hook* would be as a revision of *Castle Rackrent* in which language and narrative command are struggling in a very immediate way with murderous forces.

Michael Banim's *Crohoore of the Bill-Hook* (1825) opens at a wake, and most specifically with corpses: 'The mortal remains of old Tony Dooling and his wife, lay, the moment before interment, side by side, in the awful habiliments of the grave.' The epigraph to Volume 1 of *Tales by the O'Hara family* is from Terence's Latin play Adelphi (*c.*160bc) – *"'Quid? ille ubi est Milesius?" "What has become of the Milesian"'* – and these

---

northern nations (1823). Simpkin and Marshall were also the London publishers of the *Dublin University Magazine* from 1833. The *DUM* indicated a major engagement between Irish and German romanticism in the 1830s. As regards travel in the other direction, a checklist of fiction in the Corvey collection related to Ireland 1800–29 lists 114 items, of which 15 were quickly translated into German. See also *German popular stories: translated from the Kinder und haus Marchen*, collected by M. M. Grimm, from oral tradition (London: C. Baldwyn, 1823–6); Maria Tatar, 'Folklore and cultural identity', in David E. Wellbery (ed.), *A new history of German literature* (Cambridge: Harvard UP, 2004), pp 516–521 and Jacqueline Belanger, 'Some preliminary remarks on the production and reception of fiction relating to Ireland, 1800–1829', *Cardiff Corvey: reading the romantic text* 4 (May 2000). Online: Internet 20 October 2005): <http://www.cf.ac.uk/encap/corvey/articles/cc04_no2.html>
27 Thomas Flanagan, *The Irish novelists, 1800–1850* (New York: Columbia UP, 1959).

mortal remains, in the text's next sentence, seem to offer the first answer. From 1798 to 1848 the terrain of Irish fiction – and of Irish autobiography – is littered with corpses, intact and dismembered, before interment and disinterred, sometimes piled so deep one can hardly scramble over them to discover plot or understand characters. One commonplace account of the fiction of this period is that it is addressed to an English audience, and that the typical Irish novel attempts to lead its implied readers on an imaginary journey in which the problem of Ireland is described and (always necessarily imperfectly) explained. The imperfection of the explanation is the imperfection of language itself, given a particular emphasis by the way in which the pervasive trope of translation maps onto the landscape, the *terra incognita,* of Gaelic Ireland. Banim's epigraph – text and translation – is one indication of how he sees the job before him. There is a Shandean quality to the epigraph from Terence, since the Milesian in *Adelphi* is no Irishman (nor even a Milesian), but he is an inhabitant of an Athenian colony.

Crohoore of the billhook, the first of the *Tales by the O'Hara family* is something new in Irish fiction, but its novelty is deeply engaged with previous Irish fiction. There has been a tendency to see Michael Banim as 'correcting' earlier representations of the Irish peasantry by drawing on resources of knowledge and experience, and the Banims themselves play with notions of authenticity. One of Banim's earliest informed readers was the Irish Catholic novelist Gerald Griffin, then living in London, who admired Banim but suggested that the question of authenticity could be contested.

Griffin wrote to his brother William in 1825:

> Have you seen Banim's O'Hara Tales? If not, read them, and say what you think of them. I think them most vigorous and original things; overflowing with the very spirit of poetry, passion and painting. If you think otherwise, don't say so. My friend W— sends me word that they are *well written.* All our critics here say that they are *admirably* written; that nothing since Scott's first novels has equalled them. I differ entirely with W— in his idea of the fidelity of their delineations. He says they argue unacquaintance with the country; I think they are astonishing in nothing so much as in the power of creating an intense interest without stepping out of real life, and in the very easy and natural drama that is carried through them, as well as in the excellent tact which he shows, in seizing on all the points of national character which are capable of effect. Mind I don't speak of the fetches now. That is a romance. But is it not a splendid one?[28]

Griffin detects an implied difference here between what is 'well written' and what is 'easy and natural'. It is the Banims' selectivity as much as their realism, their 'excellent tact' which distinguishes the stories. The Banims' concept of authenticity is

---

28 Daniel Griffin, *Life of Gerald Griffin by his brother* (Dublin: James Duffy, 1874), p. 142.

much more theoretically sophisticated than has generally been credited. If the world of Maria Edgeworth and of Sydney Owenson/Lady Morgan does not prepare readers for the world of the Banims, it is not the case that Banim is writing without reference to his predecessors. On the contrary, *Crohoore of the Bill-hook* revisits aspects of *Castle Rackrent, The wild Irish girl,* and *Melmoth the wanderer* to engage with as much as to supplant their constructions of time and place. When Banim produced a preface to the James Duffy reissue of *The Croppy* in 1865 he commented on the difficulty of obtaining 'a reliable history of the rebellion of 1798'. *Crohoore of the Bill-hook* is indebted to William Godwin's *Caleb Williams* in that it poses questions as to the relaibility of earlier fictional representations in terms of describing 'things as they are' but it doesn't pose those questions in a naive or antagonistic way. It builds on Edgeworth, Owenson, and Maturin to produce a self-consciously Catholic critique that engages with rather than by-passes its predecessors.

In the first quarter of the nineteenth century three powerful Irish novelists emerged to dominate fictional representations of Ireland: Maria Edgeworth, Sydney Owenson and Charles Robert Maturin. *Crohoore of the bill-hook,* the first of the *Tales by the O'Hara family* is something new in Irish fiction, but its novelty is more deeply engaged with previous Irish novels than is generally acknowledged. One can trace significant debts to Owenson and Maturin, but the most significant influence is that of Edgeworth. Michael Banim's first novel reponds in a number of ways to incidents and themes in *Ennui, Ormond* and particularly *Castle Rackrent.* As in *Ennui* there is a 'changeling' baby. As in *Ormond* there is friendship based on fostering, and a tension as to where the Irish Catholic 'gentleman' can situate himself in relation to his compatriots. The relative influences of nature and nurture and a question mark over the essentially violent or at least unruly character of the Irish peasantry are preoccupations of both writers. Like *Castle Rackrent, Crohoore of the Bill-hook* is set in the period before the limited legislative independence of Grattan's parliament, and is thus a very particular kind of historical novel, the kind that can refer to the authority of living memory – *Sketches of Ireland sixty years ago* as J.E. Walsh called his 1847 anecdotal memoir. Its setting in the 1760s, during the Whiteboy agitation, recalls the obsessive historiography of *Captain Rock*:

> In the midst of all these transactions I came into the world, – on the very day (as my mother has often mentioned to me, making a sign of the cross on her breast at the very same time), when Father Sheehy, the good parish priest of Clogheen, was hanged at Clonmell on the testimony of a perjured witness, for a crime of which he was as innocent as the babe unborn. This execution of Father Sheehy was one of those coups d'etat of the Irish authorities, which they used to perfom at stated intervals, and which saved them the trouble of further atrocities for some time to come.[29]

29 Thomas Moore, *Memoirs of Captain Rock,* vol. 1, p. 155.

Castle Rackrent transformed the Irish novel by making servants speak out the secrets of their society and exposed its faultlines, just as Samuel Richardson's *Pamela* (1740) had done with the English novel. Edgeworth counterpoints Thady's narrative with a standard English editorial voice that tries – and largely fails – to explicate, even to translate, Ireland to its readers.

Something similar seems to be happening at first in *Crohoore of the Bill-hook*. The world of the Irish peasantry is not presented in the first person, as in *Castle Rackrent*, but with enough dialogue to make necessary frequent footnotes translating Irish phrases and explaining customs. Chapter 2 introduces Andrew Muldowney, the district piper:

> The insinuating servility of this man's voice, and the broad sychophancy of his grin, as he gave his salutation, '*Go dthogah diuyh uluig shey-an agus sunus duiv,**' bespoke his partly mendicant profession, and plainly told, at the same time, his determination to make himself agreeable and delightful in lieu of the shelter and good cheer of which he made no question.[30]

The asterisk directs the reader to a footnote: '*"God send luck and a plentiful Christmas to all in this place;" generally given shorter, but the piper will, as they say, "make a *croonawn* or song of it."' The footnote on Muldowney seems to say: 'here is a translation of the thing that is usually not said' and moreover has further recourse to Irish to explain it. *Croonawn*, 'an old song', [31] is close to Crohoore, and this is one of the ways in which the mysterious outlaw is made seem present throughout the text. Edgeworth, Owenson and Maturin had trained readers of Irish fiction to recognize footnotes as spaces for cultural translation. The borders of the page at once circumscribe their novels and draw attention to the open boundaries of history and fiction. Notes on Irish history, references to antiquarian sources, and glosses on Irish customs and beliefs suggested a textuality to Irish life that would be opaque to readers who were not equipped with knowledge of certain intertexts. In *Castle Rackrent* the two strands of annotation – the editorial footnotes, and the glossary – draw attention to Irish customs and 'idiomatic phrases' which 'could not be intelligible to the English reader without further explanation'.[32] Banim's footnotes work rather differently. They repeatedly reiterate the imperfection of translation. Banim is the first Irish writer in English to use free indirect discourse to represent the interiority of Irish-speaking characters, but in such a way as to suggest that the English translation gives only an outline, or silhouette, and that the relationship between a language and subjectivity can be understood only in its own terms. In the 1820s Louis Jacques Mande Daguerre and Nicéphore Niépce (who eventually became

---

30 John Banim and Michael Banim, *Tales, by the O'Hara family*, vol. 1, p. 15.   **31** Diarmaid Ó Muirithe, *A dictionary of Anglo-Irish: words and phrases from Gaelic in the English of Ireland* (Dublin: Four Courts, 1996).   **32** Jane Desmarais, Tim McLoughlin and Marilyn Butler (eds), *The novels and selected works of Maria Edgeworth* (London: Pickering and Chatto, 1999), vol. 1, p. 55.

partners) were working separately to capture and fix the images of the camera obscura. One might say of the Banims, deeply interested in questions of vision and visibility, that in their representations of Ireland, that they sought to replace caricatures of Irish characters with daguerrotypes.

There has been no modern scholarly edition of *Crohoore of the bill-hook*, but an initial comparison between the first edition and Michael Banim's revised edition in 1865 suggests very few changes to the text. One striking change, however, is to the title: 'Bill-Hook' loses its hyphen. That hyphen represents a fracture between Irish and English languages, Catholic and Protestant Ireland, enlightenment and counter-enlightenment attitudes to the miraculous and the supernatural. Although the tale is published as *Crohoore of the bill-hook* the character gains his celebrity and his power over the imagination of his townland under the name 'Crohoore-na-bilhogue'. The name is most strikingly inscribed in the text in Chapter 8, when Pierce and Andy capture a would-be assassin, who claims to have been sent by Crohoore. The man is locked in the cellar for the night, prior to being taken to Kilkenny jail. He escapes, leaving the name 'Crohoore-na-bilhogue' scrawled in blood on the cellar wall. The name resonates in interesting ways in both English and Irish. Samuel Johnson, in 1755, recorded two meanings for the word 'bill':

> **Bill** Beak
>
> In his bill,
>
> An olive leaf he brings, pacific sign! (Milton)
>
> **Bill** a two-edged axe

1. A kind of hatchet with a hooked point, used in country work, as a hedging bill; so-called from its resemblance in form to the beak of a bird of prey. 'Standing troops are servants armed, who use the lance and sword, as other servants do the sickle or the *bill*, at the command of those who entertain them (Temple).

2. A kind of weapon anciently carried by the foot; a battle axe.
   Yea, distaff women manage rusty *bills*;
   Against thy seat both young and old rebel. (Shakespeare)[33]

The tension here between war and peace is given a particularly Irish accent by the examples cited from Temple and Shakespeare, where it is Irish rebels who turn the billhook from an agricultural impliemnt into a weapon.

For the Irish resonances it is worth looking not only at Dineen's English for 'bileog' but also at the inflections it might take from words with which it assonates:

---

33 Samuel Johnson, *A dictionary of the English language* (London: W. Strahan, 1755); quotations from John Milton, *Paradise lost*, Book XI, lines 859–60; John Temple, *The Irish rebellion, true and impartial history* (1644); William Shakespeare, *Richard II*, Act 3, Scene 2, lines 118–9.

bile a sacred or historic tree; . . . *fig.* a scion, a progenitor; . . . a man of distinction

bile a welt; a border (of a shield); rim (of a vessel)

bileach covered with large trees

bilemhail tree-like

bileog, –oige, oga a leaf, a plant; . . . wood sorrel; . . . the 'leaf' or flat part of a table; a leaf of a book

bileogach, –aighe leafy; flaky, as snow

bille, – lí, a note; a bill

billéad, –éid, a billet; a note in writing; billeted; a children's game

billeog, –oige a bill-hook; a leaf.[34]

If the more respectable part of Clarrah suspects Crohoore of having murdered his adoptive parents with a billhook, turning back on them the instrument they had given him for labour, gratitude and self-improvement, the novella shows the creeping in of a wilder, more superstitous understanding of Crohoore, as a figure from the leaf of a book – the remarkably popular Freney, for example – or from older legend. Crohoore is not simply a figure from Irish books, however. Compared with Edgeworth, Maturin, and Owenson, the Banims' work at first seems almost naked of literary allusion, at a period when the presence of quotation and allusion in novels was of epidemic proportions. There are only three explicit quotations in *Crohoore of the bill-hook* – from William Cowper, from Walter Scott and a parody of Scott by Byron, and from an anonymous English ballad – but there are marked stylistic resemblances to Crofton Croker's *Fairy tales*. Crofton Croker's book makes newly visible in academic discourse and in print culture the kinds of knowledge and the belief systems that were part of Ireland's oral tradition. It necessarily involves acts of translation, from Irish to English, storytelling to print, local to general. He and the Banims had different kinds of access to oral tradition, the one scholarly and ethnographic, the other closer to lived experience.

Banim's story also resembles the fairy stories by Grimm, which influenced Crofton Croker, and also the fantastic tales of E.T.A. Hoffmann. Hoffmann's 'Das Fräulein von Scuderi' (1820) has a small, red-haired villain, Cardillac, whose twisted face seems to indicate his guilt, and who is apparently capable of appearing and disappearing at will, thus thwarting the Paris police force, who employ increasingly Draconian measures against what they suspect is a politically motivated secret society. In *Crohoore of the bill-hook*, the trial scene in which Pierce is found guilty and sentenced to die, poses questions not simply about the nature of law and justice in Ireland, but about the nature of literary evidence and of judgements in general.[35]

34 Patrick S. Dinneen, *Foclóir Gaedhilge agus Béarla/Irish-English dictionary* (Dublin: Irish Texts Society 1904), rev. & enl. 1927.   **35** One might elaborate with reference to the trial scene in Gerald Griffin's *The Collegians* (1829).

There has been an obvious temptation to see the difference of the Banims in terms of 'content' – their access to or insight into the *mentalité* of an emerging Catholic middle class. Willa Murphy has drawn on the work of D.A. Miller to argue that the obsession with secrecy in the work of the Banims is a particularly Irish, Catholic response to the emergence of a 'regulating narrative voice' and a 'panoptic mode of vision' in the nineteenth-century realist novel:

> Their narrative voice, like the Irish characters they write about, is split and slippery, unable to speak in an 'authentic Irish voice', because there isn't one. There is no heart, no core of identity, no authentic self in a country of supervised subjects driven into secrecy.[36]

It would be foolish not to build on Flanagan and Murphy's adumbrations of the ways in which the fact that the Bamins were Catholics – if not the first Irish Catholic novelists writing in English, then the first to make that identity their marker in the market-place – and that the subject matter of their novels signalled a marked shift in what the Irish novel would or could do. But it also worth emphasising that John Banim, in *The Fetches*, explores the terrors haunting the Protestant imagination.

PERSISTENCE OF VISION: 'THE FETCHES'

'I admit I am no casuist, Anna, and you will not therefore expect from me a very correct method; nor indeed, the good words you use with such ease to yourself; yet I can point out a particular passage. the object of the entire paper is to prove the re-appearance on earth of the dead; and history, biography, and anecdote, nay, scripture itself, are all quoted to support the now childish belief. But the essayist, having to get over one implausible common-place, namely, the rare occurrence, at present, of his supernatural visitations, has recourse to a theory of his own; he supposes' –

'that the visitation does not cease, although we are blind to it!' interrupted Anna, in a deep whisper, suddenly bending forward and taking her sister's arm – that they come and go, over and around us, and are with us, and present to us in our blindness! – that the air, and the shadows of the air, and the recesses, and the depths of place, teem with the busy and mysterious denizens of another world! – while to the eyes, made dim by the gross mind of our latter days, there has ceased to be given the seeing power of the days that are gone; though, if the primitive spirit could be reinstated within – and there is a way sister to bring that to pass – it would see, and hear, and understand, in a total

---

36 Willa Murphy, 'The subaltern can whisper: secrecy and solidarity in the fiction of John and Michael Banim', in Terence McDonough (ed.), *Was Ireland a colony? Economics, politics and culture in nineteenth-century Ireland* (Dublin: Irish Academic Press, 2005), pp 280–98, p. 281, p. 294; see also D.A. Miller, *The novel and the police* (Berkeley: University of California Press, 1988).

freedom from vulgar fear, and in the wonder of knowledge, only, such signs and whispers . . . as must redeem us out of the bondage of mere human speculation, and elevate man's soul, even while pent up in man's body, to the intelligence of angels.[37]

It is not hard to imagine why the events of 1798 might have reinvigorated a belief or at least a hope that death is not final. *The Fetches* is one of many European romantic novellas to draw on superstition and folklore for a reservoir of strategies by which to imagine possible relations between the living and the dead.[38] But memory is not the only way in which the living and the dead jostle up against one another in the 1820s. At either end of the decade Charles Robert Maturin and Jonah Barrington create extended prose works which demand that their readers look at the faces of the dead in a very direct and specific way.[39] From young John Melmoth's initial confrontation with his ancestor's portrait, looking into the face of the wanderer is a demand repeatedly made of characters in the novel. Such a gaze brings death or madness, because it forces the character in his or her notional present to recognise the undeadness of the dead, and to feel their pain. The past will not go away and leave people in peace. Since Melmoth's mission is to exchange places with a new victim of his curse, he necessarily poses as a doppelgänger in each of his encounters with putative victims. Jonah Barrington brings the Gothic crashing up against the conventions of realism by weaving it through his autobiography. He is one of many memoirists to recognize his own life as gothic. Like Maturin and many other Gothic writers Barrington is a comedian. His dead bodies engage in a macabre spectacle that has frequent notes of jubilation.

Although John Banim's *The Fetches* is very precisely situated in Kilkenny in the late 1750s, with descriptions of the town, the river, the college, and the local landscape, it is a Kilkenny out of Goethe, Hoffmann and Kleist.[40] Two young lovers, Anna and Tresham, are drawn together by an interest in (unnamed) German tales of the supernatural and by their philosophical debates on the possibility of life after death. He is a student, she is the daughter of his tutor. They read together, play music, and take gloomy twilight walks by the River Nore, frightening one another with ghost stories. Part of the narrative structure is indebted to Jane Austen's *Sense and sensibility* (1811). The romantic Anna, throbbing with sensibility, has a more sensible older sister, Maria, who confides her worries in her own lover, Mortimer, when he returns from military service in the American colonies:

37 John Banim and Michael Banim, *Tales by the O'Hara family*, vol. 2, pp 177–9. **38** In Irish romanticism 'the memory of the dead' has a very specific reference to the dead of 1798, through John Kells Ingram's ballad 'The Memory of the Dead' first published in *The Nation* (April 1843). **39** Charles Robert Maturin, *Melmoth the wanderer: a tale* (Edinburgh: Archibald Constable and Company; and Hurst, Robinson, and Co., London, 1820); Jonah Barrington, *Personal sketches of his own time* (Dublin: Ashfield Press, 1998). **40** It is possible to date the action so exactly because Mortimer has just returned from campaign with General Wolfe in North America.

'Oh! she dearly loves him; with all a pure girl's first love; and most, I believe, for the sake of his theories. I have seen them talk together of shades, and shadows, and of the world of shadows, until their voices sunk into whispers, and you could hear their hearts beating in the echo of the fear they had made contagious to one another.'[41]

The contagion of fear runs through the novella, and at first seems excessive. As in most romantic, fantastic tales the sinister atmosphere precedes and predicts subsequent events. Terrible things happen partly because the characters, and – more significantly – the reader, are expecting them to happen. It is, perhaps, worth being overly-literal at this point, and asking why *The Fetches* opens with such a degree of fatalism? Like many other Irish gothic and/or historical fictions, the pre-history of the narrative in *The Fetches* is sketched in by way of an allusion to Oliver Cromwell, and with the conceit that historical atrocities have an after-life in the places where they occurred. The action of *The Fetches* occurs when 'Ireland once more rested beneath the reflux of protestantism'. The 'reflux of protestantism' is a deeply strange phrase, of course, with its overtones of cauldrons, pressure and condensation, and signals some of the ways in which the tale will mix the vocabularies of natural science and traditional beliefs. Such 'hauntings' as that by Cromwell are the staple of the Gothic. In John Banim they take on a particular form, connected to issues of visibility.

The 'fetch' or 'döppelganger' is a very specific, very spectral manifestation of the supernatural. Tresham describes it in discussion with Anna:

'Tresham – that superstition of the Fetch, about which we spoke so much while approaching the house, interests me beyond expression. Let me hear more exactly the popular account you have received of it.'

'Thus, Anna. Of some person appointed to die, a double or counter-part becomes visible, before his or her death, at a time and place where the original could not by any possibility appear? Is this your Kilkenny creed?' –

'Exactly; with the addition that the Fetch or double must – to insure the death of the reality – be seen in the night, or evening.'[42]

In December 1824 Peter Mark Roget gave a paper to the Royal Society entitled 'Explanation of an optical deception in the appearance of the spokes of a wheel when seen through vertical apertures', published a few months later.[43] Roget's paper has often been identified by film theorists as the origin of an idea of the 'persistence of vision' although this interpretation of the essay has been contested.[44] The aspect of Roget's work relevant to *The Fetches* is his speculation that bright objects leave

41 John Banim and Michael Banim, *Tales by the O'Hara family*, vol. 2, pp 150–51. 42 Ibid., pp 160–6. 43 *Royal Society of London: philosophical transactions*, MDCCCXXV, Pt. I (London: Nicol, 1825), pp 131–40. 44 Joseph Anderson and Barbara Fisher, 'The myth of persistence of vision' in *Journal of the University Film Association* 30:4 (1978), 3–8; Joseph and Barbara Anderson, 'The myth of persistence of vision revisited' in *Journal of Film and Video*, 45:1 (1993), 3–12.

after images on the retina; and that when an image is fragmented (in Roget's case by looking at a wheel through slatted blinds) these after images can produce an optical illusion. The invention in 1825 of the thaumatrope, a parlour toy consisting of a rotating cardboard disc, with different images on each side, which – when spun – produced the illusion of movement, has been attributed to Roget, but more usually to an English doctor, John Ayrton Paris, who based his idea on work by the astronomer, William Herschel. These developments in 1825 were part of a larger set of experiments and theorisation around vision in the first quarter of the nineteenth century. There were both prototypes of early cameras and experiments in photography; developments in knowledge of the science of light; and new exhibition spaces – the diorama and the panorama – which demanded that the spectator take on board a way of viewing painting as historical narrative. The panorama was popular in Dublin, and in 1821 Marshalls' Moving Panorama of the wreck of *The Medusa*, accompanied by band music, was considerably more popular than Théodore Géricault's six-week exhibition of *The Raft of the Medusa* in the Rotunda.

It is not necessary to demonstrate that either John Banim, living in London, or Michael Banim, in Kilkenny, was aware of these developments in visual culture, any more than it is necessary to argue that the brothers were influenced by the completion of the first railway locomotive and the opening of the Stockton–Darlington railway line in 1825, to suggest that their fiction articulates a sense of subjectivity in time and motion that, for all its historical settings and preoccupation with traditional belief forms, engages with modernity in a very different way from the earlier novels of Edgeworth, Owenson and even Maturin.

Edgeworth and Owenson had long publishing careers, and their interests developed over time. It would be a mistake to suggest that they were not interested in modernity – in many ways Edgeworth's *Belinda* (1801), for example, engages with theories of vision in a quite *avant-garde* fashion through such scenes as the diagnosis carried out by Dr X. when he sees the shadow of lady Delacour projected on a wall and observes the throbbing of her ruff (she is costumed as Elizabeth I, but discussing her heroine, Mary Queen of Scots). This extraordinarily complex image is grounded in Edgeworth's own interest in the natural sciences, and the knowledge of both theory and practice she acquired in conversation with her father, Richard Lovell Edgeworth, and his friends in the Lunar Society, as well as her stay in Bristol with her sister and brother-in-law, Anna and Thomas Beddoes. Beddoes' experiences as a doctor and chemist are central to *Belinda*, as is his argument on the necessity of translating Kant into English. Luisa Calé reads Fuseli's Milton Gallery in terms of archaeologies of montage, through Sergei Eisenstein as a reader of G. E. Lessing. She produces a montage reading of the Milton Gallery informed by an exploration of eighteenth-century visual technologies and interest in the physiology of perception.[45] The Milton Gallery, other exhibition spaces, and a series of mechanical toys

45 Luisa Calé, 'Literature, montage, moving pictures: viewing Milton in 1800', a paper delivered at the University of Sussex English Graduate Colloquium on 12 May 2004. Calé is completing a book on *Henry Fuseli's Milton gallery: 'turning readers into spectators' in late*

exploiting the new theories of vision are central to the way in which Edgeworth represents urban space as the site of a troubled modernity, in which new subjectivities are invested in the denial of traditional forms of knowledge and belief. *The Fetches* illustrates a self-harming, suicidal, interiorisation of the forces of modernity as they were displaced – post-Act of Union – from public into private lives. This is a different version of different version of state terror than that narrated by Michael Banim in *Crohoore of the bill-hook*.

MEET JOHN DOE

In July 1825 Sir Walter Scott came to Ireland from 13 July to 17 August, visiting Belfast, Dublin, Limerick, Killarney, Kerry and Cork. After his return to Scotland he wrote to Joanna Baillie:

> I never saw a richer country, or, to speak my mind, a finer people; the worst of them is the bitter and envenomed dislike which they have to each other. Their factions have been so long envenomed, and they have such narrow ground to do their battle in, that they are like people fighting with daggers in a hogshead. This, however, is getting better, for as the Government temporises between the parties, and does not throw, as formerly, its whole weight into the Protestant scale, there is more appearance of things settling into concord and good order. The Protestants of the old school, the determined Orangemen, are a very fine race, but dangerous for the quiet of the country; they reminded me of the Spaniard in Mexico, and seemed still to walk among the Catholics with all the pride of the conquerors of the Boyne and the captors of Limerick. Their own belief is completely fixed that there are enough men in Down and Antrim to conquer all Ireland again; and when one considers the habitual authority they have exercised, their energetic and military character, and the singular way in which they are united and banded together, they may be right enough for what I know, for they have all one mind and one way of pursuing it. But the Catholic is holding up his head now in a different way from what they did in former days, though still with a touch of the savage about them . . . It is rare to see the Catholic rise above the position he is born in. The Protestant part of the country is as improved as many parts of England.[46]

Scott's image of the factionalism, claustrophobia and tension of Ireland in 1825 – 'like people fighting with daggers in a hogshead' – captures the mood of Irish writing in the 1820s and 1830s, an atmosphere in which dispute takes on pathological charac-

---

eighteenth-century London, in which she explores exhibition culture as a means of production, adaptation, and circulation for literary texts, and the role of practices of reading in constructing the experience of exhibitions.   **46** D.J. O'Donoghue, *Sir Walter Scott's tour in Ireland in 1825 now first fully described* (Dublin: O'Donoghue and Co., 1905), p. 74.

teristics. What justifies describing the writing of this period as pathological is the set of disjunctions between apparent causes and effects, and the excess of rage that is repeatedly released in these writings.

One might quote a number of examples of such pathological excess. In the overall histrionics of *Melmoth the wanderer* one can nevertheless isolate a particular set of disputes, including the madhouse scenes, and the tales of the Guzmanns and the Mortimers, in which contention escalates far out of the control of the protagonists. *Melmoth the Wanderer* pioneers the tropes of the glare and the howl, both of which indicate a horror beyond language; these tropes were repeatedly mined for effect in the Irish gothic of the nineteenth century.

Jonah Barrington's autobiography, *Personal sketches of his own time* (1827–32), is particularly interested in duelling as a symptom of a society in which the integrity of quarrels has replaced any call to other duties and ethics. Barrington makes the duel one of a number of practices which suggest that Ireland is a nation in which people repeatedly meet with their *doppelgängers*. E.T.A. Hoffmann's *Die Elixiere des Teufels* (Berlin, 1815–16), which introduced the German folkloric figure of the doppelgänger into the fantastic tale, was first translated into English in 1824 by Robert Pierce Gillies, and published in Edinburgh and London.[47] It is probably the German tale alluded to in *The Fetches*, which suggests that Irish folklore shares the superstition of the wraith, or double, who can be seen when someone's death is imminent.[48] Barrington repeatedly returns to the metaphoric resonance of two men facing one another, pistols raised, in a quarrel that is utterly pointless, and where quarrelling itself takes on an almost abstract quality. These duels echo other uncanny moments of self-division in the text, as in the peasant who accidentally decapitates himself.

The death of his own brother, William, in a duel, becomes the occasion for Barrington to develop a recurring motif of two young men mirroring each other, as they stand taking aim over some notional point of honour. And among his more haunting images from the rebellion is that of the priest whose body is severed by a portcullis and whose buttocks are eaten by Waddy, the terrified Protestant besieged in the old castle.

John Doe (later republished as *The Peep O'Day; or John Doe*) was praised by a reviewer for its representation of violence and low life in Ireland:

> Here is the finest description of an Irish row, at a pattern, or fair, that we have seen. Throughout the story, a perfect and profound knowledge of the Irish – the low Irish character, is evinced. As a bad specimen of that character, Jack Mullins is a master-piece. Altogether the painting is from nature – vivid, deep, and powerful, contrasting the most exquisite humour with the most thrilling pathos.[49]

47 E.T.A. Hoffmann, *The devil's elixir*, trans. Gillies. **48** John Banim and Michael Banim, *Tales by the O'Hara family*, vol. 2, p. 269. **49** *La belle assemblée*, 3rd ser., I (May 1825): 217–18.

"'Merciful God! What will become of us?'" is its theme.[50] Michael Banim, who attributes authorship of the tale to John, with the exception of the 'rout', wrote in 1865 that the original name was to have been Captain Rock, until Moore's book appeared. The final choice of John Doe, a named deployed if not invented by Blackstone to represent a plaintiff in an act of ejectment, resonates in terms of its status both as a victim of land abuse and as an everyman. In Banim's story the protagonists are eventually driven from Ireland and everything connected with them, bar the memory of their existence, erased. Scott identified the 'envenomed factions' and the 'narrow ground' of sectarianism as crowding the possibilities for imaginative literature or even realist representation. It is in this context that so many Catholic writers began to blend fantasy and realism in melodrama and sensation fiction, and so many Protestants turned to the Gothic.

For the Protestant writers of the *Dublin University Magazine,* Daniel O'Connell's speech introducing his first motion to Repeal the Act of Union on 29 April 1834, 'was devoted to the unhallowed purpose of raking from the tombs of the past, the crimes and horrors of the conquest, and evoking from the grave the unshrouded spectres of those dismal and blood-crimsoned times'.[51] One of the distinguishing features of Irish gothic is its interest in dismemberment. The discovery of a skull in a grave, as happens at the opening of Sheridan Le Fanu's *The house by the churchyard* (1863), is a favourite trope. Nineteenth-century Irish gothic engages with the generic dominance of realist fiction through a poetics of fragmentation. In the context of such atrocities as the 1798 rebellion and the famine, the 'morselization' of bodies is both ultra-realist as well as ultra-fantastic. In periodicals, particularly the *Dublin University Magazine* and the *Dublin Penny Journal* gothic texts were fragmented by serialisation and illustration and contaminated by contiguous political discourses. The Banim's blend of fantasy and realism involves an understanding of fragmentation that incorporates a sophisticated linguistic strategy for mis-representing the Irish language in deformed morsels, and challenges corporeal theories of identity.

50 John Banim and Michael Banim, *Tales by the O'Hara family,* vol. 2, p. 117.   **51** 'Emigration of the Protestants of Ireland' in *Dublin University Magazine,* 4:19 (July 1834), 8.

French connections in
Maria Edgeworth's *Ormond*

ARTHUR BROOMFIELD

In her novel, *Ormond*,[1] Maria Edgeworth's character Dora travels to Paris to enlist French support for the Irish cause. She is not the first to embark on such a mission. Unlike her predecessors Dora is seeking aid for Irish minds – those repressed, diverse voices that have been forced towards the isolation of the binarism of Catholic versus Protestant. This foreign aid may release the Irish mind from the predicament in which it finds itself. In *Ormond* Edgeworth attempted to write, a 'National Tale' which, according to Katie Trumpener, addresses questions of cultural distinctiveness, national policy and political separation.[2] However, the contradictions of Irish life, in its sharp religious divide, forbade the successful undertaking of a venture which, by definition, is a homogenous and unitary narrative. Edgeworth is not prepared to silence the strident or the contentious or to plaster over the chasm of religious division with bland ecumenism. This is one of the strengths of *Ormond*. If it is seen to challenge the credibility of the National Tale it may be because the National Tale is unable to handle the particularity of the Irish predicament. Edgeworth refuses to alter the practice to suit the theory. The real significance of *Ormond* may be read through its French connection – mainly that passage of the novel where its protagonists renew their vision through the language and culture of *légèreté*, when they are domiciled in Paris. Often dismissed as a frivolous interlude, an opportunity for the author to flesh out the alleged thinness of the Irish novel, the passage can also be read – through a post-structuralist approach – as the marginalized cornerstone that is capable of destabilizing the myth, assumptions and language of the entire project of the narrative.

This is not to ignore *Ormond's* efforts to imagine resolution at a local level. Whatever her extratextual writings may indicate, especially in relation to Spenser, in *Ormond* Edgeworth has no problem in seeing Protestantism as being comfortable with Irishness. The Protestant parliamentarian, Sir Ulick O'Shane, is a 'fine gallant off-hand looking Irishman'.[3] His speech is interspersed with terms like 'patriotic' and 'love of country'. Even the bigoted Presbyterian, Mrs M'Crule, identifies closely enough with Ireland to lament its inevitable ruination, should a particular ecumenical enterprise succeed at the local school. One can sense the author insisting on these voices' legitimacy and on their right to be heard as a distinctive identity, but from within, and relating to, the community/nation.

1 Maria Edgeworth, *Ormond* (Belfast: Appletree, 1992). **2** Katie Trumpener, *National character nationalist plots: national tale and historical novel in the age of Waverley, 1806–1830* (Princeton: Princeton UP, 1997), p. 133. **3** Maria Edgeworth, *Ormond*, p. 4.

Ormond's openness to heteroglossic theory can be read in chapter 22 of *Ormond*.[4] Mikhail Bakhtin's important – pre-post-structuralist – theoretical concept of heteroglossia identifies the multiplicity of social voices that are linked and interrelated, dialogically, within the novel, and is particularly applicable to sections of *Ormond*. An example of the dialogic exchange engages three of the voices that would make up Edgeworth's imagined nation, in what appears to be a discussion about the grazing rights of a cow. At issue is the word 'consent'. Representing the dispossessed Gael is Peggy Moriarty, whose cow is forcing her way through Sir Ulick's hedge, into his estate, in pursuit of grass. Sir Ulick, the patriotic voice who wants to make politics work, is in constructive negotiation with Peggy. They relate to each other. Marcus, his obdurate son, refuses to budge from the thinking of his planter ancestors. Marcus is marginalized because he refuses to renew the language. He insists on seeing *consent* as something to be withheld, not shared. The future, it seems, belongs to Peggy and Sir Ulick. Both renew the word consent after considerable vertical argument with their ancestral voices. Sir Ulick's porous hedge replaces the binarist estate wall. He consents to share his grass with the Gael, who consents to accept the rights and language of his ethnic class through her renewed interpretation of the word trespass (unthinkable though that would have been to her ancestors).

This passage successfully imagines a resolution to Ireland's problem only insofar as those who participate in the dialogue relate to each other and are there because they want to be there – even the neutered Marcus. But the significant absentee from the piece is the Catholic priest, Father Jos – who represents Edgeworth's greatest fear, Catholic domination and with it the marginalisation of the Protestant voice in Ireland.

Edgeworth's fear of Catholicism is suggestive of Bismarck's *Kulturkampf* of 1870s Germany. Its power base is located outside Ireland, and therefore it cannot be confined within or controlled by the geographical or constitutional boundaries envisaged by the National Tale. Unlike Marcus, Catholicism speaks a language that cannot be engaged with from within that discourse. Father Jos pronounces through speech that is deaf to others' responses. To him 'only one side . . . can be in the right'.[5] Because he abuses the position of the pulpit, from where he can avoid telling bothersome truths to his flock, his is a privileged voice, immune to interference from any possible parliamentary arrangement and so capable of undermining it. Father Jos speaks the language of authoritarianism. To him the ecumenical Father McCormuck has been 'making too free'[6] with the new Anglican parson, Dr Cambray. The key word in the lexicon of authoritarianism – into which he invests such import – is *faith*. 'I hope faith comes before reason', he admonishes King Corny.[7] The reasoned arguments of parliamentary debate will be poor opposition for the certitude of the faithful. Like Mr Ramsey in Virginia Woolf's *To The Lighthouse*, Father Jos's world works 'by abstract truths, sharp division and fixed essences'.[8] His ideology will be

---

4 Ibid., pp 163–6.   **5** Ibid., p. 111.   **6** Ibid., p. 112.   **7** Ibid., p. 113.   **8** Terry Eagleton, *Literary theory: an introduction* (Oxford: Blackwell, 1996), p. 164.

privileged over the truth even to the extent of restricting his own use of language. If faults lie on both sides of a quarrel '[i]n church quarrels it don't become a good Catholic to say that'.[9]

Edgeworth is faced with a problem particular to Ireland that did not, for example, confront Jane Austin. Nor does she evade it, as Sydney Owenson does in *The wild Irish girl*, by having her hero trade his religion for reconciliation and thus crucially, silence his Protestant voice. Edgeworth is insistent on a heteroglossic solution to Ireland's problem yet knows that the power of the faith factor, if heteroglossia is contained within the national boundary, is insurmountable. Her response suggests more a failure of the National Tale than a failure of heteroglossia. If the discourse is confined within the national boundaries it will be restricted to the language of binarism; socialism and heteroglossia in one country are prone to repression. Father Jos must be unimaginatively confronted from the polarity of a Protestant argument, or else submitted to. The possibilities of a heteroglossic solution to the Irish predicament may end at Calais but Edgeworth, in imagining a universal language that transcends national and linguistic boundaries, allows the radically different Parisian voice into the discourse. Her insistent resistance to repression, her contempt for imposed borders, allows her to precociously suggest a language that goes beyond analysis through heteroglossic theory.

The language of binarism is implicitly acknowledged in the marriage of Harry to Florence Annaly. But the marriage does not represent a resolution to the problem of religious division in Ireland. This is a homogenous union, conceded defensively, that excludes Protestants from a heteroglossic Ireland and essentially submits to the will of Father Jos. The honest Annalys, dispassionate and reserved, isolate themselves from the milieu of Irish life. By confining their social interaction to those of their own religion and class – the Misses Lardner and Durell – they reduce the possibilities of their language to petty gossip. Rather than revitalize it through dialogic exchange with the other voices of Ireland – as Sir Ulick demonstrates through colourful exchanges with King Corny,[10] they look to 'English travellers'[11] for accounts of Harry's exploits in Paris. The marriage represents the unsatisfactory preservation of a Protestant identity within the imagined Ireland of the National Tale. Harry and Florence withdraw into a language that has become 'inbred', and is sapped of its vitality. This retreat into itself can best be seen in an unconscious slip that is attributed to Dora, but that really represents beleaguered Protestantism. The slip intrudes on a discussion on Dora's upcoming marriage to White Connal. Harry, having saved her riding habit from spilled cream, is assailed by her contextually incongruous rebuttal – 'I'd rather manage my own affairs in my own way, if you'd let me Mr Ormond – if you'd leave me I can take care of myself my own way'.[12] This slip is really the voice of Protestant isolationism. It rejects Edgeworth's best efforts to construct, through the National Tale, a prescription for a heteroglossic Ireland.

9 Maria Edgeworth, *Ormond*, p. 111. **10** Ibid., p. 38–45. **11** Ibid., p. 242. **12** Ibid., p. 71.

Protestant primal fears force it to comply with the national malaise. It too will repress and reduce its vocabulary. It begs the Catholic voice to 'leave it' – clearly not a heteroglossic resolution to Ireland's problem.

Heteroglossia cannot survive in an Ireland where the faithful submit to Father Jos's logocentrism and where the dissenting voice withdraws to the periphery. It is not a situation that the author can allow to go uncontested. It is here that Father Jos comes to the rescue, for he emphasizes – ironically – the importance to Ireland of its links with the outside world. In a short – but key – passage of the novel he establishes the connection with France which will later introduce a new language to the discourse; a language that will subvert the binarist certitudes that control the language of Ireland. Father Jos has made his own of the language of absolutist France of Louis VIX. His coarse Hibernicization of the 'adict of Nantz' represents it locally as something positive rather than being the revocation of an order that had granted freedom of expression to the Huguenots. The 'Hug-e-knows' now have become the 'Hug-e-nots', if we are to follow the logic of Father Jos's revisionist French. Read from a post-structuralist position the passage highlights the role of intertextuality in the novel. The language of the passage – so astutely chosen by Edgeworth – comes from a previous centre of French culture, but has been renewed to represent the ideology of a burgeoning centre of culture in Ireland. The diachronic has become synchronic. One might here usefully recall Roland Barthes' gratitude to Julia Kristeva for shifting him away 'from a semiology of products to a semiotics of production'.[13] By importing language from outside the national boundary Father Jos creates a legitimate opportunity for Dora, Black Connal and Harry to respond in like manner. They introduce the frivolous language of pre-revolutionary Parisian society to the discourse – not as a counter but as a new voice, one that will disseminate the fixed essences of the entrenched Irish voices and that could never have emerged from within the Irish predicament as seen through *Ormond*.

That predicament is best seen through the marriage that should have taken place within a convincing National Tale – the marriage of Harry to Dora – but that cannot because of Edgeworth's fears. The union, symbolic of national unity within an autonomous Ireland, will necessitate Harry's move to the Black Islands, where the couple must contend with the hectoring interference of Father Jos – a kind of resident censor and disseminator of propaganda; a viceroy against whom Harry's voice would have little chance of survival. The ramifications of the union are imagined through King Corny's funeral. Harry, being the next-of-kin, is forced to be first to present his offering to an awesome display of clerical power – thirteen priests concelebrating the funeral mass. It is a predicament within which 'Ireland would be ruined',[14] if she were unable to release herself. The isolation of the Protestant voice will lead to the end of dialogic exchange and the attenuating of all voices.

Edgeworth's response to Ireland's predicament is, in all aspects, subversive, as one would expect from a writer who is wilfully so. Assumptions of the role of the

13 Julia Kristeva, *Revolution in poetic language* (New York: Columbia UP), 1984, pp 9–10.
14 Maria Edgeworth, *Ormond*, p. 175.

Catholic church in Irish society, of the possibilities of the National Tale, of the cultural origins and allegiances of the various Irish identities are all systematically subverted and deconstructed. However, it is her subversion of the traditionally assumed relationship between Ireland and France that is interesting from the perspective of this essay. After Spain, France has been, historically, the nation which (unsuccessfully) comes to rescue Ireland from its colonial oppressor; this is also the case in *Ormond*. But here the intervention is arguably successful. The colonizer is not Britain but Rome and it is the language not the land that has been colonized. The Irish seek liberation not by French arms but through the language of Paris. Removed from Ireland, Dora, Black Connal, Mademoiselle O'Faley and Harry are free to challenge the oppressive certitude of their language through the profusion of meanings that the same words have released in pre-revolutionary Paris. In post-structuralist terms the ground on which binarism has been built is displaced both actually and philosophically. The unnatural boundaries that limit meaning have been breached; the infinite possibilities of language are subtly uncovered.

The reality of the National Tale is not at all to Edgeworth's liking; sentimental ecumenism and polite neighbourliness mask the inevitability of segregation, parochial philistinism and dictatorial rule by the strongest voice. She consciously subverts the assumptions bound into the National Tale through international tales from the Parisian venture. Father Jos has theologised the word *faith:* he has made it the transcendental signified of national unity when he proclaims it to be above reason. But by defining it through the system of differences he is acknowledging *faith's* relationship to reason. *Faith* can only exist if it comes before, or subordinates reason. Reason is the excluded outside but is also the repressed inside. Therefore it is textually related to the marriage of Harry and Florence and to the Huguenots, all of whom are outside the myth of *faith*. *Faith* assigns a singular meaning to national identity and expects a common allegiance to it. Though the English Annalys and the French Huguenots exist outside the myth they live *inside* the national boundary. Thus they explode the idea of cultural distinctiveness, just as Father Jos does with political separateness (by being a representative of international Catholicism), both of which are intrinsic to the National Tale. Cultural distinctiveness, as enforced by Father Jos, will reduce language to the service of a given ideology – or rather his interpretation of it – as particularized in response to the Irish predicament.

Black Connal is a key protagonist in the deconstruction of the myth. Like his co-conspirators Dora and Mademoiselle O'Faley, he represents the ideal foundation blocks on which to build the National Tale. Catholic, of possible Old English stock that by now is accepted as Irish, and separated enough on class lines from his co-religionist wife, Dora, he 'proves' the unifying power of cultural identity. He has served in the Catholic Habsburg army and is an ideal officer, with the authority and status to implement culturally distinctive national policy in the politically separated Ireland of the National Tale. Alas, he has been corrupted by the intrusion of the voice of the repressed other, and thus he shares none of the singular zeal of Father Jos. Black is a kind of a fifth columnist, a trusted 'one of our own' who assaults the fable of the myth and the boundaries of its language – not from a Protestant or English position, which would still be from within the language of binarism, but from that of Paris, the libertine capital of Catholic Europe. The myth of the National Tale is built on an image of a serious community which is church-going and stable in – usually arranged – marriage. Parisian culture, however seems to get along well without these impediments. Harry does not have time to 'exclusively admire' the churches from the outside but is impressed by 'the fine façade of the Louvre':[15] and marriage, despite recurring infidelity, continues as a social norm. It is as if the interior of the word has been revolutionized while its outer form remains.

The authoritative interpretation in Ireland of the 'word' is challenged by that of Paris. Binarism is built on 'seriousness' – 'it is your national fault'[16] Black Connal accuses. But he displaces the ground beneath binarism – what Ireland wants is a certain degree of 'lightness' – rather than take sides in the Protestant-Catholic dialectic. *Lightness* however, is safely outside the discourse of Ireland, so it must be brought into association with the French *légèreté* – 'for which you have no English word', [17] a process which will renew and add to its meaning. Music and rhythm is part of the heterogeneous extra that surrounds the word. Even if *légèreté* is Hibernicised into the semantically meaningless *lay-ger-tay*, or *lay-gera-tay*, *lay-ger-ate-eh*, *lay-jer-a-tay* – or one of numerous other possibilities – it still exudes an indefinable fascination that the prosaic *lightness* cannot. It is the case, as Roland Barthes writes, that 'no thesis on the pleasure of the text is possible . . . and yet against and in spite of everything the text gives me bliss'.[18] It is this pleasurable excess over meaning that, when brought into association with *lightness,* puts the socio-symbolic representation of *lightness* under stress. Previously excluded from the socio-symbolic order of Ireland, lightness is now, because of the attraction that *légèreté* adds to it, moving towards social acceptability, towards displacing *seriousness*. The process may be understood in the light of the Kristevan term *negativity*. 'Negativity is the liquefying and dissolving agent that does not destroy but rather reactivates new organisations and in that sense, affirms'.[19] And it is this crucial challenge to the symbolic, by what it has rejected, that destabilizes, reactivates and affirms. Even if *légèreté*, to revert to the French, translates as *lightness*, Black Connal is still right when he says you have no English for it. This is because *lightness* has acquired a social status in Paris – *lightness* can no longer be dismissed by the socio-symbolic order of Ireland. The Parisian culture of floating relationships and cosmopolitan relativism is no longer exclusive to the narrow certitude of Ireland; the space that divides the two may be more symbolic than real: for it is also a link, a means of communication, between the two locations.

The indeterminate language that has created Parisian culture cannot be reduced to the weighty language of Ireland. When Dora *et al* go there they find the certitude of familiar language subverted. Since *légèreté* has added substance to *lightness* – insists that its presence within the word be recognised – it has radically altered the position

15 Ibid., p. 200.   16 Ibid., p. 103.   17 Ibid.   18 Roland Barthes, *The pleasure of the text* (New York: Hill and Wang, 1975), p. 34.   19 Kristeva, *Revolution in poetic language*, p. 109.

of lightness within the symbolic order. Being is no longer exclusively defined by seriousness. Edgeworth has transgressed logocentric absolutism by raising the rights of other possible interpretations of being and of the rights of such voices to be heard within the dominant discourse.

The word has been cleansed of corrosive grime and reactivated through the power of negativity. It is for this reason that Edgeworth relocates the language of Ireland in Paris. The exposure to the culture of *légèreté* is vital if its texture is to be made malleable. To be reorganized – like the Annalys and the Huguenots – *lightness* is linked though the system of differences with that which is privileged over it. But it can never become, or be reactivated through negative dialectic with its binary opposite. Rather its meaning must be changed through negativity, through engagement with the heterogeneous extra that 'works on moves through, and threatens it',[20] in other words, with what has been confidently rejected by the stable symbolic order of Ireland. Negativity, Kristeva claims, ultimately leads to a fading of negation: 'a surplus of negativity destroys the pairing of opposites and replaces opposition with an infinitesimal differentiation'.[21] Once *légèreté* infiltrates lightness it establishes the credibility of *lightness*. The surplus of negativity that has done this has destroyed the binarist pairing that safely excluded *lightness*. *Seriousness* has lost its supreme authority and is dragged into the debate where it is now merely another possibility in the system of differences.

Kristeva's insights on the dissolving and reactivating possibilities of negativity help the reader to understand what is going on in the Parisian interlude of *Ormond*; they help the reader to witness, in the writing of Maria Edgeworth, the process of the production of poetic language. Let us in the interests of brevity focus on one example, one word, from the text to illustrate the point: that word is *faith*.

Faith has already been proclaimed by Father Jos as the word which signifies God – the word of the social and linguistic order that Edgeworth delights in disrupting; likewise the intention to join battle with the sign of God's authority has been signalled by the *légèreté* passage of chapter 15. That battle takes places in chapters 27–30, or thereabouts – a section of the text which is located in Paris and often dismissed as an escape from the real business of the novel. Here *faith* is relieved of the social, historical and religious assumptions that identified it in the Irish context, and reduced it to a singular meaning, a single signified. It now must take its place in the system of differences, alongside the heretofore unmentionable *unfaithful*. Dragged from its pinnacle it soon loses its mystique: 'there is no mystery, no concealment'[22] (in infidelity in marriage), Mademoiselle O'Faley explains. In the capital of *légèreté*, *faith* is a matter of taste, and so a relative term. Faithful and unfaithful move freely in the salon. The unfaithful are very much in the majority and absolutism is consigned to the past. That Le Comte de Belle Chasse cannot be '*absolutely* irresistible' in libertine Paris is understood by Mademoiselle O'Faley. And even if the faithful are the distinctly uncool, 'frightfully dressed', or 'cold as any English',[23] they are still *inside*

20 Ibid., p. 81.   **21** Ibid., pp 124–5.   **22** Maria Edgeworth, *Ormond*, p. 204.   **23** Ibid., p.

the salon and *inside* the language. Importantly that salon scene is not a reversal of the faithful flock who inhabit Father Jos's church to the exclusion of all others. In the salon the faithful have a voice, even if it is – at the moment – unfashionable. What has been excluded is absolutism, not just that of Louis XIV, who represents it polit- ically, but the French precursors of Father Jos's language are 'banished [from] France'[24] through dissemination. Reference to Gayatri Spivak's explanation of dissemination as the seed that neither inseminates nor is recoverable by the Father, but is scattered abroad,[25] may help us better understand what is going on in this passage. Edgeworth is aware of the passions engendered by absolutist centres of culture when language is appropriated to serve the singularity of its cause. King Corny wouldn't give a farthing for a man that couldn't be in a passion on a 'proper occasion'.[26] But, as the passions that united the culture dissipate, meaning comes under attack. King Corny likes himself for being 'rasonably passionate' but, however, frequently repents. So, as the passion experienced by absolutist France in the moment of dissemination dissipates, the certitude of the language that accompanies it is chal- lenged and its meaning becomes engaged in the play of textuality between Ireland, where it is scattered, and Paris. Thus Father Jos's certitude fastens onto *Hug-o-nots* but the semen, the meaning, cannot impregnate Ireland's culture. It is now a bastard child of the *Hug-e-know* of Parisian language that has lurched along the endless chain of signifiers. So when the text of Ireland is engaged with the text of libertine Paris, as in *faith*, instead of reassurance in the absolute singular meaning of the father, it meets and is in turn disseminated within a play of endless meanings: instead of passion it meets a void where passion had been. Harry can now hope to pursue Dora – his former obsession – 'without feelings, without scruple'.[27]

If the text of this passage yields a reading that explodes the myth of the National Tale and disseminates the singularity of its language, if it represents an ideal of language liberated from ideology and from meaning, it may represent the semiotic in the Kristevan sense. But of course that semiotic is in crisis within the symbolic order. Just as the whole passage can be read as the gap that enlightens the narrative, the gap between *faith* that is before reason, and faith Parisian style, represents the crucible wherein poetic language is being forged; where meaning is transforming and reacti- vating. Dora in Paris cannot suddenly leap from valorized *faith* and stable marriage to the fecklessness of *à la carte faith*. Black Connal's advice, 'don't aim at correctness',[28] is attempted by Dora. Thwarted opportunity may have preserved her from infidelity with Harry; she rejoices in having the Compte 'in her chains'; she is numbered among those faithful to their husbands but not among the 'uncool'. She neither bends too low nor holds herself too high. Dora may struggle to rid herself of the hold of 'old' *faith* but her singular vision is illuminated by the salon 'blazing with lights, reflected on all sides'[29] and she still faints when she first meets Harry in Paris.

205. **24** Ibid., p. 111. **25** Gayatri Spivak, 'Preface', in Jacques Derrida, *Of Grammatology* (Baltimore: The Johns Hopkins UP, 1976), pp xiv–xv. **26** Maria Edgeworth, *Ormond*, p. 48. **27** Ibid., p. 203. **28** Ibid., p. 205. **29** Ibid., p. 201.

The representation of the symbolic order of Ireland exerts as powerful a pull in one direction as does the temptation to be unfaithful with Harry, in the other. Dora represents not hybridity but the stage where both senses of *faith* are of valid meaning and equal in their attraction; the absolutist *faith* of Ireland on the one hand opposed to *légèreté,* the *faith* of Parisian society on the other. Dora may be nostalgic for meaning but the pull of the liberated word is scarcely resistible. She is the crucible, the embodiment of *différance*, the disseminated seed moving through time, that can neither return to the father, nor impregnate an uncertain destination.

Could the accusation of hybridity be levelled against Edgeworth at the end of chapter 28? Is she here closing off the possibilities of a deconstructive reading and settling for a *stable* compromise to the predicament of Ireland? 'Riding was just coming into high fashion with the French ladies' and it was their ambition 'to ride on a side saddle'.[30] A horse and English side-saddle is procured for Dora who impresses all and sundry with her 'horsemanship'. The English decentred saddle could well unconsciously represent a resolution to the Franco-Irish dilemma – an agreed point between the certitude of the Irish logos and Parisian libertine ways. Her seat signals her rejection of the logos but also her intent to fight to change it from within. It may even suggest the freezing of the meaning of *faith* at a certain point in its struggle for renewal. This is not however the end of the matter. Hybridity may seem to imply an end to the task of deconstruction but it also inherently suggests, in Homi K. Bhabha's phrase, 'a third space'[31] where binary differences will be continuously broken down. We should recall that Edgeworth delights in how 'we like to see how strangers play with our language'[32] and this should distance us from falling for a static model of hybridity. In any case, to reach a compromise, to bring closure to the Irish predicament, seems out of character with the subversive drive that compels Edgeworth. She is a permanent revolutionary rather than a deal-fixer. Hybridity infers stasis. Rejecting it we should look for movement in the text: movement that suggests the continuous reactivating process taking place within the word *faith*. The language in this paragraph sparkles with movement: '[t]he spring was now appearing'; '[r]iding was just coming into high fashion'; Dora 'was ambitious to show her . . . horsemanship'.[33] It is clear from her seat on the horse that she is contemptuous towards the logos. But of equal significance the rolling action of the horse on which Dora is seated suggest the continuous movement or rolling over of meaning, of its formation, dissolution, re-formation – its infinite futile attempts to catch up with the present. Moreover it demonstrates, of course, the rejection of '*Faith* above reason' but also, of far greater significance, a subtly told understanding of dissemination. While Black, Mademoiselle O'Faley and Harry embrace *légèreté,* Dora is holding back, conscious that it is of the past.

In *Ormond* Maria Edgeworth acknowledges and then confronts the religious divide that is central to the problems of Ireland. By so doing she allows herself the

freedom to give names to the positions, to represent the passions of the moment, and
to then demolish their certitude. She permits what Julia Kristeva calls the 'completion of the thetic phase'.[34] This recognition in turn releases her creativity. She
imagines new possibilities for Ireland that must be explored through a language that
has been forged beyond its boundaries – language that contemptuously asks questions of Ireland's binarism. The French connection in *Ormond* is, to paraphrase
Adrienne Rich, the passage that asks the questions.[35] No doubt Edgeworth sees
Catholicism as an oppressive force and greatly fears its power. But the battle against
the myth and language through which that power is projected is not an end in itself
– this would deny her the earned status of subversive – but one more strategy in the
war against her constant quarry, fixed meaning. The narrative of Ormond makes a
valiant attempt to justify the National Tale: that it has survived for so long and been
accepted by so many is a tribute to Edgeworth's skills. And of course, the argument
for is never overthrown, just subverted. After all, most of the protagonists live happily
ever after. That subversion is at work through the novel, but is orchestrated from the
off-centre cornerstone of the Parisian venture. From here tension is exerted. Sleepers
like *légèreté* and *faith* are summoned to duty. They prove, not the supremacy of the
cornerstone – this would be merely binarist – but the inherent instability of the
structure of which they are already a part. Both are in flux, disseminated, in the
process of becoming, incessantly asking questions – deconstructing the language that
makes up the National Tale.

34 Kristeva, *Revolution in poetic language*, p. 63.   35 Adrienne Rich, 'Notes towards a
politics of location', in Julie Rivkin and Michael Ryan (eds), *Literary theory: an anthology*
(Oxford: Blackwell, 1998), p. 645.

'Raparees' or 'refugees'?: the normative image of involuntary displacement in nineteenth-century Irish literature

JASON KING

'What a fuss they're making all over the world about these "raparees", or refugees, or whatever they call them', remarks the Irish family matriarch, Jemima Dodd, in Charles Lever's novel *The Dodd family abroad* (1852). 'My notion', she adds, is 'that we who harbour them have the worst of the bargain', because 'we have our own [Irish] villains' and 'considering how plentiful the blackguards are at home, I think it's nothing but greediness in us to want to take Russian and Austrian ones' as well!'[1] Jemima's Dodd's confusion between 'raparees' and refugees is clearly intended for comic effect, but it brings into focus a variety of Continental European and Irish images of political exile and involuntary displacement that span a period from the Williamite conquest to the mid-Victorian era. Her conflation of 'raparees' and refugees, or Irish and Continental European political exiles also, points up an ideological contradiction at the heart of what Bernard Porter terms the 'refugee question' in mid-Victorian Britain: namely, that while London was 'the refugee capital of Europe after the revolutions of 1848 [where] exiles of every nationality congregated', were accorded remarkably 'generous treatment' and given refuge as proof of British liberty against Continental despotism,[2] at the very same time Irish political agitators and Young Ireland rebels were actively repressed after 1848 and driven into exile.[3]

1 Charles Lever, *The Dodd family abroad* (London, 1898 [1852]), vol. 1, p. 333. 2 Michael Marrus, *The unwanted: European refugees from the First World War to the Cold War* (Oxford, 1985), p. 15. 3 On the one hand, European political outcasts fleeing from despotic regimes were not only tolerated but publicly recognized as 'refugees' in mid-Victorian Britain, the beneficiaries of a durable, humane, and remarkably liberal British tradition of granting asylum that reached its apogee in the aftermath of the failed rebellions of 1848, when a host of exiles from across the European Continent found protection on English soil. According to Bernard Porter, 'the general image or stereotype which attached to [these] refugees . . . in the popular magazines and novels of the time' was 'especially sympathetic towards their causes'. There was 'very little sign', he adds 'that when Victorians thought of . . . political refugee[s], the picture which came to their minds was anything like that which Continental reactionaries would like to have placed there'. And yet, clearly the Victorian public did not extend the same sympathy towards 'the causes' espoused by displaced groups of Irish emigrants in the aftermath of the Irish rebellion of 1848, or regard Irish political agitators and Fenian sympathizers in the decades that followed as a refugee community. Nor did Irish emigrants and Italian refugees in mid-Victorian London always make common cause with one another, but rather tension simmered between them and occasionally broke out into

The question of whether these Irish and European 'raparees' and refugees were perceived to be engaged in similar national struggles or to represent fundamentally different social types in mid-Victorian Irish literature is the starting point for the discussion which follows.

More broadly speaking, I want to examine the social construction of the figure of the 'refugee', and the normative image of involuntary displacement, as it evolves and develops in the period between the late Romantic and mid-Victorian Irish novel, especially as reflected in the works of Charles Maturin, Lady Morgan, Charles Lever and Joseph Sheridan Le Fanu. My primary argument here is that the normative image of involuntary displacement and the very term 'refugee' itself was highly unstable and over-determined by its political and religious connotations in nineteenth-century Irish writing, because even as the emergent figure of the Continental European political refugee was becoming recognizable as a secular social type, it was already fore-shadowed by and failed to fully supersede the residual image and half-suppressed remembrances of its indigenous Irish equivalent, the dispossessed raparee of centuries earlier. More specifically, these political and religious connotations of the terms 'raparee' and 'refugee' appear to be in a state of flux in nineteenth-century Irish literature, encapsulating within their layers of meaning alternative historical experiences of religious persecution and political dispossession suffered first by Irish Catholics in the wake of the Williamite conquest in the late seventeenth-century – from which the term 'raparee' originates – as well as the arrival of Protestant French Huguenots in Ireland, including the forebears of the Maturin and Le Fanu families, who were fleeing Catholic persecution in Continental Europe. Indeed, it is only in 1796 that the very term 'refugee' itself acquired wider connotations than that of 'expelled French Protestants' to signify 'all such as leave their country in times of distress'.[4]

By contrast, the term 'raparee' is derived from seventeenth-century Gaelic roots, and signifies, according to the *Oxford English dictionary*, 'an Irish pikeman or irregular soldier, of the kind prominent during the war of 1688–92; hence, an Irish bandit, robber, freebooter' or 'recusant' or 'vagabond'. The term 'raparee' still had resonances, though, in nineteenth-century Irish literature, especially in Sydney Owenson or Lady Morgan's novel *The O'Briens and the O'Flahertys: a national tale* (1827). In her novel, Owenson invokes folk remembrances of the figure of the 'raparee' which she likens to 'smugglers' or 'other lawless persons' in the historical present of nineteenth-century Ireland, as 'the successors of the Raparees of Queen Ann's and George the

open hostility, culminating in the eruption of the Garibaldi riots of 1862. Nevertheless, there would appear to be a considerable degree of resemblance between these displaced communities of Irish and Continental European migrants as fellow 'refugee peoples' living alongside one another and engaged in similar national struggles to liberate their homelands from their respective 'imperial masters', whether it be Great Britain, Rome, Moscow or Vienna. See Bernard Porter, *The refugee question in mid-Victorian politics* (Cambridge, 1979), pp 80–1; and Sheridan Gilley, 'The Garibaldi riots of 1862', in *Historical Journal*, 5:16 (1973), 697–732. **4** Cited in Marrus, *The unwanted*, p. 8.

First's day'.[5] As Ina Ferris notes, the novel's protagonist, Murrough O'Brien, 'is brought to tears' after 'reading the final entry of the annals [of his ancestors] by the account of the brutal extermination during the reign of William of Orange of the outlaw Irish figures known as "raparees"', [6] who happen to prefigure and bear an uncanny resemblance to the character of his Gaelic foster-brother Shane, whom O'Brien 'has been remembering' in the historical present. Indeed, Murrough O'Brien's foster-brother Shane is explicitly described by Lady Morgan as the 'last specimen of the Raparees of the earlier part of the last century', because like them he too has 'the true Irish spirits, formed for every excitement, to madden into riotous gaiety, to sink into gloomy despondency'.[7]

This tension between the political and religious connotations of the terms raparee and refugee, as well as Irish Catholic and Protestant historical memories of religious persecution and political dispossession, would become predominantly registered in nineteenth-century Irish literature, I would suggest, in a gothic narrative mode, particularly as reflected in the literary works of Joseph Sheridan Le Fanu. In the short stories collected in his *Purcell papers* (1880), and especially 'Ultor De Lacy: a legend of Capercullen', [8] Le Fanu would deliberately juxtapose and over-layer these Irish Catholic and Protestant Huguenot historical memories of religious persecution and political dispossession and conflate both of their reminiscences of conquest and involuntary displacement into a singularly overdetermined and temporally blurred and fluid gothic narrative format. More to the point, it is my contention that these Irish Catholic and Huguenot historical memories of conquest and displacement appear purposely interwoven in Le Fanu's adaptation of the gothic convention of the unveiling of the ancestral familial portrait: one that bears a likeness not only of the progenitor of the protagonist's family line, but also attests to the perpetration of an ancestral act of violence, the repercussions of which can only be expiated by his descendants in the historical present. This convention of the unveiling of the ancestral familial portrait is prefigured in both Charles Maturin's gothic novel *Melmoth the wanderer* (1820)[9] as well as Lady Morgan's *The O'Briens and the O'Flahertys* (1827); but it is only in Le Fanu's short story 'Ultor De Lacy' that both Irish Catholic and Protestant historical memories of religious persecution and political dispossession appear mutually implicated in the shape of a gothic plotline, where they are conflated together into a seemingly singular, trans-historical experience of involuntary displacement.

Le Fanu's version of the Protestant Gothic thus features a particularly heightened form of 'political unconscious'[10] that is predicated upon his social position as a bene-

5 Lady Morgan, *The O'Briens and the O'Flahertys: a national tale* (London, 1988 [1827]), p. 57. 6 Cited in Ina Ferris, *The Romantic national tale and the question of Ireland* (Cambridge, 2002), p. 91. 7 Morgan, *The O'Briens and the O'Flahertys*, p. 253. 8 Joseph Sheridan Le Fanu's short story 'Ultor De Lacy' was first published in the *Dublin University Magazine*, 58:348 (December, 1861), 694–707. All quotations are taken from the *DUM*. 9 I am grateful to Dr Patrick Maume for suggesting this to me. 10 In *Heathcliff and the Great Hunger: studies in Irish culture* (London, 1995), Terry Eagleton discusses at length the idea of

ficiary of the Williamite conquest who nevertheless sympathizes and enters into an imaginative engagement with its victims in his writing. As Norman Vance remarks in *Irish literature since 1800*, Joseph Sheridan Le Fanu, 'like Charles Maturin, was of Huguenot stock, with an hereditary claim on folk-memories of Catholic persecution in Continental Europe'.[11] And yet, despite his Tory Unionist sympathies and public persona as a defender of conservative Protestant interests while editor of the *Dublin University Magazine*, Le Fanu 'concerned himself as a writer', notes W.J. McCormack, 'with the defeated heirs to the wars of William and James rather than with the wars themselves. His attention was always drawn', McCormack adds, 'to the displaced and exposed figures who' – like the raparees dispossessed by Le Fanu's own ancestors – 'become representatives of his own class and sect'[12] which are themselves threatened with dispossession and disestablishment as a result of the Tythe War, Repeal Campaign, and Land War over the course of Le Fanu's own lifetime. Le Fanu's short stories exhibit a highly complex form of historical imagination, in other words, whereby the collective angst suffered by his Protestant contemporaries appears mediated and sublimated into an objective historical correlative of Jacobite Ireland.

Through a process of elision of confessional and historical memories of persecution and dispossession, the figures of the 'raparee' and the 'refugee' thus become deliberately conflated in Le Fanu's fiction to heighten the sense of isolation and exposure which are integral aspects of his Gothic sensibility. Furthermore, in 'attributing to a [seventeenth or] eighteenth-century Catholic the anxieties of a nineteenth-century Protestant', notes McCormack,[13] Le Fanu collapses both communities' collective fears of persecution in order to create a pretext for crises and transgressions that had occurred in the distant past only to be re-enacted and expiated in the historical present, as one of the primary means for the resolution of narrative tension engendered in the development of his gothic plotlines. Yet, having said this, while it is one thing to claim that memories of 1685 and the Revocation of the Edict of Nantes were as important an imaginative stimulus for the Protestant Gothic as was 1690 and the battle of the Boyne in the Irish Catholic historical imagination, it is quite another to exemplify and provide detailed textual analysis of the specific ways in which these historical memories of persecution and dispossession actually influence and shape the unfolding narrative plotlines and content, or appear implicated in particular patterns of imagery, in the works of writers like Le Fanu.

I would like to propose a close reading, then, of Joseph Sheridan Le Fanu's short story 'Ultor De Lacy' (1861) which examines both its adaptation of the stock motifs of gothic fiction while also drawing upon his nephew Thomas Philip Le Fanu's *Memoir of the Le Fanu family* (1924)[14] in order to illustrate a biographically and historically specific inter-connection between his ancestral memories of persecution and

'Protestant Gothic [which] might be dubbed the political unconscious of Anglo-Irish society, the place where its fears and fantasies most definitely emerge' (p. 187). **11** Norman Vance, *Irish literature since 1800* (Edinburgh, 2002), p. 72. **12** W.J. McCormack, *Sheridan Le Fanu and Victorian Ireland* (Dublin, 1991), p. 83. **13** Ibid., p. 98. **14** Thomas Philip Le Fanu, *Memoir of the Le Fanu family* (Manchester, 1924).

dispossession and the ways in which they are implicated in the content and shape of his narrative's development. In fact, J.S. Le Fanu's nephew Thomas Philip Le Fanu himself felt an abiding interest in his Huguenot family heritage and was a distinguished scholar in his own right, contributing articles on the history of the Huguenot community in Ireland as well as prominent individual Huguenots such as Abraham Tessereau to the *Huguenot Society's Proceedings*,[15] in addition to compiling the *Memoir of the Le Fanu family*. In his *Memoir*, T.P. Le Fanu recalls a family 'tradition handed down' of religious persecution and flight from the depredations of Louis XIV in their native France, including anecdotes of encounters with French war vessels on the high seas which, he notes, are 'common to many Huguenot families';[16] but the *Memoir of the Le Fanu family* also records that the original forebear of the Le Fanu family in Ireland, namely, Charles Le Fanu de Cresserons – whom J.S. Le Fanu's chief protagonist in *Wylder's hand* (1864) is modelled upon – arrived in Ireland from France not only as a Huguenot refugee but also as a warrior directly in the service of William III. As Thomas Philip Le Fanu recounts in his *Memoir*:

> Charles Le Fanu de Cresserons was one of the numerous refugees who escaped immediately before or after the revocation to Holland . . . Joining the army of the Prince of Orange, he served during the Irish campaign as a captain in La Meloniere's regiment of foot . . . He fought at the battle of the Boyne in that regiment which was the first to ford the river at Oldbridge, and a portrait of William III, said to have been given to him by the King, is still in possession of the family. It is referred to as having belonged to him in the will of Joseph Sheridan Le Fanu, who died in 1873, but the story of its presentation is purely traditional.[17]

Whether or not the story is 'purely traditional' or apocryphal in origin, there can be no doubt that Joseph Sheridan Le Fanu was familiar with it because the idea of the presentation of the portrait at the moment of conquest is reproduced as the central, underlying motif in his short story 'Ultor De Lacy'. Like the 'white plump hand' in *The house by the church yard* (1863), or the 'spirit-monkey' in 'Green tea' (1872), the familial portrait of an ancestral conqueror functions metonymically as a disembodied icon – at once a supernatural agent and stock gothic device – that increasingly haunts the narrative's protagonist and precipitates a sense of crisis, whereas it is the discovery of its underlying significance which brings about a resolution of the narrative's fundamental conflict.

Sheridan Le Fanu was hardly the first writer, of course, to have conceived of this gothic premise of the narrative's plot 'matching characters to ancestral portraits or prophecies to fix their identities'[18] in relation to the perpetration of ancestral acts of

15 See T.P. Le Fanu, 'The Huguenot churches of Dublin and their ministers' in *Huguenot Society Proceedings*, 8:2 (1905); 'Archbishop Marsh and the discipline of the French Church of St Patrick's Dublin, 1694' in *Huguenot Society Proceedings*, 12:4 (1922). **16** T.P. Le Fanu, *Memoir*, p. 37. **17** Ibid., p. 28. **18** Katie Trumpener, *Bardic nationalism: the romantic novel*

transgression or violence committed in the distant past which can only be expiated by them in the historical present; for the very same premise lies behind the unfolding of the labyrinthine plotlines of Charles Maturin's gothic novel *Melmoth the wanderer* (1820). Accordingly, before I proceed to examine Le Fanu's short 'Ultor De Lacy' in more detail, I want to consider the evolution of this gothic narrative convention of the unveiling of the ancestral familial portrait as prefigured in the Irish novel in the earlier part of the nineteenth century.

In the case of *Melmoth the wanderer*, then, it is the protagonist John Melmoth's discovery of a portrait of his ancestor, 'Jno. Melmoth, anno 1646',[19] on his dying uncle's Wicklow estate that shifts the narrative into a gothic register and provides the first intimation of the transgressive figure of the Wanderer himself, 'a Faust [who] is a Mephistopheles at the same time'.[20] After he enters his uncle's closet:

> John's eyes were in a moment, and as if by magic, riveted on a portrait that hung on the wall, and appeared, even to his untaught eye, far superior to the tribe of family pictures that are left to moulder on the walls of a family mansion. It represented a man of middle age. There was nothing remarkable in the costume, or in the countenance, but *the eyes*, John felt, were such as one feels they wish they had never seen, and feels they can never forget.[21]

Furthermore, despite the fact that this ancestral portrait which captivates John Melmoth is over one hundred and fifty years old, it is no mere 'family picture', according to his uncle, but rather a supernatural image which bears an uncanny likeness of their demonic predecessor, Melmoth the Wanderer, whose countenance continues to haunt Old Melmoth as he lies 'dying of a fright' because 'the original is still alive'.[22] After the death of Old Melmoth, John Melmoth becomes similarly transfixed with terror when he too momentarily catches sight of the figure of the Wanderer and discovers 'in his face the living original of the portrait'.[23] Nevertheless, he carries out 'the injunction of his uncle to destroy the portrait'. Thus:

> he tore it from the frame with a cry half terrific, half triumphant . . . He expected to hear some fearful sounds, some unimaginable breathings of prophetic horror follow this act of sacrilege, for such he felt it, to tear the portrait of his ancestor from his native walls.[24]

Accordingly, John Melmoth's attempt at expiation here takes the form of a symbolic renunciation of his ancestry through the 'sacrilegious' destruction of the familial portrait of his own progenitor, in order to make amends for the ancestral family crime that it is deemed to represent.

and the British empire (Princeton, 1997), p. 152.   **19** Charles Maturin, *Melmoth the wanderer* (Oxford, 1989 [1820]), p. 18.   **20** Chris Baldick, 'Introduction' to *Melmoth the wanderer* (Oxford, 1989), p. xvi.   **21** Maturin, *Melmoth the wanderer*, pp 17–18.   **22** Ibid., pp 18–19. **23** Ibid., p. 20.   **24** Ibid., p. 60.

The motif of the unveiling of the ancestral familial portrait thus provides the cornerstone of the frame-tale in *Melmoth the wanderer* which links its numerous gothic subplots and diverse settings of nineteenth-century Ireland and counter-Reformation Spain together across wide swathes of space and time. The ancestral familial portrait of Melmoth the Wanderer also attests to the power of generational memory, not so much in the specific features it records as the sense of foreboding it engenders in those who behold it and then 'feel they can never forget': the portrait itself provides a presentiment of the Wanderer, in other words, which becomes indelibly marked in the mind of the protagonist, even after its physical likeness and 'wrinkled and torn canvas'[25] are consigned to the flames. Thus, long before John Melmoth learns of his ancestor's pact with the devil whereby he elongates his natural life span by one hundred and fifty years in exchange not only for his own soul but also his ultimately fruitless endeavours to convert the souls of others' to the devil's cause, the protagonist intimates the Wanderer's sinister past from beholding his lineaments and semblance in the portrait he destroys.

Furthermore, Terry Eagleton argues that it is not only the remembrances of the Wanderer but also those of his creator, Charles Maturin, whose sense of generational and historical memory informs the subject matter of his Gothic novel. As Eagleton notes, 'Maturin, like Le Fanu, came of Huguenot stock, and hailed from a history of religious persecution. The dungeon and locked chamber, the sequestered castle from which there is no escape, is for Maturin Ireland itself, a land thronged with the spectres of the past and haunted by the memory of ancient crimes.'[26] 'It is not hard to read this as a metaphor', Eagleton adds, 'of the original crime of forcible settlement and expulsion, which belongs to the period in which Melmoth's bargain with the devil takes place, or to see his preying upon the dispossessed as a nightmarish image of the relations between the Ascendancy and the people.'[27] Maturin's own historical memories of religious persecution and political dispossession, in other words, as well as his anxieties about the increasing clamour for Catholic Emancipation, and perceived threats to his own social position as an Anglican curate in the service of the Protestant Ascendancy, would appear to be sublimated and to find an outlet in his flourishes of gothic imagination. Whatever his anti-Catholic animus, however, the sheer convoluted structure and labyrinthine Gothic plotlines of *Melmoth the wanderer*, the spiritual instead of political nature of the Wanderer's 'aboriginal crime . . . in search or expiation';[28] and the very tenuous geographical and historical links the novel constructs in its variegated portrayals of displacement between seventeenth-century Spain and nineteenth-century Ireland – as exemplified, not least, in the unlikely flight of the dissident Catholic Monçada from the dungeons of the Inquisition to the coast of Wicklow: all function to obfuscate rather than illuminate the actual legacy of Huguenot flight and Protestant conquest which brought the Maturin family from Europe to Ireland in the first place.

By contrast, the portrayal of displacement and motif of the unveiling of the ances-

---

25 Ibid.   **26** Eagleton, *Heathcliff*, p. 189.   **27** Ibid., p. 190.   **28** Ibid.

tral familial portrait are explicitly invested with political overtones in Lady Morgan's novel *The O'Briens and the O'Flahertys*. In the final chapter of the second volume of the novel, entitled 'The Raparee', the protagonist Murrough O'Brien is momentarily overcome after reading in the 'Annals of St Grellan' which record his own family history a harrowing account of the Williamite conquest: especially the entry marked '1691. – King William's army plunder and murder the poore Irish at pleasure . . . so that they now began to turn raparees, hiding themselves in the bog-grass . . . and in the glens and crannies of . . . mountainses. And others of the better sort of papists, being driven out of the towne to go upon their keepinge, turn raparees, being forced to unquiet means'. Moreover, Morgan emphasizes the pathos rather than political implications of raparee displacement, noting that 'those who were then called "raparees," and executed as such, were, for the most part, poor harmless country people, that were daily killed in vast numbers, up and down the fields, or taken out of their beds and shot immediately'.[29] The figure of the raparee in *The O'Briens and the O'Flahertys* is thus divested of political agency and imagined as a type of internal exile involuntarily displaced by the spread of colonial terror, which only afterwards becomes invested with the stigma of banditry, outlawry, and recourse to 'unquiet means'.

In reading the Annals of St Grellan, Murrough O'Brien is deeply moved, however, not only by the antiquity but also the seeming *contemporaneity* of its portrayals of displacement. Although a committed republican, a member of the 'brotherhood of United Irishmen'[30] on eve of the uprising of 1798 when the novel is set, and a veritable successor of the Wild Geese as a refugee-warrior who has distinguished himself in the military service of the Catholic Hapsburg Austrian empire rather than remaining in his native land, Murrough O'Brien nevertheless experiences the shock of self-recognition and an unexpected sense of continuity upon his return when he discerns in the annals' portrait of a raparee the lineaments of his own family line. The motif of the unveiling of the ancestral familial portrait thus leads to a 'blurring of temporal boundaries'[31] in *The O'Briens and the O'Flahertys* between 'its graphic delineation [of] the wretched outlawed Irish gentleman, and the hound-hunted Irish peasant of Cromwell's time',[32] on the one hand, and Murrough O'Brien's presentiment of personal vulnerability as a descendant of this colonial legacy of raparee displacement in the historical present. Like John Melmoth in Maturin's novel, O'Brien is transfixed when he first discovers the portrait of his ancestor in the annals:

> Twice he passed his hand across his humid eyes . . . when, in the next page to the melancholy description that had so deeply affected him, he found its illustration, in the full-length drawing of

> A raparee
> Or wild Irishman,
> Of the 18th century.

29 Morgan, *The O'Briens*, pp 241–2.   **30** Ibid., p. 303.   **31** Ferris, *The Romantic national tale*, p. 91.   **32** Morgan, *The O'Briens*, pp 243–4.

It was evidently a portrait, being marked by all that truth, which a close copy of nature alone preserves. It represented a man in rude vigorous senility. The figure was gaunt, powerful, and athletic; but the countenance (the true phys- iognomy of the western or Spanish race of Irishmen), was worn, wan, and haggard, and full of that melancholy ferocity, and timid vigilance of look, which ever characterizes man, when hunted from civilized society; or when in his savage, unaccommodated state, ere he has been admitted to its protec- tion. A dark, deep, sunken eye, with the Irish glib, cumhal, and prohibited coolun, or long, black matted lock, hanging down on each side, added to the wild and weird air of a figure, still not divested of manly comeliness. The dress, if the garb so tattered could be called a dress, was singular. It was still worn at the time, by the natives of the isles of Arran: . . . the whole giving a most perfect picture of a *wild Irishman*, as he was called, and exhibited on the stage in his traditional dress and deplorable humiliation, from the time of Charles the Second almost to the present day.[33]

In beholding in this ancestral familial portrait 'a most perfect picture of a *wild Irishman*' – 'A raparee or wild Irishman, of the 18th century', singularly conflated with contemporary 'natives of the isles of Arran' – Murrough O'Brien experiences a presentiment of the past, an apprehension of the potential recrudescence of primor- dial acts of violence that threaten to recur unless the aftershocks of these ancient crimes be expiated in the historical present: no less intensely than John Melmoth in Maturin's text divines the curse of the Wanderer in the lineaments of a portrait that similarly transports him from 'the present day' to 'the time of Charles the Second'. Moreover, whereas the unveiling of the ancestral familial portrait of Melmoth the Wanderer presages his multiple acts of displacement between Ireland and Spain from the era of Charles II until the present day, the portrayal of the figure of the raparee in Morgan's text is inversely represented to impress an even earlier, sixteenth-century legacy of Spanish visitants into the recesses of Irish folk-memory, as manifested in 'the true physiognomy of the western or Spanish race of Irishmen'. Yet unlike the figure of the Wanderer who is the feared transgressor and hunter of souls, the raparee is 'hunted from civilized society' whose 'protection' he does not enjoy 'in his savage, unaccommodated state'.

More to the point, *The O'Briens and the O'Flahertys* differs fundamentally from *Melmoth the wanderer* in so far as the 'memory of ancient crimes' it recollects is polit- ically rather than spiritually inflected. Moreover, the portrait of the figure of the raparee elicits not just Murrough O'Brien's historical memory of the traumatic displacement of his ancestors but also his personal recollection of the public execu- tion of his foster-brother Shane, a native Gael, 'a genuine peasant',[34] and an 'Irish Caliban',[35] seven years beforehand for a crime that he did not commit. 'The recol- lection suffocated him with emotion', Morgan writes; 'he flung down the book, and

33 Ibid.   34 Ibid., p. 408.   35 Ibid., p. 525.

rose to change the subject of his thoughts'.[36] But once again, like John Melmoth before him, O'Brien begins to perceive that the ancestral familial portrait is no ordinary painting but invested with a preternatural significance:

> Doubting his senses, and as one spellbound, he stood fixed, gazed intensely, and breathed shortly, but spoke not – for before him, on the threshold of the door, stood the object of his melancholy reminiscence, the awful original of the fearful and affecting picture, which had curdled his blood even to look upon. It was indeed 'the raparee,' not as he had seen him in the prime of manhood, but the same in form, in dress, in attitude, as the vignette represented him, and in the half-crouching position, the habitual posture of vigilance and fear.[37]

Like in *Melmoth the wanderer*, the unveiling of the ancestral familial portrait in *The O'Briens and The O'Flahertys* seems a prelude to the actual appearance of 'the awful original of the fearful and affecting picture', but this 'classic gothic moment' is immediately foreclosed in Morgan's text, notes Ina Ferris, as 'the narrative goes on to naturalize the apparition'[38] and explain that Shane had escaped the hangman's noose only to become an internal exile living in the guise of a raparee of centuries earlier in a 'habitual posture of vigilance and fear'. As a vestigial raparee suffering internal exile at the end of the eighteenth century, Shane embodies 'the continuation a century later of a subculture of political outlaws and guerrilla fighters, based in the same hills and engaged in the same struggle, [which] makes it difficult to dismiss the chronicle's portrait of "the raparee, or wild Irishmen, of the 18th century" either as mythology or historical aberration'.[39] Unlike the republican hero and committed United Irishman Murrough O'Brien, in other words, his foster-brother Shane represents a residual image of involuntary displacement that appears not only co-extensive with the 'raparee or wild Irishman, of the 18th century' or 'hound-hunted Irish peasant of Cromwell's time', but also devoid of any form of historical or political consciousness beyond the blinkered perceptions of a perpetual fugitive.

Between the characters of Shane and Murrough O'Brien there is thus a doubling of the image of involuntary displacement: one that conflates internal and external types of exile, the figures of the raparee and the refugee they represent, and the residual confessional and emergent national forms of conflict they take flight from until the very face of displacement itself in the novel becomes one of an 'equivocal countenance'.[40] In recent discussions of *The O'Briens and the O'Flahertys*, Ina Ferris, Katie Trumpener, and Julia M. Wright have all noted the effects of temporal disruption that the interpolation of the Annals of St Grellan and appearance of Shane have on the shaping of different types historical consciousness that correspond with emergent and residual or 'inaugural' and 'antiquarian' forms of nationalism exhibited in

36 Ibid., p. 245. **37** Ibid. **38** Ferris, *The Romantic national tale*, p. 91. **39** Trumpener, *Bardic nationalism*, p. 153. **40** Morgan, *The O'Briens*, p. 506.

the novel:[41] but none of them fully consider the extent to which this temporal disjunction itself is specifically focalised through the figures of the 'raparee' and the refugee and the dichotomised forms of involuntary displacement they represent. Shane's internal exile and fugitive existence is inversely related, in other words, to Murrough O'Brien's more overtly politicized form of displacement and embrace of the republican ideals of revolutionary France, where he ultimately distinguishes himself in the service of Napoleon after taking flight from Ireland in 1798 in order to escape 'beyond the reach of persecution' as a would-be refugee.[42] Indeed, even as a youth, O'Brien enacts almost exactly in reverse the flight of the Huguenots, when he recalls being 'dragged by intolerance from my seagirt isles, and forced by that protestant Jesuitism, so similar in its means and ends to the system of Loyola, into a seminary of the established church, – kidnapped into protestantism, as my father had been before me, – witnessing the persecution . . . I escaped from the horrors which bewildered my young imagination, by playing the truant, and embarking on board a French vessel . . . work[ing] my passage to Bordeaux'.[43] As a victim of 'protestant Jesuitism' seeking liberty in revolutionary France, Murrough O'Brien explicitly inverts the historical image of Huguenot persecution and dispossession from which the very notion of the refugee originates.

The ancestral crime that the novel explores and the protagonist seeks to expiate is thus not simply one of colonial violence but confessional indoctrination as well. Murrough O'Brien, and the novel's heroine Beauvoin O'Flaherty both seek to escape the cloistered existence of a religious vocation where they would atone and become 'answerable for [their] fathers' sins',[44] very much in the same mould as Monçada in *Melmoth the wanderer,* but only the former are able to convert their 'expiatory offerings on the altars [their parents] had violated'[45] into more pragmatic and political forms of service to the would-be Irish nation. It is the act of displacement itself, in other words, that precipitates the mobilization and politicization of a form of national consciousness in the novel: but one that does not extend to the vestigial figure of the raparee, who remains entrapped within an anachronistic and feudal ideology of a 'barbarous people, checked in their natural progress towards civilization by a foreign government'[46] which he himself comes to emblematise. In the end, the unveiling of the ancestral familial portrait in *The O'Briens and the O'Flahertys* brings together the figures of the observer and the observed, the vestigial raparee and the would-be refugee, who between them disclose a panoply of images of exile from Ireland and move along a geographical and historical continuum of types of involuntary displacement: one which culminates in the flight of O'Brien from Ireland to

41 See Ferris, *The Romantic national tale,* pp 89–92; Trumpener, *Bardic nationalism,* pp 152–153; and Julia M. Wright, '"The nation begins to form": competing nationalisms in Morgan's *The O'Briens and the O'Flahertys*' in *ELH,* 66 (1999): 939–963. Julia Wright, in particular, argues that 'Morgan's protagonists in *The O'Briens* promote a [progressive or inaugural] brand of nationalism specific to the United Irishmen while devaluing and even mocking, the idealization of the Irish past' (p. 940). **42** Morgan, *The O'Briens,* p. 546. **43** Ibid., p. 301. **44** Ibid., p. 515. **45** Ibid., p. 519. **46** Ibid., p. 231.

seek refuge once again in Continental Europe, where his place of asylum itself now appears troubled by the spectre of authoritarianism in Napoleonic France.

If Morgan's novel politicises the unveiling of the ancestral portrait motif, however, and if 'Morgan's and Owenson's historical Gothics describe a political and historical repetition compulsion'[47] in their various portrayals of acts of displacement, then it is only in Josesph Sheridan Le Fanu's short story 'Ultor De Lacy' (1861) that these gothic narrative techniques would be self-consciously extended into an explicitly imperialist pattern of 'repetition compulsion' which is premised upon the culpability of his own family history and forebears in the conquest, religious persecution and political dispossession of Catholic and Gaelic Ireland. Moreover, unlike Maturin and Morgan for whom the motif of the unveiling of the ancestral familial portrait is but a stock convention of Gothic fiction, the presentation of the portrait of William III to Charles Le Fanu de Cresserons after the battle of the Boyne in 1690 consecrates a foundational moment in Le Fanu family history on the occasion of their first arrival on Irish shores. Thus, in Le Fanu's short story 'Ultor De Lacy', the narrative features a typical gothic plotline that centres on a family, which, like the Le Fanus', originated in France – albeit 'in the reign of Henry VIII' – but has been 'long naturalized in Ireland'.[48] In the first chapter, entitled 'The Jacobite Legacy' and set in 1705, the protagonist Ultor De Lacy is presented with 'a black box containing' a family portrait by his father as he lies dying, like Old Melmoth in Maturin's text, which 'constituted the most important legacy bequeathed to his only child by the ruined Jacobite'.[49] Ultor De Lacy himself follows in the footsteps of his father to become 'one of the few Irishmen implicated treasonably in that daring and romantic insurrection[,] the Rebellion of '45'.[50] Although hunted as a fugitive, Ultor De Lacy remains surreptitiously in Ireland to raise his two daughters in a ruined castle in 'the romantic glen of Capercullen near the point where the counties of Limerick, Clare, and Tipperary converge'.[51] A number of fantastic and supernatural incidents follow, and then the story concludes with the elopement of Ultor De Lacy's youngest daughter Una, who was engaged to another and destined to preserve the family line, with a supernatural apparition of an 'outlawed Irish soldier'[52] – a composite figure of a raparee, a member of the sidhe, and an incubus which has haunted the De Lacy family since the seventeenth century. More to the point, this apparition itself appears highly reminiscent of the 'wild and weird air' depicted in the portrait of the raparee in Morgan's text: its strange 'figure . . . being that of a tall, lean, ungainly man, dressed in a dingy suit, somewhat of the Spanish fashion, with a brown laced cloak and faded red stockings'.[53]

It is only in the final chapter of the story, however, that the significance of this apparition as well as the unveiled ancestral portrait is finally revealed 'in the plenitude of its sinister peculiarities'.[54] The narrative concludes with Ultor De Lacy's other daughter, Sister Agnes, examining his possessions after his death, when she comes

---

47 Trumpener, *Bardic nationalism*, p. 152.   48 'Ultor De Lacy', p. 694.   49 Ibid., p. 695.
50 Ibid.   51 Ibid., p. 694.   52 Ibid., p. 705.   53 Ibid., pp 701–2.   54 Ibid., p. 706.

across the family portrait that 'faithfully portrayed the phantom which lived with a vivid and horrible accuracy in her remembrance',[55] the very apparition of the raparee who stole away her sister. Furthermore, 'folded in the same box' as the family portrait 'was a brief narrative stating that':

> A.D. 1601, in the month of December, Walter de Lacy, of Cappercullen, made many prisoners at the ford of Ownhey, or Abington[56] of Irish and Spanish soldiers, flying from the great overthrow of the rebel powers at Kinsale, and among the number one Roderick O'Donnell ... who, claiming kinship through his mother to De Lacy, sued for his life with instant and miserable entreaty ... but was by De Lacy, through great zeal for the queen ... cruelly put to death. When he went to the tower top, where was the gallows, finding himself in extremity and no hope of mercy, he swore ... that he would devote himself thereafter to blast the greatness of the De Lacys, and never leave them till his work was done. He hath been seen often since, and always for that family perniciously, insomuch that it hath been the custom to show the young children of that lineage the picture of the said O'Donnell, in little, taken among his few valuables, to prevent their being misled by him unawares, so that he should not have his will, who by devilish wiles and hell-born cunning, hath steadfastly sought the ruin of that ancient house, and especially to leave that *stemma generosum* destitute of issue for the transmission of their pure blood and worshipful name.[57]

The revenant that haunts the De Lacy family is thus a representative of Catholic and Gaelic Ireland who prefigures the raparees displaced by Le Fanu's own ancestor Charles Le Fanu de Cresserons during the battle of the Boyne some ninety years later, just as Le Fanu substitutes the Oldbridge Ford for the very place of his childhood at Abington as the original site of an ancestral act of violence that brought his family to Ireland in the first place. The narrative's unfolding sense of crisis is only resolved, in other words, in typical gothic fashion, with the disclosure of an ancestral crime and transgression, the repercussions of which haunt the protagonists because it can only be expiated in the historical present. Indeed, the expiation of this ancestral act of violence can only be achieved in the narrative through the ultimate extermination of the conqueror's family line, even though Ultor De Lacy like Le Fanu himself is not personally but only genealogically implicated in the perpetration of this ancient crime. Le Fanu thus inverts the motif of the presentation of the family portrait at the moment of conquest so that it is the likeness of the vanquished rather than the victor that is handed down to subsequent generations, as a kind of talisman

---

55 Ibid.   56 'In 1823', writes W.J. McCormack, when Joseph Sheridan Le Fanu was nine years old, his father 'Thomas Le Fanu was appointed rector of Abington, a parish on the borders of counties Limerick and Tipperary, on the edge of the Slieve Felim Mountains . . . Abington, by all accounts, was a place to avoid in 1823' (*Sheridan Le Fanu and Victorian Ireland*, pp 18–19).   57 'Ultor De Lacy', p. 706.

to ward off and guard against supernatural visitations from 'the said O'Donnell', who would threaten 'the transmission' of his conqueror's 'pure blood and worshipful name'.

Yet behind the narrative's apprehension of elopement with the revenant of a raparee lie the much more contemporary anxieties of Ascendancy Protestants like Le Fanu about interbreeding with the oppressed and about the increasing politicisation of the masses of Roman Catholicism in Ireland, who might eventually 'blast the greatness' of the Protestant Irish nation not through the pollution of its bloodline or 'devilish wiles and hell-born cunning', but the more imminent means of Disestablishment and Repeal which haunted the Protestant political unconscious. The unveiling of the ancestral portrait in Le Fanu's narrative thus leads to a genealogical and fictional doubling of the ancestral and imaginary figures of Charles Le Fanu de Cresserons and Ultor De Lacy's ancestor Walter De Lacy, both of whom represent the perpetration of ancestral acts of violence as reflected in the obverse images of the victor and the vanquished engraved in the portraits they receive, whereby the visage of the Protestant conqueror William of Orange becomes conflated with the ghostly impression of a revenant of a raparee. These inverted images of William of Orange and the revenant of a raparee blend together into the likeness of one another, in other words, through the gothic convention of the unveiling of the ancestral portrait: but it is the defining experience of religious persecution and political dispossession that ultimately binds the respective legacies of the Le Fanu family of Huguenot refugees and the raparees they subjugated into a singular, highly complex, and historically over-determined image of involuntary displacement. Put another way, it is the recrudescence of the threat of persecution and dispossession initially suffered by Irish raparees that Le Fanu revisits as a source of gothic narrative tension that is projected in his short stories such as 'Ultor De Lacy' into the historical present of Ascendancy Ireland, which is itself threatened with a form of involuntary displacement already prefigured by the fate of those their forebears dispossessed. Thus, there is a highly complex historical imagination and political unconscious at work in Le Fanu's short story 'Ultor De Lacy' which becomes a meditation on the social position of exposed and isolated conservative Irish Protestants in the mid-Victorian period that is at the same time infused with a sense of Williamite guilt; but it is also a form of political unconscious that is specifically, thematically, and verifiably rooted in Le Fanu's own family history that brought his Huguenot refugee forebears to Ireland and into conflict with Irish Catholic raparees who they dispossessed.

If the image of the refugee was highly over-determined by its residual political and religious connotations in nineteenth-century Irish writing, and in Morgan's and Le Fanu's literary works in particular, however, then it must also be interpreted against the backdrop of the emergence of the secularised political exiles engaged in nationalist struggles across the European Continent after 1848. This was increasingly becoming the normative image of involuntary displacement in nineteenth-century Irish writing, against which the figure of the raparee had long since calcified into an archaic seventeenth-century mould of recusant aspirations and Jacobite revenge.

Thus, it is not the works of Lady Morgan or J.S. Le Fanu, which exist very much in a state of suspended animation between these two worlds, that one must turn to in order to trace the emergence of the secular nationalist revolutionary and political exile as normative images of involuntary displacement, but rather to the fiction of Charles Lever.

By way of conclusion, I want to offer a few points of comparison between Lady Morgan and Le Fanu's works, on the one hand, and Charles Lever's novel *The Dodd family abroad*, in order to sketch out more fully this normative image of involuntary displacement as it develops in nineteenth-century Irish writing, because in contrast with Morgan's national tale and Le Fanu's Gothic narrative constructions, Lever's *The Dodd family abroad* was the first Irish novel to feature the modern 'refugee' or secular political exile as not only an object of satire but a recognizable social type. Through its use of the epistolary form, or what Lever terms a 'story in letters',[58] *The Dodd family abroad* both foregrounds and invites the reader to make comparisons between different types of travel and a diverse array of traveller types, including Irish and Italian political discontents, as one of the most complex literary portrayals of human mobility in the Victorian period. Indeed, the novel brings together various elements of the aristocratic 'Grand Tour', the rise of recreational travel and the burgeoning popularity of institutionalized mass-tourism in the form of Cook's and Murray's tours (against which Lever would publicly fulminate in *Blackwood's* in 1865), as well as more involuntary forms of movement and political displacement, all of which circulate alongside the itinerant and frequently belligerent Dodd family as they make their way through Continental Europe. More to the point, *The Dodd Family abroad* also tacitly points up the ideological contradiction underpinning the refugee question in mid-Victorian Britain, by acknowledging the similarities between Young Ireland and Young Italy, that in spite of Great Britain's much lauded tradition of extending tolerance to European political exiles in the aftermath of 1848 as proof of British liberty, they actually appear to have a lot in common with their Irish counterparts.

For the most part, Lever treats both Irish and Continental European political exiles, such as the Polish refugee Kossuth, the Italian Mazzini, or the French Ledru-Rollin as objects of satire and figures of fun. For example, the novel's protagonist, Kenny James Dodd, remarks that: 'Whenever we have a grudge with a foreign state we should not begin to fit our fleets or armaments, but just send a steamer off to the nearest port with one of [these] refugees aboard. I'd keep Kossuth at Malta; . . . Ledru Rollin at Jersey; . . . and have Mazzini and some of the rest cruising about for any service they might be wanted on. In that way, we'd keep these Governments in order, and . . . be turning our vermin to a good account besides'.[59] Unlike most of his contemporaries, however, Lever's character also recognizes that the nationalist movements sweeping across Europe leading up to the 1848 rebellion have their equivalent in Ireland, and that those Irish political agitators who fled or were expelled after the

58 Lever, *The Dodd family abroad*, vol. 1, p. xvii. 59 Ibid. vol. 2, p. 245.

uprising are refugees themselves in all but name. Thus, he remarks from his vantage point in Italy that: 'These Italians . . . are very like the Irish', for between them 'there is the same blending of mirth and melancholy in the national temperament, the same imaginative cast of thought, the same hopefulness, and the same indolence'.[60] More to the point, the 'national temperament' of both 'peoples' have been similarly warped by the experience of colonization, he avows, because 'for centuries [they] have been subjected to every species of misrule'.

Finally, then, I would suggest that in at least recognizing the outward affinities and convergent interests between these discontented groups of Irish and Italian subject populations under the auspices of British and French or Austrian colonial rule, Charles Lever's novel *The Dodd family abroad* begins to expose the ideological contradiction at the heart of the 'refugee question' in mid-Victorian Britain, and that it is the exposure of this contradiction which provides the novel with one of its many sources of comic irony. By contrast, it is in the writing of Lady Morgan and Joseph Sheridan Le Fanu that one might begin to discern a narrative movement towards the resolution of this contradiction, in their repeated insistence that the disparate figures of the 'raparee' and the 'refugee', as well as the divergent histories of Catholic and Protestant religious persecution and political dispossession they figuratively represent, are in effect one and the same, brought together in a set of actual and fictional family portraits that attest to the likeness of Irish Catholic raparees and Protestant Huguenot refugees in a singular, historically over-determined image of involuntary displacement. Whatever the degree of resemblance, then, between the types of displacement experienced by Irish Protestants or Catholics in the distant past or the historical present, as reflected in the works of either Lady Morgan, Le Fanu or Lever, it is only by adopting a sweeping perspective that examines the outflow of the unwanted between both Ireland and Continental Europe that one can begin to trace the emergence of the normative image of involuntary displacement in nineteenth-century Irish writing as it was both constructed and contested.

60 Ibid., p. 387.

William Monsell: a Roman Catholic Francophile Anglo-Irishman

MATTHEW POTTER

William Monsell, first Baron Emly (1812–94), is a major figure in the history of County Limerick. Indeed, he is a significant figure in the history of Ireland, although his prominence has only recently begun to be acknowledged.[1] He was born into a wealthy Protestant landed family, whose principal residence was Tervoe House, near the village of Clarina, about five miles from Limerick city. He was reared in an atmosphere of devotion to the Union with Britain, loyalty to the Church of Ireland, and adherence to the Tory Party. He was educated in England, at the public school of Winchester (1826–30), and at Oriel College Oxford (1831–3). In 1836, he inherited the family estates from his grandfather. Monsell was a serious, conscientious, and just man. In 1850 he converted to Catholicism under the influence of his great friend and mentor, John Henry Newman (1801–90). This process of conversion occurred over a long period in the late 1840s, and coincided with a change in his political allegiance from Tory to Whig.

In the 1840s Monsell had flirted with Federalism and even Repeal; but from the early 1850s onward his religious and political views remained fairly fixed. He became a staunch Unionist, and broke with the Liberals over Home Rule in 1886; however he gave long and valuable service to the Liberal cause for many years, serving as the party's Liberal MP for County Limerick from 1847 to 1874. During this period he became one of Ireland's leading political figures. He served in several British administrations, under four prime ministers, between 1853 and 1873. He was Clerk of the Ordnance (1853–7), President of the Board of Health (1857), Paymaster-General and Vice-President of the Board of Trade (1866), Under-Secretary for the Colonies (1868–71) and Postmaster General (1871–3). He was a close friend of such prominent figures as Newman, Manning, Cullen and Gladstone. In 1874 he was raised to the peerage with the title Baron Emly of Tervoe. He is one of the most fascinating figures in the history of nineteenth-century Ireland; but what sets him aside from the bulk of Irish political figures over the past two centuries was his major engagement with the political, cultural, social and religious life of the Continent of Europe. To

---

1 The chief accounts of Monsell's life are Matthew Potter, *The life and times of William Monsell, 1st Baron Emly of Tervoe (1812–94)* (Limerick, 1994); Matthew Potter, 'A Catholic Unionist: the life and times of William Monsell, 1st Baron Emly of Tervoe (1812–94)' (PhD thesis, NUI Galway, 2001); and Dermot Roantree, 'William Monsell M.P. and the Catholic question in Victorian Britain and Ireland' (PhD thesis, University College Dublin, 1990).

understand his life fully it is first necessary to examine the three great strands of his political philosophy: patriotism, Unionism and Liberalism.

Monsell always considered himself Irish. On 1 March 1870, while addressing the House of Commons, he described himself as 'an Irishman'.[2] His public utterances throughout the 1850s, 60s and 70s are filled with references asserting that Ireland was a separate nation from England or Scotland; on 26 July 1867 he told the Commons that the Irish and the English were 'two distinct races'.[3] The best summary of his sense of nationhood is to be found in a remark of his close friend, David Moriarty, bishop of Kerry (1814–77). In 1868 the bishop told Gladstone that 'there does not breathe a purer patriot than Monsell, and what is rare in Irish patriotism, he is heart and soul attached to [the] British connexion'.[4] Linda Colley has described the development of the concept of a dual nationality between the years 1707 and 1837, when a British nation was constructed from the four component countries of the United Kingdom. She describes the half-century between 1776 and 1815 as 'one of the most formative periods in the making of the modern world and – not accidentally – in the forging of British identity'. There emerged 'a new unitary ruling class in place of those separate and specific landed establishments' that had existed in the four countries in the sixteenth and seventeenth centuries. However, the Scottish, Welsh and Anglo-Irish nobilities did not become absorbed into the English élite. Instead, according to Colley, they 'became British in a new and intensely profitable fashion, while remaining in their own minds and behaviour, Welsh or Scottish or Irish as well'.[5] Monsell subscribed to this dual nationality. On 2 January 1881, he wrote to Gavan Duffy: 'I think the entire union of hearts between the three kingdoms may be arrived at without the sacrifice of one grain of our national feeling'.[6] Any attempt to deny the authenticity of this claim infuriated him: in 1893 he angrily attacked Gladstone and his supporters for their 'monstrous' accusation, that of 'not loving our country' because 'we are Unionists'. Warming to the theme he continued:

> I confess I have a strong feeling on this subject – an intense feeling – I feel bitterly the accusation. I declare before God that from the time I first entered Parliament some fifty years ago my earnest desire was . . . to raise up my fellow countrymen that were then downtrodden and give them every advantage and every privilege that the citizens of the rest of the United Kingdom enjoy.[7]

In short, Monsell was a Unionist because he was an Irish patriot, not despite it.

The third strand in Monsell's ideology was his Liberalism. This term requires

2 *Hansard's Parliamentary Debates, Third Series*, 199.1023 (1 March 1870).   3 *Hansard*, 189.222 (26 July 1867).   4 Moriarty to Gladstone, 28 November 1868, in Gladstone Papers, British Library Add. MSS 44416.   5 Linda Colley, *Britons: forging the nation 1707–1837* (New Haven and London, 1992), pp 7, 13.   6 Emly to Duffy, 2 January 1881, Gavan Duffy Papers MS 800S/23, National Library of Ireland.   7 *A Roman Catholic Liberal peer on the Irish Home Rule bill: speech by Lord Emly* (Dublin, 1893).

some explication, as it meant a great deal more than being a member of a particular political party. Liberals believed that constitutions, laws and political proposals should promote individual liberty, based on the exercise of rational will. Government, they held, should be carried on with the consent of the governed, and be responsive to public opinion. The state's function was to create the conditions within which individual liberty could find its fullest expression. It was there to make laws, not to meddle in the economy, or direct people's lives. The state, they believed, is an institution established by rational individuals to deal with the public business of society in order that each person might be free to pursue his own concerns. Liberals believed in freedom of speech, of worship, of association, and of the press.[8]

Monsell worked throughout his career for civil and religious equality, and upheld the classic Liberal freedoms: speech, religion, and the freedom to engage in political activity. He gradually emerged as the unofficial leader of the Catholic Whigs, a sub-group of the Irish Liberal Party which combined Irish patriotism, Unionism and Liberalism in an interesting political experiment that lasted from 1847 to 1874.[9] The Catholic Whigs were moderate reformers, opposed to Toryism on the one hand and separatism on the other. They constituted one of the largest categories of Irish MPs in parliament throughout the 1850s and 60s, but were virtually obliterated in the home rule landslide at the 1874 general election. Monsell's chief policy interests were in education, and in advancing the civil and political rights of Roman Catholics. In this, he resembled his fellow Catholic Whigs.

As well as being a Catholic Liberal, Monsell was an adherent of the Liberal Catholic movement, which had arisen as an offshoot of Ultramontanism in both France and Germany. As Ward notes: 'In the hands of Lamennais, the Ultramontane movement was destined to undergo a violent change of direction, a change which opened the way for the movement of the Liberal Catholics'.[10] Hugues Félicité Robert de Lamennais (1782–1854) was one of the most significant figures in the Catholic revival of the nineteenth century. His aim was to 'baptise the revolution', to reconcile the teaching of political liberalism with the Roman Catholic Church, and thus to bridge one of the great ideological divides of the nineteenth century. The movement that he founded grew and prospered in the France of the July Monarchy (1830–48). During this period it was led by Lamennais' two chief disciples, Jean-Baptiste Henri Lacordaire (1802–61), and Charles Forbes René, Comte de Montalembert. Lacordaire was responsible for re-establishing the Dominican Order (to which he belonged) in France, and he electrified congregations in Notre Dame

8 For Liberalism see Harry K. Girvetz, *From wealth to welfare: the evolution of Liberalism* (Stanford, 1963) and William A. Orton, *The Liberal tradition: a study of the social and spiritual conditions of freedom* (New Haven, 1945).   **9** See David Thomas Horgan, 'The Irish Catholic Whigs in parliament, 1847–74' (PhD thesis, University of Minnesota, 1975).   **10** Wilfrid Ward, *William George Ward and the Catholic revival* (London, 1912), pp 101–2. For the Liberal Catholics see also Joseph Altholz, *The Liberal Catholic movement in England: the Rambler and its contributors 1848–62* (London, 1962), and Hugh A. MacDougall, *The Acton-Newman relations: the dilemma of Christian Liberalism* (New York, 1962).

de Paris with the eloquence of his preaching. Montalembert (1810–70) was a politician, publicist, historian and author. He was a member of the French parliament for
most of the period 1837–57, straddling the successive regimes of Louis-Philippe, the
Second Republic and the Second Empire. As France's leading Liberal Catholic political figure, he campaigned on two fronts: firstly, he tried to persuade liberals that
Catholics could be loyal to the Liberal political regimes that ruled France after 1830;
secondly, he sought to wean Catholics away from their attachment to the *ancien
régime*. Above all, 'he aimed also to train [the Catholics] to win their rights in and
through parliamentary processes'.[11]

The chief aim of the French Liberal Catholics was to obtain what they called 'free
education', that is, freedom for secondary education, which was under the strict
control of the *Université* (in effect, the Ministry for Education). In 1846, 140 deputies
supporting Catholic schools were elected to the French parliament, with
Montalembert as their leader. While the 1848 revolution at first seemed to doom
their efforts to failure, it eventually provided the occasion of their greatest victory.
On 20 December 1848, a leading Liberal Catholic and friend of Montalembert,
Frédéric Alfred, Comte de Falloux (1811–86) was appointed Minister for Public
Instruction; the hour for the establishment of 'free education' had come. The *Loi
Falloux* of March 1850 gave members of religious orders the right to open schools
without requiring any further qualification, and introduced councils with strong
clerical elements to control the *Université*. The restrictions on the total number of
pupils allowed to attend Catholic secondary schools were abolished. However, the
Université retained the monopoly of conferring degrees.[12]

This stunning victory was in some ways a pyrrhic one for the Liberal Catholics.
It led to a sharp split with the Ultramontanes, so that the French Catholics became
polarized into two increasingly hostile factions. Montalembert, Falloux and
Lacordaire continued to be the most prominent Liberal Catholics. They were joined
by Jacques Victor Albert, fourth duc de Broglie (1821–1901) who belonged to one of
France's greatest families and had a distinguished political career.[13] Among the French
bishops, the leading Liberal Catholic was Félix-Antoine-Philibert Dupanloup
(1802–78), bishop of Orléans (1849–78). *Le Correspondant* became their newspaper,
with Falloux and others at its head. At the same time, the Ultramontanes acquired
formidable leaders especially the fiery journalist Louis Veuillot (1813–83), editor of
L'Univers. The split between Ultramonanes and Liberal Catholics spread from France
to Germany, England, Ireland and indeed over much of the world.

The Liberal Catholic movement, which had much in common with the
Tractarian movement, had obvious attractions for Monsell and his fellow Oxford

---

11 J.C. Finlay, 'Charles Forbes René de Montalembert' in *New Catholic Encyclopaedia*, vol. 9
(New York, 1967), p. 1075. See also Margaret Oliphant, *Memoir of Count de Montalembert: a
recent chapter of French history* (2 vols, Edinburgh, 1872). 12 Alfred Cobban, *A history of
modern France, volume two: 1799–1871* (London, 1961), p. 154. 13 He was French ambassador
to London, 1871–2; minister for Foreign Affairs, 1873; deputy prime minister and minister
for the Interior, 1873–4; and prime minister and minister for Justice, 1877.

converts, the third earl of Dunraven, and the de Vere brothers. It appealed to them as Liberals, and as pragmatists; it provided them with an ideology, and a model of how a Catholic parliamentary body should operate. The chief difference between the Irish Liberal Catholics and the Irish Ultramontanes was that the former elevated their Liberalism to a principle, while the latter, operating in a parliamentary system, saw it as a necessary expedient.[14] Two other aspects of French and German Liberal Catholicism appealed to Monsell and his friends. Firstly, it was strongly Anglophile: both Johann Joseph Ignaz von Döllinger (1799–1890) and Montalembert idealized the English constitution and English culture. England was the nursery of parliamentary democracy, of intellectual freedom, of modern civilization; this strongly appealed to the English-educated Monsell. Secondly, the French Liberal Catholics had shown how a successful Catholic parliamentary agitation could win 'freedom of education', and throw off the domination of a non-Catholic state bureaucracy over Catholic schools. The parallels with Ireland, and the lessons to be drawn from this example, were obvious. It must be remembered that throughout his life Monsell's chief political interest was in the question of education – at primary, secondary and tertiary level.

Monsell soon became Ireland's leading Liberal Catholic. He favoured the Church's reconciling itself to parliamentary government, freedom of thought and worship, and religious toleration – all of which were core Liberal beliefs, but which did not find favour with Catholic conservatives who saw Church and state in Catholic countries as having a much more '*intégriste*' relationship. He believed that Christianity could survive and prosper only by embracing the modern world. He also wanted to reconcile religion and science. Besides the de Veres and Dunraven, the other principal Liberal Catholic in Ireland was Bishop Moriarty, who was a lone Liberal voice in the Irish hierarchy.[15] Such individuals were opposed to the Ultramontanism of the archbishop of Dublin, Cardinal Cullen (1803–78), and clashes between the two sides became frequent in the 1860s, especially over the vexed issue of Catholic education.

All of this demonstrates how very much an international figure Monsell was in his outlook. It is worth emphasizing how much Monsell's consciousness of being a citizen of the world was both strikingly modern, and not at all typical of his time and place. Irish politicians (with some notable exceptions) from the early nineteenth century to the present day, tended not to have a strong European sense of themselves and of their world. Their universe generally and increasingly consisted of Ireland, Britain and the United States – an anglophone world. Also, the class to which Monsell belonged, and specifically the Anglo-Irish élite, tended to become more isolated from Europe as the nineteenth century progressed. The previous age had been that of French cultural supremacy in Europe; it was also the era of the Grand

14 Roantree, 'William Monsell M.P.', pp 5–6, 169–70. For the Anglophilia of the French and German Liberal Catholics, see Matthias Buschkuhl, *Great Britain and the Holy See, 1746–1870* (Dublin 1982), pp 133–45. 15 See Kieran O'Shea, 'David Moriarty (1814–77)', in *Journal of the Kerry Archaeological and Historical Society*, 5 (1972), 86–102.

Tour and of great interest, on the part of Britain and Ireland, in European fashion in
art, architecture, costume and furniture. Then, the nineteenth century became the
age of England's 'complacent arrogance' and 'England, not Europe was the loser',
writes the prominent historian J.H. Plumb; he continues: 'the maintenance of
English ways, the insistence on the superiority of English ideas, led to a withdrawal
from European culture as a whole, and England in the nineteenth century developed
its art and its literature almost uninfluenced by foreign examples'.[16] Among the
Protestant Anglo-Irish this became even more marked: their disproportionately large
service in the British armed forces and their belief in British superiority were among
the factors that orientated their vision away from Europe, and towards the Empire.[17]
Similarly, the rising Catholic masses had strong ties with their emigrant kin in North
America, Britain and Australasia, but little contact with the mainland of Europe. The
Catholic religious orders, with their links to Rome and to the Continent, remained
the strongest link with the European mainland.

Monsell's world view, on the other hand, was more reminiscent of Ireland's in the
seventeenth and eighteenth centuries, when the Irish diaspora spread throughout
Europe, and links with Continental Catholicism were strong. His conversion to the
Catholic Church had made him a member of a world-wide organization (in contrast
to the anglo-centric Church of Ireland) while his wealth and connections enabled
him to travel widely on the Continent. The British nobility, despite the insular
tendencies already mentioned, 'formed part of a linked French-speaking aristoc-
racy'.[18] 'The polite of every country seems to have but one character', as a
mid-eighteenth-century Englishman put it. 'Like artists and intellectuals, but in
much greater numbers, they moved about Europe, in search of education, pleasure
and employment'.[19] Monsell was not only a Francophile, but a fluent French speaker;
his facility gave him the *entrée* into the entire cosmopolitan European and
Europeanised élite.

Three great world cities formed the capitals of Monsell's universe. Paris was, in
many ways, the centre of Western civilization in the nineteenth century; Monsell, like
so many others, succumbed to its charms. He visited it frequently and became a
familiar figure at one of the great salons of the time, that of Anne Sophia Swetchine
(1782–1857).[20] She was a Russian aristocrat, and a convert to Catholicism, who had
arrived in Paris in 1816 and made it her home in 1825. She resided in a mansion on
the Rue St Dominique, in the very fashionable Faubourg St Germain; there she

16 J.H. Plumb, *The first four Georges* (London, 1956), p. 35.   **17** See Michael McConville,
Ascendancy to oblivion: the story of the Anglo-Irish (London, 1986), pp 242–52.   **18** Philip
Magnus, *King Edward VII* (London, 1964), p. 97.   **19** Quoted in Jonathan Dewald, *The
European nobility, 1400–1800* (Cambridge, 1996), p. 3.   **20** The salon was a centre of
discussion on such topics as art, literature, politics and even religion. Of the three greatest
salons in Paris of the first half of the nineteenth century, one was hosted by a Frenchwoman,
Madame Recamier, and the other two by Russians, Princess de Lieven and Madame
Swetchine. See M.V. Woodgate, *Madame Swetchine (1782–1857)* (Dublin, 1948), p. 95. This
remains the best work in English on this enigmatic woman. See also 'Madame Swetchine
and her salon' in *The Month*, 1 (July-December 1864), 163–76.

hosted her salon for some thirty years until her death. It was claimed that '[in] religion, she was a strict Catholic and in philosophy Christian. In politics, she preferred a Liberal monarchy.'[21] It was not surprising, therefore, that while she welcomed all parties, Madame Swetchine's salon became a centre for the Liberal Catholics. Montalembert, Falloux, Lacordaire and Broglie were regular attenders, and Monsell met them all there. Around 1850, he first met Montalembert, and they became very close friends; he also befriended the other three. In addition, Monsell became a very warm friend of a number of prominent French clerics; these included Bishop Dupanloup and Cardinal Louis-Edouard-Désiré Pie, bishop of Poitiers (1815–80) as well as Cardinal Charles-Martial-Allemand Lavigerie (1825–92) who became archbishop of Algiers, and of Carthage, as well as primate of Africa. The intellectual brilliance of Monsell's French friends was notable: Montalembert, Falloux, Broglie and Dupanloup all became members of the French Academy.[22]

Rome was another city that Monsell grew to love; he often stayed there for months at a time. Indeed, his familiarity with Rome was such that he could casually remark in a letter to Newman, concerning a mutual acquaintance, that 'he does not speak French well enough to enjoy Roman society thoroughly'.[23] Also, he befriended the city's most prominent resident – a circumstance referred to by Aubrey de Vere at the time of Monsell's death: 'He was very intimate [with] Pius IX,' de Vere told a correspondent; the pope 'often sent for him, and had long private conversation with him, without any ceremony'.[24] The troubles of the pope and of the church were a matter of high priority for Monsell. He took a keen interest in Catholic affairs throughout the world. In 1860 and 1861 he spoke on a number of occasions in parliament, condemning the massacres of Christians in the Lebanon.[25] In 1863 he denounced Russian oppression of Catholic Poland.[26] Indeed one of his last sallies into public life was a letter to *The Times* concerning the slaughter of Catholics in Uganda in 1893.

The third great city with which Monsell was familiar was London; as a member of parliament, he was obliged to spend half of each year living there. The sittings of parliament commenced in late January or early February, and continued until late July or early August; sometimes there were additional sittings in October, November and December.[27] During his English sojourns, Monsell would meet his many friends there. These included Gladstone, successive dukes of Norfolk (particularly the fifteenth duke) and successive archbishops of Westminster: Nicholas Wiseman (1802–65), and Henry Edward Manning (1808–92).

21 'Madame Swetchine and her salon', p. 166. **22** Another giant of the Liberal Catholics, Johann Joseph Ignaz von Döllinger, also befriended Monsell. **23** Letter from Monsell to Newman, 16 March 1861, in *The letters and diaries of John Henry Newman*, vol. 19, ed. Charles Stephen Dessain (London, 1969) p. 484. **24** Aubrey de Vere to Robin O'Brien, 26 April 1894, De Vere Papers, Trinity College Dublin, MS. 5053–4, no. 276. **25** *Hansard*, 160.1479–86 (17 August 1860), 1583–6 (20 August 1860); 161.1229–31 (1 March 1861); 162.250–2 (22 March 1861). **26** *Hansard*, 170.1406–10 (24 July 1863). **27** Chris Cook and Brendan Keith, *British historical facts, 1830–1900* (London, 1975), p. 100.

During one of his frequent visits to France, Monsell (whose first wife had died in 1855) was introduced to a young French noblewoman, Marie Louise Ernestine Berthe de Montigny (1835–90). Her father, Philippe August Comte de Montigny-Boulanvilliers (1789–1866), was a noble of the *ancien régime* who had served in the Grand Armée and was decorated with the Legion d'Honneur. After a short courtship they were married on 23 February 1857, in Madame Swetchine's private chapel.[28] Monsell's second marriage was as happy as his first had been. Berthe was a pretty young woman, who quickly learned to speak English. On 5 March 1858 she gave birth to the long-awaited son and heir, Thomas William Gaston, later the second Lord Emly. A little girl, Mary Olivia, quickly followed, in 1859; both were born in France.

Berthe brought renewed joy into her husband's life. She was his equal in piety, and introduced the new devotion to our Lady of Lourdes into her Irish home. The apparitions at Lourdes occurred in 1858, and Berthe erected the first Lourdes grotto built in Ireland at Tervoe;[29] she also strengthened and deepened his attachment to France. When the Comte de Montigny died in 1866, his inheritance was shared between his three daughters (he had no son). In this way, Monsell came into an estate near the town of Montoire, in the Loire Valley, which had been the playground of the French kings and nobles for centuries. The estate featured the Chateau de Drouilly, which remained in the ownership of the Monsell family until the middle of the twentieth century; it was to be Monsell's second home for the rest of his life. Intermarriage between the Irish and French élites was uncommon at this time;[30] thus he had a fairly unique and intimate relationship with France and came to identify closely with the country. He was there in 1870, when the great crisis of the Franco-Prussian War broke upon the country. In 1880 he described himself, when addressing the House of Lords, as a French landlord.[31] His residence in Montoire also deepened his connections with French Liberal Catholicism. Bishop Dupanloup lived in Orléans, sixty-five miles away, while Falloux's residence in Angers was fifty miles from Montoire. Bishop Pie's diocese of Orléans also lay nearby, while Berthe's cousin was archbishop of the neighbouring diocese of Bourges. Above all, he gained a unique insight into the culture of another land. Montoire is in the département of Loire-et-Cher, and Monsell witnessed at first hand the apex and decline of the Second Empire (which enjoyed strong support there), as well as the battle between clericals and anti-clericals under the Third Republic, and the effects that economic depression in the 1870s and 1880s had on landlord-tenant relations there (they curiously parallelled contemporary developments in Ireland).

Monsell was also intimately involved in the Ultramontane-Liberal Catholic struggle on the mainland of Europe which climaxed in 1863 and 1864. In August 1863 a congress of Belgian Catholics was held at Malines, the seat of the Belgian

28 Monsell to Dunraven (1857), Dunraven Papers. D3196/F/10/No. 40. 29 Potter, 'A Catholic Unionist', p. 45. 30 Coincidentally, Monsell's friend and neighbour, Eyre Massey, third Baron Clarina (1798–1872) was married to Susan Elizabeth Barton (1810–86) of the Anglo-French wine producing dynasty, whose estates were divided between Ireland and France. 31 *Hansard*, 254.1866 (3 August 1880).

primate.[32] Montalembert delivered two very important speeches there. His first, 'A Free Church in a Free State', urged that the church should not be established, but that it should operate freely and without state support. His second, 'Liberty of Conscience,' rejected religious intolerance in principle, and condemned persecution in all its forms. The importance of this exposition of Liberal Catholic political ideology by Montalembert was that it was an articulation of the same position as that held by both Newman and Monsell. The question of religious intolerance in Spain came before parliament, and Monsell asked Newman's advice on the matter. Newman wrote back, and took his stand on practical grounds, stating that 'the question is not so much an ecclesiastical one, or a political or legal or constitutional one in Spain, but a social one'. The tide of public opinion was the determining factor, and 'the Spanish laws are Anti-protestant [*sic*], because the people is such . . . the Spanish government is more liberal than the people, just as our ministries have been more liberal, and our representatives, than the constituency'. He promoted religious toleration on pragmatic grounds 'as, a fact, persecution does not answer. It does [*sic*] against men's feelings; the feelings of the age are as strongly against it as they were once for it. The age is such, that we must go by reason, not by force'. He fully accepted Montalembert's thesis: 'I am not at all sure that it would not be better for the Catholic religion every where [*sic*], if it had no very different status from that which it has in England.'[33] Monsell echoed these sentiments in his speech on Spain to the Commons on 17 July; he stated that the issue was not a religious one, but rather 'simply a political and social one'. He believed that the policy of the Spanish government, like that of Britain, was determined by public opinion. The Catholic Church in Ireland, he said, 'had no privileges, she had liberty. This was the source of her vigour, and of that zeal and energy which made her victorious over all her assailants'. He concluded by stating that privilege 'often palsied' the church, and that its triumph would be brought about in an atmosphere of religious liberty for all. This speech met with a very favourable reaction in parliament.[34]

It was not, however, Westminster's good opinion that was uppermost in Monsell's mind. The leading Ultramontane, William George Ward (1812–82), coupled Montalembert's Malines addresses and Monsell's speech to the Commons in a fiercely critical pamphlet which he published soon after.[35] By January 1864 Monsell was seriously alarmed by denunciations in Rome of Montalembert's Malines speeches. He wrote to Dunraven:

> We are engaged here in a conflict far more serious than about Model Schools. On the one side are the Bishop of Orleans with whom I am with constantly [*sic*], and a few more obscure persons including myself – I have spoken in the

32 Altholz, pp 219–20. Malines is the Belgian ecclesiastical equivalent of Armagh or Canterbury. **33** Letter from Newman to Monsell, 17 June 1863, in *The letters and diaries of John Henry Newman*, vol. 20 (London 1970), pp 476–7. **34** *Hansard*, 172.1008–13 (17 July 1863). **35** [William George Ward], *Civil intolerance of religious error: M. De Montalembert at Malines* (London, 1863).

strongest language to the Pope – on the other, a host of persons, among whom are many English, strange to say, denouncing Montalembert, and pressing as I am told, for his condemnation – as yet the blow has been averted, and I trust it will not fall.[36]

Monsell was quite right, for Pope Pius IX, according to Newman, ordered Cardinal Antonelli to send private letters of complaint and censure to Cardinal Sterckx, archbishop of Malines, where Montalembert had delivered his discourses, and to Montalembert himself.[37] While some commentators attributed this successful outcome solely to Dupanloup, it is reasonable to suppose that the pope also took into account the opinions of his friend Monsell.[38] A public condemnation of Montalembert would have been disastrous: both Newman and Monsell would have been tainted in the process.

Nevertheless the pope himself moved decisively to crush Liberal Catholicism throughout the world. He followed up his condemnations of the speeches of Montalembert by sending to the bishops of the world an encyclical, *Quanta Cura*, with an accompanying 'Syllabus of Errors'.[39] The latter was regarded with dismay amongst the Liberal Catholics and caused a storm of protest everywhere when it appeared on 8 December 1864. It was a list of eighty propositions which had already been condemned by the pope in previous documents. Many of these were obvious targets for papal condemnation, such as rationalism, pantheism, indifferentism, socialism and communism. However, as Altholz has written concerning the last condemnation on the list, 'the last proposition condemned in the Syllabus is an almost perfect statement of the Liberal Catholic creed: the Roman Pontiff can and ought to reconcile himself to and come to terms, with progress, liberalism and modern civilisation'. The encyclical itself condemned the principle of freedom of conscience and worship, and the principle of 'the sovereignty of the people considered as supreme law independent of all human and divine rights'.[40] It seemed as if the pope was declaring war on the modern world.

Predictably, Monsell was horrified. He recorded his reaction in a letter to Newman on 10 January 1865:

Our Catholic papers and the Dublin review [*sic*] all seem to maintain that 80 new propositions are added to the creed ... But what are we to do in Parliament when the encyclical is thrown in our faces? – our respect for the Pope must tie our tongues – I am told that several French and Belgian bishops will write to Rome to point out the difficulty in which they who have sworn to the constitution of their respective countries are now placed – Would it be

36 Monsell to Dunraven, 22 January 1864, Dunraven papers, (DP) MS D3196/F/10/43.
37 *The letters and diaries of John Henry Newman*, vol. 21 (London, 1971), note to p. 41.
38 Ibid., p. 41.   39 See Damian McElrath, *The syllabus of Pius IX: some reactions in England* (London, 1964). See also Altholz, and MacDougall.   40 Altholz, p. 231.

possible to get any English or Irish bishops to do something of the same sort? The Bishop of Orleans is in despair.[41]

Quanta Cura and the Syllabus constituted a major victory for the Ultramontanes. As Altholz notes, 'Henceforth Liberal Catholicism was capable of little more than a rear guard action'. He adds: 'The Munich brief and the Syllabus had sounded the death knell of Liberal Catholicism. Its agonies were prolonged until 1870, however, as the Liberal Catholics struggled to salvage some fragments of accomplishment from the wreckage of their movement.'[42] Monsell, a practical politician, had to soldier on, realizing that, in the world of largely Protestant politicians in which he had his field of operation, the pope's actions had made his task immeasurably more difficult.

Monsell was also active at the time of the Vatican Council in 1869.[43] The main issue was the proclamation of the doctrine of Papal Infallibility. This was the last occasion on which the Liberal Catholics (who opposed this dogma) rallied in their losing battle against the Ultramontanes. They became known as Inopportunists – that is, they tended to believe in the concept itself, but felt that it was inopportune to have it proclaimed a dogma of the Church at that moment. To them it was a continuation of the retrograde policy of *Quanta Cura* and the Syllabus. Newman, Monsell, Montalembert, Acton and Döllinger were among the most prominent Inopportunists.[44] Dupanloup and Moriarty were among the minority of bishops taking that line, while, predictably, Cullen and Manning were among those who campaigned hardest for a definition.[45] Monsell played two major roles in the drama. Firstly, he tried to persuade Newman to attend the Council as theologian to Dupanloup. The latter was willing to take him, but Newman declined the offer.[46] Secondly, Monsell was given a document which was a French translation of a memorandum written by Döllinger (originally in German) to be circulated to the German-speaking bishops who would attend the Council. Roantree notes that it argued 'in strong and urgent language for the inopportune-ness of a definition of the Pope's personal infallibility'.[47] Monsell translated it into English, and Newman had it printed.[48] It was then distributed to the English-speaking bishops who were due to attend the Council. As Roantree says, 'it is impossible to say what kind of impact it could have had';[49] Papal Infallibility became a dogma in 1870, and Monsell accepted it reluctantly, as he had already accepted the Syllabus. The Vatican Council represented the final defeat of Liberal Catholicism.

41 Letter from Monsell to Newman, 10 January, 1865, in *The letters and diaries of John Henry Newman*, xxi, p. 383. **42** Altholz, pp 233–4, 235. **43** For the Irish bishops at the Council, see Emmet Larkin, *The Roman Catholic Church and the home rule movement in Ireland, 1870–1874* (Chapel Hill, NC, 1990). **44** See Dermot Roantree, 'William Monsell and Papal Infallibility: the workings of an Inopportunist's mind', in *Archivium Hibernicum*, 43 (1988), 118–34. **45** Larkin, pp 4–7. **46** Roantree, 'William Monsell and Papal Infallability', pp 123–4. **47** Ibid., p. 125. **48** *Is it opportune to define the infallibility of the pope? Memorandum addressed to the bishops of Germany. respectfully offered in translation to the bishops of the United Kingdom and its colonies and to the bishops of the United States* (London 1869). **49** Roantree, 'William Monsell and the Catholic Question', p. 243.

In the final analysis, Monsell's enduring historical interest may rest not principally on his political impact on the affairs of state or the systems of governance of his time, nor even on his role as a local grandee among the Limerick and Irish gentry. His significance may, rather, reside in the very particular combination of religious and political views and positions which he firmly held, and which represent an ideological strand in Irish political life that was virtually obliterated in the polarized world of Nationalist–Unionist contestation in Ireland from the intrusion of Home Rule to the settlements of 1920–2.

Catholic, Liberal and Unionist, Irishman, Briton, adopted Frenchman and European, friend of Gladstone and Duffy, of Pope Pius IX and Newman, of Acton and Cardinal Paul Cullen, Monsell represents conjunctions of belief and loyalty which were to be eclipsed by the ideological fervour and the traumatic conflicts of the twentieth century. The fact that he was neither an O'Connell nor a Parnell should not mean that what he was, and the political disposition he represented, should be ignored; his political position on the spectrum of Irish politics in the Union era provides historians with a valuable, distinctly European vantage point from which to consider the full complexity of political life in Victorian Ireland, and from which to contemplate those other political possibilities which Monsell and his contemporaries entertained but which, in the event, were never realized.

Ireland, Britain, and mass literacy in nineteenth-century Europe

PADDY LYONS

In 1859 a detailed government return recorded that of around nine million reading-lesson books ordered for elementary schools in mainland Britain between September 1856 and May 1859, some five million were direct reprints of what were known as *The Irish readers*: textbooks which had earlier been developed in Ireland on the basis of a series first devised and published by the Dublin-based Kildare Place Society.[1] In the years of this return, the report continued, most other series purchased were by and large cloned from *The Irish readers*, and of those few which were not, none achieved sales beyond 10,000. In other words, when State schooling for all was instituted in mainland Britain in the middle decades of the nineteenth century, the new network of British elementary schools was largely reliant on reading books developed a generation previously in the ongoing colonisation of Ireland; the materials whereby the diffusion of mass literacy in English was undertaken for Britain were not native or indigenous, but were imported from Ireland. From this nineteenth-century innovation would emerge a new linguistic base for twentieth-century literary production.

Budgetary comparison confirms that the diffusion of mass literacy on the two islands was not synchronic or in phase, and was first advanced in Ireland; indeed, the relative spend on schooling for Ireland and Britain in the first half of the nineteenth century seems notably biased in Ireland's favour.[2] Between 1815 and 1832, London governments dispensed more than £300,000 to the Kildare Place Society in Dublin (later the Irish Commissioners of National Education), but meanwhile spent nothing at all on elementary education for the children of England and Wales. Some of this money was used for building schoolhouses and training teachers; but a significant portion was earmarked for research and development projects, including work on textbooks and the curriculum. Although an annual expenditure of £20,000 for England and Wales is recorded from 1832, throughout the remainder of the 1830s that amount, plus half as much again was dispensed in Ireland, even though the population of Ireland at the time (roughly 8 million) was only half that of England and Wales (roughly 16 million). To the end of the 1840s this disproportion between budgets

---

1 James Tilleard, 'On elementary schoolbooks', in *Transactions of the National Association for the Promotion of Social Sciences* (London, 1859), pp 387–96. 2 Extrapolated from tables established in J.M. Goldstrom, *The social content of education, 1808–1870* (Shannon, 1972), pp 193–5.

continued, and it was not until 1850 that the amount spent on education for Ireland (in that year, £120,000) was exceeded by the spend for England and Wales (£193,000); by then famine had taken its grim toll, and the population of Ireland had dropped to barely a third of that of England and Wales. It could be argued that this unequal expenditure amounts to no more than another instance of the readiness of imperial powers to treat colonized peoples as guinea-pigs, and later to appropriate whatever advantage or profit emerges from these laboratory experiments. Alternatively – and perhaps less severely – their implementation in Britain might be viewed as belonging to what Emmanuel Todd describes as the phase when an imperial centre moves to 'treating ordinary citizens like conquered peoples'.[3] The question of how Britain benefited still remains.

Before the nineteenth century, mass literacy had been at best a dream project, championed across Europe by progressive enlightenment intellectuals, whose plans were realised only in the family circles of an international bourgeoisie. Wider development was hindered by the absence of suitable state educational apparatuses; this was an effect of divisions then underlying all acquisition of skills in reading and writing. For the privileged of Europe, literacy was learned co-linguistically, that is to say with a dimension of reasoned translation, mostly (though not invariably) in relation to Latin. On the one hand, grammatical competence and rhetorical know-how came about – for this élite few – though the study of one language alongside another; this was the backbone of the curriculum in colleges, grammar schools and universities. However for those outside these circles of power, who perhaps attended dame schools, dominie schools, village schools or hedge schools, there existed instead a diversity of almanacs and alphabet primers, chapbooks and hornbooks from which to take the first steps in deciphering letters, along with slate and chalk with which to practise forming letters, but, crucially, without any abstract or co-linguistic aspect to underwrite these achievements, or to place these linguistic skills on a par with those common among lawyers, doctors, clergy and higher administrators. Change only came through the democratic project crystallised in the French Revolution, which was to launch a new type of textbook promoting general literacy and mass academicization, the type of textbook exemplified in – for example – *The Irish readers*.

Thomas Paine's *Declaration of the rights of man*, propounded by the French revolutionaries of 1789, drew together the democratic aspirations of Enlightenment Europe, and was in itself an initiative of some originality in the spread of mass literacy. It presented itself as a founding document, prior and apart from legislation. It began with 'ARTICLE I: Les hommes naissent et demeurent libres et égaux en droits', thus shifting the complex meaning of the term 'droit' away from the sense of law to be obeyed and towards that of a right to be enjoyed. Published on its own, as a set of guiding principles that were to hold sway regardless of what policy decisions might be advanced later, it proclaimed a new republic that was to rest on universal suffrage,

3 Emmanuel Todd, *After the empire,* trans. Michael Lind (New York, 2003), p. 77. This phase occurs in the course of Todd's analysis of the Roman Empire.

and then promptly spelled out that for such a utopian goal to be realized, universal literacy in a common language was an essential prerequisite. It is notably forthright in declaring, in Article IX, that 'Free communication of thoughts and opinions is one of the most precious rights of man: every citizen should therefore be able to speak, write, and publish freely'.

In moving on towards practical measures, the *Decrees of Year 2* (1794) represent a further turning point, projecting a system of state education whereby all citizens could acquire literacy and communicative skills.[4] As Renée Balibar, historian of the French language, has observed, 'a new linguistic practice was created'; she elaborates:

> Under the Ancien Régime, the king and the privileged held linguistic power . . . The revolutionary novelty of the *decrees of Year 2* [*sic*] . . . consisted in the fact that the new citizens, themselves the creation of the political revolution which they were achieving, could now participate directly, without inter- preters, in affairs of state and in public affairs in general, without the constraints imposed by the old barriers of language . . . Poor peasants from the smallest communes, throughout the departments of the Republic would manage in spite of tremendous linguistic difficulties to defend their own vital interests by writing letters to the Convention . . . or a soldier would find it impossible to obtain the smallest promotion in the army unless he could read and write French. This transformation in the use of French had both a qual- itative and a quantitative side to it: before the Revolution one-third of the king's subjects had access to the privileged forms of monarchic French; after ten years of the revolutionary usage of the national language, three-quarters of the population were able to communicate on an equal footing and to keep abreast of public affairs.[5]

One early outcome of the *Decrees of Year 2* was the entry into general circulation of a series of school-readers, small books comprising short narratives and dialogues designed to forward general literacy; these were in essence adaptations for French children of the *Lessons for children* (1778), which has been devised by an English dissenting educationalist, Anna Laetitia Barbauld (1743–1825), for use in her school in Palgrave in London. Extensively reprinted throughout the nineteenth century, these French textbooks came to be known as '*berquinades*', after their translator, the

---

4 For a more detailed account, see Albert Soboul, *The French Revolution, 1787–1799,* trans. Alan Forrest (London, 1974), especially i, pp 175–9, ii, pp 602–5. 5 Renée Balibar, 'An example of literary work in France: George Sand's *La Mare au Diable/The Devil's Pool* of 1846,' in Francis Barker et al. (eds), *1848: the sociology of literature* (Colchester, 1978), pp 30–1. This essay condenses arguments from Balibar's earlier works, *Le français national: politique et pratiques de la langue nationale sous la Révolution française* (Paris, 1974) and *Les français fictifs: le rapport des styles littéraires au français national* (Paris, 1975). Her later work includes *Le français republican* (Paris, 1985), and *L'institution du français: essai sur le colinguisme des Carolingiens à la République* (Paris, 1985).

journalist Arnaud Berquin (1747–91).[6] Although developed under the auspices of colonialism, *The Irish readers*, soon to be launched by the Kildare Place Society were, in a crucial sense, an anglicization of Berquin's French versions of Barbauld's text-books.

In stark contrast to revolutionary France, state policy in Britain was highly unfavourable to democratically inspired movements promoting mass literacy; as the historian Edward Thompson has remarked, 'a reading public which was increasingly working class in character was forced to *organise itself* '.[7] Thompson's great study *The making of the English working class* (1963) chronicles in chilling detail the ruthless scrutiny and state suppression met with by the Corresponding Societies of the 1790s, and by the artisan movements of the 1810s and 20s, which sought to foster reading and writing among adult working people. Even the most conservative improvers and reformers, such as Sarah Trimmer (1741–1810) and the founders of the Sunday School movement, met with intense suspicion from those who held power: the bishops would only consent to children gaining access to limited literacy as part of their Bible study, insisting that instruction should be restricted to reading and not extend to writing; they believed that learning to write was unlikely to advance the poor in virtue or devotion. The secular doctrine is spelled out clearly in William Wordsworth's translation of the *Decrees of Year 2* into downright counter-revolutionary discourse:

> O for the coming of that glorious time
> When prizing knowledge as her noblest wealth
> And best protection, this Imperial Realm,
> While she exacts allegiance, shall admit
> An obligation on her part to teach
> Those who are born to serve her and obey;
> Binding herself by statute to secure
> For all the children whom her soil maintains
> The rudiments of letters . . .[8]

Here, empire takes up a missionary position; any inclination towards egalitarianism that might undermine hierarchy has flown out the window. General education is admitted as tolerable if it can guarantee the security of the state ('her . . . best protection'), and literacy is recommended as a means to enforce a social contract between explicitly *un*equal partners ('exact allegiance . . . admit an obligation . . . to . . . those who are born to serve . . . and obey'). Equal access to free communication is not in prospect; instead, linguistic practices are sharply differentiated, and the underclass is

---

6 For a fuller account of Berquin, see Renée Balibar, 'National Language, Education, Literature', in Barker et al. (eds), *The politics of theory*, pp 134–47.   **7** E.P. Thompson, *The making of the English working class* (London: Penguin, 1980), p. 799.   **8** *The excursion,* book 9, lines 293–301, in *The poetical works of Wordsworth*, ed. Thomas Hutchinson, rev. Ernest de Selincourt (London, 1950), p. 692.

to have no more than the 'rudiments of letters', which would hardly be adequate for devising or indeed comprehending the supple structure of legalistic abstractions and qualifying clauses that comprise this piece of poetry. In short, the arguments of democracy have been hijacked, and realigned to underwrite hegemony and class dominance.

Because of Britain's readiness to import and exploit cheap labour from Ireland, these strictures were not applied with the same rigour to her neighbouring colony, where educational policy was conceived otherwise than in the homeland. The schoolbooks prepared in this context by the Kildare Place Society were, of course, far from subversive or radical in sentiment; indeed, as John Logan notes, these short dialogues and narratives, 'domestically situated tales from everyday life',

> conveyed a world view that emphasised respectful deference to hierarchy, the justice of a divinely sanctioned social structure and the appropriateness of the modest rewards that accrued to honest labour.[9]

Althusser has, however, taught us to view ideologies not so much in terms of sentiments, and to attend particularly to how they function;[10] in terms of the practices they incited, these little books make a clear break with the past, offering new empowerment to their users. Their originality becomes most evident if we consider what they did *not* do. In stern and very deliberate avoidance of conflictual material, these readers were resolutely non-denominational, and non-sectarian, and this in turn was to determine which idioms they would *not* utilise: even while drawing on the work of Sarah Trimmer and the Sunday School movement, they were cautious not to foreground the cadences of the King James Bible, as that could lose the support of the Catholic clergy; nor did they give space to Latin or Latinisms, which could seem to favour Roman Catholic over Protestant clergy, and which too would open a door on internationalism and on the powerful discourses of law and medicine. Because it was no part of their goal to maintain old associations between Ireland and the international community, and because they came into existence to sever such bonds and to further the subjugation of the Irish to and through English, these little books became the first mass circulation readers to teach reading and writing in English without a co-linguistic dimension. Moreover, they set out to facilitate written composition,[11] teaching writing through the use of model sentences,

9 John Logan, 'The dimensions of gender in nineteenth-century schooling', in Margaret Kelleher and James H. Murphy (eds), *Gender perspectives in nineteenth-century Ireland: public and private spheres* (Dublin, 1997), p. 45. 10 'Ideas have disappeared as such (insofar as they are endowed with an ideal or spiritual existence), to the precise extent that it has emerged that their existence is inscribed in the actions of practices' (Louis Althusser, 'Ideology and ideological state apparatuses', in *Lenin and philosophy*, trans. Ben Brewster [New York, 1970], pp 169–70). 11 Logan notes in passing that 'data collected by the two great official surveys of the early nineteenth century curriculum, carried out in 1824 and 1834 respectively, . . . show that reading instruction formed its core. Writing was almost as widely available [as

employing what is now known as the 'direct' or 'Berlitz' method. Thus, although the modest volumes that comprised the Kildare Place series would later be displaced by more sectarian versions (when the Catholic Church became strident in its demands for denominational education in mid-nineteenth century Ireland) by then these readers had already installed a pedagogy which was to prevail as primary to instruction in written communication,[12] and which would have special consequences for literary work.

As if in tacit acknowledgement of what these little books and associated pedagogy might represent, their arrival into state education in Britain was hedged with containment. To meet the demands of advancing industrial production, a network of elementary schools was in the course of the 1840s established in mainland Britain, under the guidance of the newly appointed HM Schools Inspectors Matthew Arnold (1822–88) and Sir James Kay-Shuttleworth (1804–77). It was in these schools that Kildare Place reading-books and Irish classroom practices were adopted and extensively deployed. It might at first seem surprising, as the state took on responsibility for mass education in mainland Britain, that the home or mainland text-book market should be dominated by reading-books specifically developed in Ireland to foster the linguistic subjugation of the Irish. Although the establishment of elementary schools was undertaken so as to provide schooling for all, putting an end to social divisiveness in Britain was not on the agenda, and it was not the entirety of British children who attended the elementary schools. Rather, *The Irish readers* were adopted in what were effectively underclass schools, in a system founded on a two-tier basis of class bias.

By a sequence of changes to their charters during the late eighteenth and early nineteenth centuries, what were known as 'grammar schools' had come more and more to exclude all but children of the middle and upper classes. From their establishment at the end of 1830s, the new elementary schools formed a separate, parallel, and segregated system, drawing its pupils almost exclusively from the proletarian classes; there was to be little crossover. In ratifying and approving this arrangement of segregated schooling for discrete social classes, the *Schools Inquiry Commission* advocated the reproduction of class difference in, as well as through, the educational apparatus:

literacy] and absent only from the scriptural Sunday schools . . . and from a small number of . . . "hedge" schools' ('The dimensions of gender', p. 42). **12** It had become so entrenched that this pedagogy which made Irish people literate in English would be adopted by early twentieth-century educationalists attempting to introduce Gaelic as the linguistic medium of the Irish Free State. In his study of *Compulsory Irish: language and education in Ireland, 1870s–1970s* (Dublin, 2002), Adrian Kelly observes that the First National Programme of Primary Instruction (1922) recommended the practice of 'composition', defined as 'teaching pupils how to "form short consecutive sentences"' (p. 23). It may be that the evident success of a method which had brought literacy without a co-linguistic dimension in turn encouraged the Irish language revivalists in a less fruitful avoidance of co-lingualism in their own endeavors.

> Indiscriminate gratuitous education we view as invariably mischievous . . .
> and class distinctions within any school are exceedingly mischievous, both to
> those whom they raise and those whom they lower.[13]

Until 1909 the British government appointed no separate minister for Education,
and Robert Lowe (1811–92, later Viscount Sherbrooke; Gladstone's first Chancellor
of the Exchequer and in command of schooling) was in tune with the commissioners: a split, segregated system was the core of his fearsome manifesto for a national
curriculum, *Primary and classical education* (1867). Lowe's vision was stark and unam-
biguously anti-egalitarian:

> The lower classes ought to be educated to discharge the duties cast upon
> them. They should be educated that they might appreciate and defer to a
> higher cultivation when they meet it, and the higher class ought to be
> educated in a very different manner, in order that they may exhibit to the
> lower classes that higher education to which, if it were shown to them, they
> would bow down and revere.[14]

Nevertheless, to sustain privilege and deference, and keep in check the democratic
potential of mass literacy, policy had to become practice, and this brings us to the role
of the schools inspectors.

Echoing his masters' voices, Matthew Arnold's annual inspectorial reports were
ample in appropriately ungenerous pedagogic recommendations. As so often in his
poems and critical essays, in these reports Arnold constantly appears to be giving with
one hand while actually snatching back with the other. His *General report* for 1872,
for example, considers how and why Latin should be taught differently in elementary schools and in grammar schools. While recommending Latin universally as 'the
best of languages to learn grammar by', with an airy gesture he stigmatizes the
elementary school pupils as unfit to benefit from what Latin might have to offer: 'But
[in elementary schools] it should by no means be taught as in our classical schools;
far less time should be spent on the grammatical framework'.[15] In what Arnold,
following Lowe, designated as 'classical schools', children who were to form the élite
– and later govern – were to continue to acquire literacy co-linguistically, through
translation from and into classical languages. There, because classical schooling was
co-linguistic, grammar would facilitate the management, manipulation, and possession of language. The situation was, however, different in the elementary schools:
what would be acquired by elementary pupils was, relatively speaking, a dispossession. In the elementary schools grammar became parsing, introduced as a set of rules
that were their own justification, to be accepted and unquestioningly obeyed. What

---

13 Report of the Taunton Commission (1858–65); cited in Brian Simon, *Studies in the history
of education, 1780–1870* (London, 1960), p. 325. **14** Robert Lowe, *Primary and classical
education* (Edinburgh, 1867), p. 32. **15** Matthew Arnold, *Reports on the elementary schools,
1852–1882*, ed. Francis Sandford (London, 1899), p. 165.

was to be learned was the practice of obedience. Without a co-linguistic dimension, the effect of grammar would not be to facilitate, but to regulate. This aim is quite explicit in the patronising syllabus set out by Arnold for the training of would-be teachers:

> For the ordinary pupil-teacher the text-books of grammar . . . are much too elaborate. These aim at showing the rationale of grammar and of the terms and laws of grammar; but this is a stage of the doctrine for which the pupil is, in this case, seldom ripe; he has the memory to master the rules of grammar, but seldom the understanding to master its metaphysics . . . What the pupil-teacher wants is the rule as a positive fact before him, as a rule, not as a theorem.[16]

This was the rule as a positive fact: to learn literacy in the elementary schools would be to learn obedience to rules while being denied any glimpse of a rationale: literacy for workers instead of literacy for management. By a curious contradiction, what is presented as a single 'national language' – in this instance, 'English' – is not understood as unitary, but as comprising quite separate linguistic practices. Cut off from the co-linguistic work it facilitated in classical schooling, for the elementary pupils grammar's dictats were to remain arbitrary: 'metaphysics', 'law'. The plan is familiar to any student of colonial policy: recruit some aspiring souls – here, the pupil-teachers – into the lower ranks of administration, induct them in the mechanisms of oppression, and then sit back and wait for a cascade effect.

But, disregardful of Arnold's unrelenting efforts, history took its own course. Debates on late-nineteenth-century education in Britain featured a broad range of rebellious voices opposed to the framework that Lowe championed and that Arnold had sought to maintain. Though they had been its pupils, working-people and trades-unionists did become empowered, and spoke out vigorously against its undemocratic stranglehold. Their rebelliousness was possible because, like much social engineering since the early nineteenth century, external intervention such as Arnold's failed to think along with the process it aimed to control from outside: the diffusion of mass literacy. This same deficiency was evident in Jeremy Bentham's approach to signification which, as Lacan observes, set its focus 'prior to the moment when the subject puts his head through the holes in the cloth'. Hence a blindness as to how subjects actually enter into signifying practices, and this, as Lacan sarcastically continues,

> wouldn't mean anything if things didn't start functioning differently . . . [if it wasn't that] there is from the beginning something other than use value. There is its *jouissance* use.[17]

Jouissance was Lacan's term for pleasures that reach outside the symbolic system: those taken in disobedience rather than conformity to law. The pedagogy that developed

---

16 Arnold, General report for 1861, in ibid., p. 92.   **17** Jacques Lacan, *Seminar VII: the ethics of psychoanalysis,* trans. Dennis Porter, ed. Jacques-Alain Miller, (London, 1992), p. 229.

with the *Irish readers* invited – even incited – such creative defiance. At the core of the method was the model sentence, and this always had a dual aspect: such sentences were at once concrete and direct, establishing communicative usage (though 'domestically situated tales from everyday life') while at the same time abstract, being exemplary of and related to larger, generative linguistic schemas, and thereby breaking with the immediate communicative context. Removed from the practical context of colinguistic translation, grammar's abstractions introduced not only rules that could easily seem arbitrary, but also paradigms that opened doors through which substitutions and alternatives were to enter. Hence the defiant *jouissance* observable in nonsense-rhymes and in playground graffiti, early triumphs over the frustrations attendant on entering into communicative structures; and hence, later, the glee which opponents could take in forthright denunciation of a system from which they had started out. Hence, too, the new possibilities for literary production.

The word 'literature' underwent a shift in meaning around 1800.[18] Whereas its earlier usage had covered reading materials indiscriminately – a sense still present in a phrase such as 'literature on double glazing dropped through the letter-box today' – its primary use since the early nineteenth century has been to designate a limited field, so that (for example) the works of Thomas Hardy might be said to belong to literature, while those of Ian Fleming quite likely might not. What sets 'literature' apart nowadays is that, just as with the model sentences promulgated in *The Irish readers*, the literary effect is understood as at once participating in and breaking off from simple communication. Nineteenth-century criticism summarised this doubleness by viewing literature as engaged in both statement and suggestiveness. Twentieth-century neo-formalism drew a line between the directness of cookery books and car repair manuals (which lead to activity) and the relative indirectness of a song, a play or a novel. Roland Barthes expanded the distinction in poststructuralist terms, as fundamental to literary pleasure:

> Language is redistributed. Now, *such redistribution is always achieved by cutting.* Two edges are created: an obedient, conformist, plagiarising edge (the language is to be copied in its canonical state, as it has been established by schooling, good usage, literature, culture), and *another edge,* mobile, blank (ready to assume any contours), which is never anything but the site of its effect: the place where the death of language is glimpsed. These two edges, *the compromise they bring about,* are necessary. Neither culture nor its destruction is erotic; it is the seam between them, the fault, the flaw, which becomes so.[19]

Co-linguism had long enabled this double-edged effect, but most usually among an élite, and occasionally more widely, as in sixteenth-century macaronic poems, or *Commedia dell'Arte* – fruits of cultures where migrancy and multilinguism were not

---

18 'Literature lost its earliest sense of reading ability and reading experience, and became an apparently objective category of printed works of a certain quality' (Raymond Williams, *Marxism and literature* [Oxford, 1977], p. 48). **19** Roland Barthes, *The pleasure of the text,* trans. Richard Miller (London, 1976), pp 6–7.

targets for negative discrimination.[20] Thanks, however, to the new pedagogy of mass literacy, literary possibilities became generally accessible to newly literate pupils, many of them Irish.

To look at how the new pedagogy facilitated literary effects, establishing and breaking communication, it would be useful to introduce some brief comments on a short poem by W.B. Yeats, himself an exemplary nineteenth-century Irish child of the *Readers*, whose *Autobiographies* remark ruefully on his lack of capabilities in Latin and modern languages.[21] Though very obviously written in English, this poem exhibits a diversity of linguistic practices, a diversity that would be veiled so long as a language were imagined as unitary. It takes up the fourteen-line unit of the classical sonnet, and then draws, with rebelliously Lacanian *jouissance,* on the colloquial cabaret-like idiom of stage-Irish Victorian parlour songs ('Malachi Stilt-Jack am I') to rewrite its model in rhyming couplets. Ostensibly, it declares that no language fit for literature is available to a modern writer; in effect it gives the lie to that declaration, through pitting the underlying logic of the school-readers against their own strictures and models.

High Talk

Processions that lack high stilts have nothing that catches the eye.
What if my great-granddad had a pair that were twenty foot high,
And mine were but fifteen foot, no modern stalks upon higher,
Some rogue of the world stole them to patch up a fence or a fire.

Because piebald ponies, led bears, caged lions, make but poor shows,
Because children demand Daddy-long-legs upon his timber toes,
Because women in the upper stories demand a face at the pane,
That patching old heels they may shriek, I take to chisel and plane.

---

20 'A single national language did not exist as yet . . . The dialects became complete images and types of speech and thought; they are linguistic masks . . . The role of Italian dialects in the commedia dell'arte is well known. Each mask features a dialect of the Italian language' (M.M. Bakhtin, *Rabelais and his world,* trans. Hélène Iswolsky [Bloomington, 1984], pp 468–9). **21** 'My father had wanted me to go to Trinity College . . . I did not tell him that neither my classics nor my mathematics were good enough for any examination' (W.B. Yeats, *Autobiographies,* ed. William O'Donnell and Douglas Archibald [New York, 1999], p. 90). Although by the time he reached 30 years of age, Yeats 'had been a good deal in Paris', his ability to communicate in French was, he records, more limited than his survival skills, as is apparent from an incident following on a squabble with his fluent French-speaking friend, Arthur Symons: 'we found ourselves in some café – the Café d'Harcourt, I think – and when I looked up from my English newspaper, I found myself surrounded with painted ladies and saw [Symons] was taking vengeance. I could not have carried on a conversation in French, but I was able to say, "That gentleman over there has never refused wine or coffee to any lady", and in a little they had all settled about him like greedy pigeons' (Yeats, *Autobiographies,* p. 256).

> Malachi Stilt-Jack am I, whatever I learned has run wild,
> From collar to collar, from stilt to stilt, from father to child.
>
> All metaphor, Malachi, stilts and all. A barnacle goose
> Far up in the stretches of night; night splits and the dawn breaks loose;
> I, through the terrible novelty of light, stalk on, stalk on;
> Those great sea-horses bare their teeth and laugh at the dawn.[22]

The remarkable final line exemplifies the principal sentence constructions recommended by the *Readers*, and can be parsed as a subject-verb–object construction followed by a version that illustrates the pattern subject-verb-indirect object. But these manifestations of the models appear at the end of a maze of very deliberate-looking deformations which ensure that the preceding syntax does read not at all smoothly. The complex sentence that constitutes the poem's opening line is built on a double negative, which in a school-exercise book would merit reprimand in red pencil. The second sentence, which continues over lines 2 to 4, shifts its drift midway, and even shifts it again, so that it is not immediately evident whether the 'them' of line 4 refers to the great-granddad's stilts, or to 'mine', or indeed – as is implicit from what follows – to both. The third sentence, lines 5 to 8, plays equally fast and loose with the school-book rules, beginning on three subordinate clauses that each start out with the word 'because', a word with which, it was decreed (though for no necessarily good reason), no sentence could properly open. Like the stilt-walker they talk about – who thrills the public by appearing awkward in his defiance of gravity, yet succeeds in clumping onwards – each of these sentences first court opaqueness that seems about to breach communication, but does at last march into clarity. The gravity they defy is that of Matthew Arnold's pseudo-grammarians, whose rulings they depart from ('whatever I learned has run wild'), turning potential nonsense into sense regardless of the rules, and foregrounding struggle with the communicative medium.

Through the pedagogy of the model sentence, the school-readers incited and encouraged their pupils in paradigmatic substitutions, while licensing only figuration that referred to the known existing world. The metaphor which opens this poem speaks defiantly, however, of absence rather than of presence, and then is extended until it begins to spiral into a chain of equivalences which seem ready to undermine all direct signification: 'From collar to collar, from stilt to stilt, from father to child'. According to school-book rules, a sequence of verbless syntactic units can have coherence as a listing of symmetrical elements, and it remains open whether or not a reader takes the 'barnacle goose' of line 11 as after all in apposition with and identifiable with metaphorical Malachi. As the syntax modulates back towards sentence structure – 'night splits and the dawn breaks loose' – there is, for a moment, a break with that enchained list, and even a return to school-book syntax, and the stilt-walker reappears as a separate element in line thirteen. But the final line gives this another twist and, as one recent editor puts it, 'an impressive incoherence: the poet's figures

22 W.B. Yeats, *The Poems,* ed. Daniel Albright (London, 1992), pp 390–1.

of speech have become so elevated they seem to have lost their referents, to mean nothing at all'.[23] What gives rise to this notion of 'impressive incoherence' is the prefixing of a demonstrative adjective at the start of the last line '*Those* great sea-horses bare their teeth . . .' – a move that a school-master would have to mark as incorrect, on the grounds that the word 'those' can only qualify elements that had been already mentioned in a discourse.[24] It introduces a breach, gesturing outside the discursive frame, breaking with established communication. If the literary effect is at least as much produced through the struggle with syntax and figuration as through symbolization,[25] what is most remarkable about the final line of the poem is that it shares the structure of the model sentences which taught the basic authoritativeness of subject-predicate-object to the pupils of the *Irish readers* and their successors. As with other such nonsense sentences in modern literature (for example, 'I carry the sun in a golden cup')[26] it acquires a coherence and impressiveness from the larger abstract structures of language to which it reaches, while also as here, pointing surrealistically beyond the horizon of the directly communicable.

The school readers that enable mass literacy are barely two centuries with us; and so long as literary criticism has mostly been fascinated with issues of discourse and the symbolic, investigations into their imaginative potential remain somewhat tentative. The British spy novelist John Le Carré, when questioned about the springs of his story-telling, recalled the school readers by remarking that while 'The cat sat on the mat' is in no way an interesting story, it's only necessary to change one element, and write 'The cat sat on the dog's mat', and then things start looking up.[27] These comments may be taken as an indirect homage to the *Irish readers,* and to the new possibilities that have made their way into English, from democratic Europe, thanks to their development in nineteenth-century Ireland.

---

23 Albright, ibid., p. 836.   **24** The opening line of Yeats's poem 'Sailing to Byzantium' makes similar use of the demonstrative: 'That is no country for old men'. The line prompts Albright to propose reductively: 'the country is Ireland, famous for salmon-streams' (ibid., p. 630): a pertinent illustration of the unconscious grip the strictures of the school readers can exercise over academic editors!   **25** In his *Autobiographies,* when describing himself walking home from the 'cheap school' he attended in London, Yeats recalls 'a small green-covered book given to my father by a Dublin man of science; it gave an account of the strange sea creatures the man of science had discovered among the rocks at Howth or dredged out of Dublin Bay. It had long been my favourite book; and when I read it I believed that I was growing very wise, but now I should have no time for it nor for my own thoughts' (p. 59). If the seahorses of the final line do come out of a book from which he recalled his schoolmasters had distracted him (and which has not been traced by Yeats's editors), they would hold a personal appeal for Yeats, as a fitting signifier for a horizon beyond the struggles and frustrations of schooling.   **26** Part of the refrain to Yeats's poem 'Those Dancing Days Are Gone'; the phrase was borrowed by Yeats from Ezra Pound's *Canto 23;* see Albright, pp. 317, 740.   **27** Le Carré made these remarks in a talk at Warsaw University, while on a lecture tour of Central Europe in the late 1990s; he returned to this example in a television discussion of the Iraq war, for the programme *Hard Talk*, broadcast by BBC World at various times during January 2004.

A transnational nation–building process: philologists and universities in nineteenth-century Ireland and Germany

ANDREAS HÜTHER

Contact between Ireland and Germany existed since the Middle Ages, but it was not until the later nineteenth century that substantial intellectual exchange took place. This exchange was made in two, at first sight, extremely disparate areas: philology and nationalist agitation. German philologists were among the most industrious in their field, advancing the knowledge of both the linguistic and literary heritage of Ireland. In the first two decades of the twentieth century, Ireland was briefly of interest to Germany as a potential trouble-spot that would tie-up English troops or even serve as a bridgehead for a German invasion of England. Both areas became intertwined through the active participation of German Celtic scholars in cultural nationalist agitation in Ireland and in the build-up of support for the Irish cause in Germany and America. Albeit on the fringes, German Celtic scholars became voluntarily involved in the Irish revival movement and the German war effort, lending their academic expertise to both causes. My argument here is that philologists played a more important part in nation-building and nationalism than has hitherto been acknowledged in literature. I will also argue that universities as institutions and the transnational network of Celticists were a factor in late nineteenth- and early twentieth-century nation-building processes in Ireland and that their role in this regard has so far been neglected.

Traditionally, France, America, Australia, and Great Britain are the primary international contacts that Ireland enjoyed and enjoys. Emigration dominated the relation to the outer-European countries. A long, intertwined and in many ways unhappy history is shared with the neighbouring island – a relation which was successively and unsuccessfully undermined by the closest Continental neighbour. Military assistance in several rebellions and educational training for the outlawed religious caste formed a positive picture of France in Ireland, especially in the nineteenth century. Despite missionary efforts in medieval times and the foundation of the so-called *Schottenklöster* (Scottish monasteries) by Irish monks throughout Europe, contact between Ireland and Germany was for a long time scarce and limited. The earliest account of 'Travel Literature' by German travellers in Ireland dates from the sixteenth century. However, only the decades between 1830 and 1870 have generated a substantial number of travel writings.[1] This was also the period when contacts on a

---

1 This slump only reverted from the 1950s onwards. Gisela Holfter and Hermann Rasche, 'German travel literature about Ireland: the saga continues', in Jane Conroy, *Cross-cultural*

larger scale, in areas such as trade and commerce, were made.[2] The social and political difficulties arising out of the respective situations regarding the religious divides
within the two countries in the nineteenth century seemed to have created a
common ground of interest.[3] In German newspapers Daniel O'Connell's campaign
for Catholic emancipation in the 1820s was followed closely, as was the plight of
Catholics in Protestant-dominated Prussia and the *Reich* after 1871 in Irish papers.[4]
Predictably, the Catholic emancipation movement received both admiring and negative comments. O'Connell was celebrated as a great reformer by some and as an
untrustworthy charlatan by others.[5] In literary terms, the connection between
Ireland and Germany was initially dominated by the Ossianic 'discovery'. Among the
most prolific literary encounters was the reception and translation of Thomas
Crofton Croker's *Fairy legends and traditions of the south of Ireland* by the brothers
Grimm. And while the respective interest in the denominational struggles illuminated domestic problems, the German reaction to French occupation in the early
nineteenth century inspired the Young Irelanders in the 1840s on a larger scale. The
historicist and *Volk*-oriented national revival sparked off by Johann Gottfried Herder,
Johann Gottlieb Fichte and Gotthold Ephraim Lessing presented a way out of the
denominational trap of Irish nationalism at the time. The literary-minded Romantic
idealists also introduced Germany to Ireland through their translations of poems by
German poet-patriots such as Theodor Körner, Friedrich Rückert and Ferdinand
Freiligrath.[6] Conversely, German interest in Ireland was of a more passive and
academic nature. The main figures on the German side of the academic parenthood
to modern Celtic philology – Franz Bopp and Johann Kaspar Zeuss – were not
acquainted with Irish scholars. As they left no notes to the contrary, it can be assumed

travel: papers from the Royal Irish Academy International Symposium on 'Literature and Travel'
(Frankfurt/Main: Lang, 2003), pp 459–68. For further research on nineteenth-century
German travel literature on Ireland see among others Andreas Oehlke, *Die Iren und Irland in
deutschen Reisebeschreibungen des 18. und 19. Jahrhunderts* (Frankfurt/Main: Lang, 1992);
Hermann Rasche, 'A strange spectacle: German travellers in the west of Ireland, 1828–1858'
in *Journal of the Galway Archaeological and Historical Society*, 47 (1995), 87–108. **2** Additionally,
some research has been undertaken into the unusual economic success story of William
Thomas Mulvany (1806–85), a civil engineer for the Board of Works, who retired to
Germany in 1849. In his retirement he established several coalmines in the Ruhr area
(Shamrock, 1856; Hibernia, 1857), founded a mining company – Erin – which was bought
by the Prussian state in 1882, and was involved in planning and building several canals in the
area as well as founding the stock exchange in Düsseldorf. See among others Olaf Schmidt-
Rutsch, *William Thomas Mulvany – Ein irischer Pragmatiker und Visionär im Ruhrgebiet,
1806–1885* (Köln: Stiftung Rheinisch-Westfälisches Wirtschaftsarchiv, 2003). **3** Links
between Irish 1798 rebels and Hamburg are discussed in Paul Weber, *On the road to rebellion:
the United Irishmen and Hamburg, 1796–1803* (Dublin: Four Courts Press, 1997). **4** Joachim
Fischer, *Das Deutschlandbild der Iren 1890–1939: Geschichte, Form, Funktion* (Heidelberg:
Winter, 2000), p. 29. **5** Eoin T. Bourke, 'Daniel O'Connell: Ein Riese unter Zwergen oder
ein echter Lump? Der irische Agitator in deutscher Vormärzperspektive', in Helmut
Koopmann and Martina Lauster (eds), *Vormärzliteratur in europäischer Perspektive I* (Bielefeld:
Aisthesis, 1996), pp 159–74. **6** Joachim Fischer, *Das Deutschlandbild der Iren 1890–1939*, p. 25.

that neither was aware of or at least not particularly interested in the political and social problems of Ireland in the nineteenth century. Zeuss and Bopp single-mindedly followed their paths through a textual Ireland in much the same way as their compatriots Karl Marx and Friedrich Engels.[7] These encounters highlight the gist of the nature of the German-Irish relation: while both sides were aware of each other and of some of their cultural achievements, active contact was rarely made. It took the rise of Celtic philology in the nineteenth century and its peak at the time of political turmoil to change this.

Looking back from our vantage point, philology, like many academic disciplines, was in its early stages a hit-and-miss affair with laymen and hobby researchers outnumbering the few serious scholars. Early research into the Celtic languages and ruminations of their derivation produced numerous figments of imagination.[8] The establishment of comparative linguistics by Franz Bopp and his subsequent inclusion of the Celtic language within the Indo-European language family, paved the way for serious academic research.[9] However, the case of Zeuss shows that philology was prone to be utilized for popular and political purposes. Zeuss's first scholarly works were written consciously in German rather than the scholarly *lingua franca* Latin.[10] This, combined with the fact that he opposed the generally accepted view that Bavarians were descendants of Celts rather than Germans made it difficult for Zeuss to pursue an academic career.[11] It was only in the 1850s that one interpretation – that the languages were part of the Indo-European language family – became the widely accepted scholarly orthodoxy. After the publication of Johann Kaspar Zeuss' seminal *Grammatica Celtica* (1853),[12] the first movements towards the establishment of a Chair

7 See Patrick O'Neill, *Ireland and Germany: a study in literary relations* (New York: Lang, 1985). 8 For examples of such imaginative excesses during the early Irish revival see among others Tony Crowley, *Language in history: theory and texts* (London and New York: Routledge, 1996), p. 107. 9 Bopp had excluded the Celtic languages in his initial work *Ueber das Konjugationssystem der Sanskritsprache in Vergleichung mit jenem der griechischen, lateinischen, persischen und germanischen Sprache* (1816), but later followed James Cowles Prichard, *Eastern origin of the Celtic nations* (1831) and Adolphe Pictet, *De l'affinité des langues Celtique* (1837) by including the languages within the Indo-European language family in *Ueber die celtischen Sprachen vom Gesichtspunkte der vergleichenden Sprachforschung* (1838). See Reinhard Sternemann, *Franz Bopp und die vergleichende indoeuropäische Sprachwissenschaft: Beobachtungen zum Boppschen Sprachvergleich aus Anlaß irriger Interpretationen in der linguistischen Literatur* (Innsbruck: Innsbrucker Beiträge zur Sprachwissensachaft, 1984). 10 *Die Deutschen und ihre Nachbarstämme* (1837) and *Die Herkunft der Baiern von den Markomannen* (1839). 11 A historian following his thesis, Johann Nepomuk Sepp, encountered similar problems. Hans Halblitzel, 'Zur Biographie von Professor Dr Johann Kaspar Zeuß (1806–1856)', in Bernhard Forssmann (ed.), *Erlanger Gedenkfeier ür Johann Kaspar Zeuß* (Erlangen: Univ.-Bibliothek, 1989), pp 60–1, 63. 12 The full title reads *Grammatica Celtica: e monumentis vetustis tam hibernicae linguae quam britannicarum dialectorum, cambricae, cornicae, armoricae comparatis gallicae priscae reliquiis*. For Zeuss see Myles Dillon (ed.), *Zeuß memorial volume* (Dublin: Dublin Institute for Advanced Studies, 1956), Hans Halblitzel, *Prof[essor] D[okto]r Johann Kaspar Zeuss: Begründer der Keltologie und Historiker aus Vogtendorf/Oberfranken; 1806–1856* (Kronach: Stürzel & Fehn, 1987), and Bernhard Forssmann (ed.), *Erlanger*

of Celtic Studies in Berlin were made. Although the study of the Irish language was not formally institutionalized until 1901, it was taught at German universities throughout the second half of the nineteenth century.

The most prolific teacher of Irish was the Sanskrit scholar Ernst W.O. Windisch in Leipzig. Amongst his students were Heinrich Zimmer, who received the first chair of Celtic in Berlin in 1901, and Kuno Meyer. With this and the subsequent generation of German Celticists – namely Heinrich Zimmer (Greifswald and Berlin), Kuno Meyer (Liverpool and Berlin), Rudolf Thurneysen (Freiburg and Bonn) Julius Pokorny (Vienna and Berlin) – the scholarship of Irish linguistic and literary study in Germany peaked. Their industriousness and diligence and – through extensive travel – their contacts in Ireland, Wales and elsewhere made German universities the centre of Celtic research, and for a while it became almost a necessary prerequisite for a successful career in the discipline to have studied at least one term at a German university. Several Irish Celticists studied in Freiburg, Berlin, and Bonn in the 1900s and 1910s, some of whom received their the PhDs from these universities. But the involvement of the German Celticists in propaganda and agitation arguably gave this this undeniable achievement an ideological as well as scholarly slant.

The embroilment of university professors with the military and propaganda machinery in Imperial Germany has received extensive attention from historians. Initial historical interest focused on the failure or unwillingness to speak out against the rise of fascism in the 1930s. It was initially the reluctant acceptance of historical continuity between Imperial Germany and Nazi-Germany in many societal areas which triggered a plethora of research into the development of universities and the social position of academics.[13] The intrinsic link between professors, political elites and public opinion was originally explained as a shared fear of modernization and thus a drift into an ever-increasing exclusive and defensive nationalism.[14] As the most vociferous and widely-published advocates of Imperial state-policy, the focus of research was on the role of academic historians and economists, theologians, and philosophers who explained and justified the war to both administrative elites and the public on the basis of their academic credentials.[15] University professors were held in high esteem in German Imperial society and thus their publications and speeches had considerable impact. The exclusivist and elitist education system meant that universities created a self-perpetuating class of civil servants and university professors, whose public position was akin to that of army officers.[16] And from their exalted position and intimacy with the ruling elite, academics were accorded a public

Gedenkfeier für Johann Kaspar Zeuss (Erlangen: Univ.-Bibliothek, 1989).   **13** For the origin of the argument see Fritz Fischer, *Griff nach der Weltmacht: die Kriegszielpolitik des kaiserlichen Deutschland 1914/18* (Düsseldorf: Droste, 1961).   **14** Fritz Ringer, *The decline of the German mandarins: the German academic community, 1890–1933* (Cambridge: Harvard UP, 1969). **15** First in Klaus Schwabe, *Wissenschaft und Kriegsmoral. Die deutschen Hochschullehrer und die politischen Grundfragen des Ersten Weltkrieges* (Göttingen: Musterschmidt, 1969).   **16** See Hans-Ulrich Wehler, *Das Deutsche Kaiserreich 1871–1918* (Göttingen: Vandenhoeck & Ruprecht, 1994), pp 122–31.

and political function as shapers of public opinion.[17] Their academic expertise thus spread into the realm of politics and influenced the political process. Prior to the foundation of the Reich in 1871, Germanists – and this included academic lawyers, philologists, and historians – debated the issue of what constituted the German nation at academic congresses. A great number of these professors were also members of the Frankfurt parliament of 1848 in which the unification of Germany was debated.[18] As academic congresses and meetings were held across state borders, these created a community of students and scholars who acted out the political ideal of a unified Germany and thus, by operating beyond the boundaries of the patchwork of German states, universities contributed to the nation-building process in Germany.[19] After the foundation of the Reich, nation-building in Germany assumed the task of creating a unified nation within its borders, including non-German speakers in the north (Danes), east (Poles), and west (French). The Germanisation of non-German speaking provinces was attempted by educational matters at primary and secondary school level, and also by the foundation of universities in these areas, such as Breslau (Wroclaw) in the east and Straßburg (Strasbourg) in the west.[20]

Professors close to the Kaiser pushed for the recognition of Ireland, and its national movement, as a potential ally – in whatever form – in the struggle for European hegemony. With ethno-linguistic minorities at home striving for some form of autonomy from the Reich, the Kaiser as ultimate decision-maker regarded such movements abroad as inappropriate partners. By the mid-1880s any serious endeavours by such groups to achieve autonomy were suppressed and Germanisation attempts were increased.[21] Consequently, although 'the Irish situation' was recognized as a potential trouble-spot in England's side, this was largely a passive acknowledgement and no or little action was taken by the well-informed political decision-makers.[22] In favour of revolutionizing ethnic minorities in enemy states – Irish in the United Kingdom, Poles in Russia, and so on – was the military and a number of politically active professors. The Irish case had two particularly strong advocates: Theodor Schiemann and Kuno Meyer. Schiemann was an accomplished historian of Eastern European and Russian history and a popular writer of weekly articles about foreign policy in the widely-read conservative *Kreuzzeitung* (from 1911 *Neue Preußische Zeitung*). He also had connections to revolutionary Irish-American circles in the person of George Freeman.[23] Schiemann in general opposed the right

17 See for example Rüdiger vom Bruch, *Wissenschaft, Politik und öffentliches Meinung: Gelehrtenpolitik im wilhelminischen Deutschland, 1890–1914* (Husum: Matthiesen, 1980).   **18** See various articles in Frank Fürbeth (ed.), *Zur Geschichte und Problematik der Nationalphilologien in Europa: 150 Jahre Erste Germanistenversammlung in Frankfurt am Main, 1846–1996* (Tübingen, Niemeyer, 1999).   **19** Thomas Nipperdey, *Deutsche Gechichte 1800–1866: Bürgerwelt und starker Staat* (München: Beck, 1998), p. 480.   **20** Bonn served a similar function when it was founded in 1851 as a Prussian university in the newly acquired Rhineland territories. **21** Wolfgang Hünseler, *Das Deutsche Kaiserreich und die Irische Frage 1900–1914* (Köln: Lang, 1978), pp 22–3.   **22** Ibid., pp 66–7.   **23** Hans-Dieter Kluge, *Irland in der deutschen Geschichtswissenschaft, Politik und Propaganda vor 1914 und im Ersten Weltkrieg* (Frankfurt/Main:

to independence of 'smaller ethnic groups' which, he argued, would bring no cultural advancement.[24] However, he was convinced that Russia and especially England, with whom he sought an alliance as late as July 1914, would stand in the way of German aspirations, and he lobbied with the Kaiser to support the Irish independence movement with the outbreak of war. Together with Kuno Meyer, he aided Roger Casement in his missions to Berlin, and published – without naming him as original author – German translations of a number of Casement's articles, while continuously detailing the position of the radical factions of the Irish national movement in German newspapers and within the Imperial administration.[25] In a tactic similar to that of the Celtic scholar Heinrich Zimmer, who opposed the right of the Polish minority for education in their own language, Schiemann endorsed the right to cultural and linguistic independence of small nations, at least in the case of Ireland.[26] While this pragmatic application of policies might be easy to understand, a closer look at the involvement of German Celtic scholars in both the Irish and German politics and agitation, gives a deeper insight into universities and disciplines within the nation-building processes.

As has already been indicated, there are few studies of the role of philologists involved in nationalist agitation before and during the First World War. The importance given to historians in the nineteenth century as those best qualified to explain the present on the basis of the past has left its mark on the twentieth century. Only slowly, with the recent increase in 'cultural studies', has attention been diverted to the role of philologists. This is exemplified in the historiography of German Celtic scholars and their involvement in German-Irish connections in the First World War. While both early standard works on Ireland and Germany in the early twentieth century[27] concentrate on historians within the German administration and treat Celtic scholars as more (Hünseler) or less (Kluge) important aides, Joachim Lerchenmueller recently based a whole study on academic historians of the period. He shows that they were instrumental and pro-active in helping the Irish cause and influencing the German administration and public opinion through lectures and lobby groups.[28] The inclusion of philologists, in this case Celticists, in understanding the processes of nation-building and nationalism in general is enhancing our understanding of these processes for several reasons. The most important point here is that

Lang, 1985), pp 174–5. For Schiemann's connection with Ireland see also Hünseler, *Kaiserreich und Irische Frage* passim and Joachim Lerchenmueller, *'Keltischer Sprengstoff': Eine wissenschaftsgeschichtliche Studie über die deutsche Keltologie von 1900 bis 1945* (Tübingen: Niemeyer, 1997), passim. **24** Kluge, *Irland in der deutschen Geschichtswissenschaft*, p. 176. **25** Ibid., pp 177–179. For Casement and Germany see among others Jürgen Elvert, 'Sir Roger Casement and Germany', in Joachim Fischer, Gisela Holfter Eoin Bourke (eds), *Deutsch-Irische Verbindungen: Geschichte – Literatur – Übersetzung/Irish-German Connections. History – Literature – Translations* (Trier: Wissenschaftlicher Verlag, 1998), pp 77–86 and Reinhard R. Doerries, *Sir Roger Casement in Imperial Germany* (London: Cass, 2000). **26** Kluge, *Irland in der deutschen Geschichtswissenschaft*, p. 180. **27** Hünseler and Kluge. **28** Joachim Lerchenmueller, *'Keltischer Sprengstoff'*, passim.

through their studies, philologists were assumed to have an intrinsic knowledge of a national culture in all its aspects from the beginning of recorded times. As their social position gave them access to the relevant military and political circles, they were in a position to hand down knowledge about potential allies and enemies through their research and first hand experience. Additionally, their research into the cultural and linguistic relationships made philologists the foremost experts in intellectual nation-building. Lerchenmueller's detailed study of the greats of German Celtic philology – most notably Kuno Meyer, Heinrich Zimmer, Julius Pokorny, and Rudolf Thurneysen – has not only lifted the veil from such marginalized figures but also further deepened our knowledge about the intertwined nature of academics and the Imperial power structures.

The Celticists' involvement in political affairs, however, was not only limited to Germany. In the Irish quest for a national university and the 'university question', but also in the setting up of research institutions and distributing knowledge about the Irish language, culture, and customs, they contributed immensely to positive Irish nation-building efforts in the late nineteenth century, while at the same time creating a negative image of England as the anti-German and anti-Irish.

The most prolific case of political activity among Celtic scholars at the time can be ascribed to Kuno Meyer.[29] In 1911 Meyer was appointed to the chair of Celtic in Berlin to succeed Heinrich Zimmer. Before this appointment Meyer was a lecturer and professor at the University of Liverpool for 27 years from 1884 to 1911. Very early on in Liverpool, he gave lectures on the importance of the Celtic languages to academic and non-academic audiences, such as the Liverpool Gaelic League branch. He was sympathetic to the cause of the Irish national movement with whose leaders – many of whom were also philologists – he was in constant contact. In 1903 Meyer founded the School of Irish Learning in Dublin with the help of Alice Stopford Green. In the opening speech Meyer made clear that the establishment of the school was not only an important step towards securing the survival of the Irish language, but that it was a matter of 'national concern. To provide . . . students with the necessary instruction, to initiate them into the study of the older stages of the language, is, in my opinion, a question of national importance'.[30] A year previous to the establishment of the School, Meyer wrote to Lord Castletown:

> It is rare to find anyone who cares for Irish literature and yet I feel all the time that this neglected field will one day be invaded by hosts of workers . . . What would not France & Germany give if they had [tales] from such early times . . . I have often wished to be able to do something more practical for Ireland and the Irish, to throw myself more into the Irish movement and I hope to be able to do so yet. Meanwhile I try to contribute as much as possible to a

29 See Seán Ó Lúing, *Kuno Meyer (1858–1919): A biography* (Dublin: Geography Publications, 1991).   **30** Kuno Meyer, 'A school of Irish research: lecture by Prof Kuno Meyer' in *Celtica* (May-June 1903), 82–6. Quoted in Lerchenmueller, *'Keltischer Sprengstoff'*, p. 15.

juster connection of the part which Ireland has played in the History of Mankind, and perhaps I can best do so from my study.[31]

Meyer was fully aware that language and the distribution of language knowledge via language learning institutions had a positive effect on the development of a nation. He continued to marry scholarship and political nation-building during his lecture tour in America. At the outbreak of war in 1914 Meyer drew up a plan with his brother Eduard[32] and Schiemann to go to America, under the guise of a lecture tour about Irish literature, to rally German-American and Irish-American support for American neutrality. Meyer cleverly linked his academic expertise with political propaganda: the speeches and lectures given at Gaelic League rallies and universities in the USA usually started with a description of the glory of ancient and middle Irish poetry, only to mourn its demise during 800 years of Anglo-Saxon oppression – a situation that was about to be changed.[33] Returning from America in 1917, Meyer instantly got in touch with Field Marshal Helmut Graf von Moltke whom he asked to intervene with the Kaiser and the army leadership to assist Ireland against the common enemy, Great Britain.[34] As the aged officer held only little sway in the army, all he could achieve was a short lecture tour for Meyer at the western front, throughout which he lectured about Ireland's plight and Germany's gain by assisting Ireland. He even lectured to the Kaiser on one occasion.[35] Meyer was also part of the attempted establishment of a battalion of Irish soldiers amongst those held as prisoners of war near Berlin.[36] Meyer can thus be seen as the prototype of a conservative academic who in the increasingly nationalist and chauvinist environment of the German state and society applied his expertise in an increasingly nationalist and chauvinist manner in line with the *Zeitgeist*.

Another eminent German Celtic scholar, Julius Pokorny, who specialized in monastic Ireland, gave a rhetorically beautiful speech at a Gaelic League meeting in 1910 in which he crafted the academic facts of his trade – the language and culture of the Irish past – into identity markers for the emerging Irish nation: a heroic past or 'Golden Age', which was communicated through the ancient Irish language, promising a bright future on the nation's soil:

31 Kuno Meyer–Lord Castletown 10 June 1902. NLI Lord Castletown Papers MS 35,313 (10).   **32** A distinguished ancient historian and member of the ultra-nationalist Pan-German League.   **33** Manuscripts of these speeches seem not to have survived. The Staatsbibliothek in Berlin which held Meyer's estate has a great number of newspaper cuttings from American newspapers summarizing the lectures given by Meyer.   **34** Meyer–Moltke 27 October 1917 and 29 November 1917. Moltke refers to Meyer's letter from the 27th in his reply from 31 October 1917. Berlin-Brandenburgische Akademie der Wissenschaften, Nachlass KM 11.   **35** Moltke–Meyer 10 December 1917. Berlin-Brandenburgische Akademie der Wissenschaften, Nachlass Kuno Meyer 11.   **36** David Thorne, 'Celtic Studies at the "University of Ruhleben" 1914–1918' in Sabine Heinz (ed.), *Die Deutsche Keltologie und ihre Berliner Gelehrten bis 1945* (Frankfurt/Main et al.: Lang, 1999), pp 59–70.

Are you blind, men of Ireland, that you cannot see the native soil red from blood of fallen martyrs, that you cannot read the inscription on every stone, on every hillside, telling about the deeds of your heroic ancestors?

Are you deaf, men of Ireland, that you cannot hear the voice of your great poets resounding through mountains and glens, that you cannot hear the war-trumpets of Brian Boru, echoing along the plains of Clontarf?

Are you dumb, men of Ireland, that everyone of you does not arise, a speaker for his people, crying out his distress and needs, so that the very foundations of Westminster are shaken in trembling terror?

It was long since the nations of Europe had begun to awake, that they began to feel that there was something else in the world besides business and fashionable life. In Germany no one esteemed, no one honoured, him who was not a Nationalist. And in years to come historians would judge with harsh contempt those nations that gave up their national tongue.[37]

Language carried with it history, literature, and character, and only the national language was able to give a full expression to the national character.

Material culture, literary, and linguistic evidence are employed to fill the abstraction 'nation' with substance – language, history, customs, heroes, villains, friends, foes – thus becoming 'real' and creating a community of those belonging to the nation. Those like Pokorny and Meyer who wanted to could and did see the links between the cultural and political realms, and they instrumentalized those links for their own purposes. As F.M. Barnard states, the significance of culture within the nation-building process lies 'in directing attention to a profound change in the source of national legitimation'.[38] Culture, and above all language, became the rallying point around which nationalists gathered. Language classes as well as the university provided a meeting place and forum for networking and the exchange of ideas,[39] becoming pools from which revolutionary nationalists were recruited.[40]

Closely connected to the language issue was the university question in the 1890s. While it was never at the forefront of national agitation, the university question had occupied Irish nationalists since the 1840s. The first success was the establishment of the Catholic University of Ireland in 1854. Endowment of the Catholic University was among the popular topics of his election campaign when Isaac Butt (of the Home Rule party) stood and was elected in Limerick City in 1871, and it was again part of the agitation in the 1898 revival.[41] That education, university education and

37 Julius Pokorny, 27 July 1910. Quoted in Lerchenmueller, *'Keltischer Sprengstoff'*, p. 18.
38 F.M. Barnard, 'National culture and political legitimacy: Herder and Rousseau' in *Journal of the History of Ideas*, 44 (1983), 250.   **39** Thomas J. Morrissey, *Towards a National University: William Delany SJ (1835–1924): an era of initiative in Irish education* (Dublin and Atlantic Highlands: Wolfhound Press and Humanities Press, 1983), p. 166.   **40** Seán Cronin, 'Nation-building and the Irish revival movement' in *Éire-Ireland*, 13 (1978), 10.   **41** Alan O'Day, *Irish home rule, 1867–1921* (Manchester and New York: Manchester UP, 1998), p. 33 and p. 189.

the Irish language had primary relevance to Irish cultural nationalists shows the urgency with which Douglas Hyde and others pursued the point in the intermediate education debates in 1899 and the 'compulsory Irish' campaign in 1908/9.[42] In a letter as part of the campaign Hyde enlisted the elite of European Celtic scholars, asking them to testify to the value of the Irish language.[43] The overwhelming responses in the affirmative of European scholars gave a great boost to the Irish culture and its proponents. Mahaffy's argument that texts in Irish had no value and were on the contrary immoral, and thus not worthy of scientific study at university level, was scientifically thrown out. It was thus not merely affirmed that it was worth studying the Irish language, but that culture in the Irish language was on a par with the other European cultures. In the process of finding their own place among the nations, this was an important victory as it not only confirmed Irish as a literary language but it 'scientifically' confirmed a distinguished ancient Irish culture. Hyde himself admitted that the struggle for compulsory Irish was a front for the more important issue of Irish national life:

> The real question that is at stake under the cloak of (compulsory) Irish in the new university – the real question that is at stake is this – is Ireland going to be Ireland or is it going to be Irelandshire . . ., or is it going to become a poor little miserable imitation third-rate English county? . . . The fact is universally admitted . . . that now has been put into the hands of the Irish people, for the first time in three hundred years, the power of *saving their national life* through the new university . . . By making Irish essential or compulsory, you will be impressing upon it – marked and stamped upon it – the hall-mark that every nation loves to impress upon what is nearest and dearest to it . . . The university should lay down the law that nobody can enjoy its privileges except the man who proves he is an Irishman having learnt the language of his native country.[44]

The university here is put at the centre of national revival and made the institution to form the future nation and future Irishmen. The university plays a threefold role in the nation-building process. First, universities are the educational centres of the future administrative, political, and cultural élites.[45] Second, universities provide the institutional background for these future élites to meet seminars, debating societies, student papers, and social functions, resulting in the nucleus of a national network and the creation of a national spirit.[46] Third, universities provide the frame

42 Morrissey, *Towards a National University*, pp 321–44. **43** Hyde-Windisch [1899] University Archive Leipzig, Windisch estate 2.III.2. **44** *Munster News* 7 July 1909. Quoted in Morrissey, *Towards a National University*, pp 337–8. **45** Senia Pašeta, *Before the revolution: nationalism, social change and Ireland's Catholic élite, 1879–1922* (Cork: Cork UP, 1999), p. 1. **46** The premises at 86 St Stephen's Green hosted students such as Tom Kettle, James Joyce, Hugh Kennedy, William Magennis, Arthur Clery, Eamon de Valera, John M. O'Sullivan, T.F. Rahilly, Alfred T. O'Rahilly, and Patrick H. Pearse to name but a few.

for research into the cultural and political past and thus have the monopoly on scientifically verified knowledge and truth about the cultural and political past.[47] The struggle for a Catholic university in Ireland throughout the nineteenth century thus was not, as often dismissed in literature, only a pastime of the middle classes. Through the university, access to administration could be controlled and research channelled into appropriate directions. Under the auspices of humanities subjects and specifically the study of the cultural past and present, a truly national university held the key to the interpretation of past, present, and future and this was essential in the cultural argument for an independent Ireland. A complete genealogy of an older and richer civilization would give Ireland prestige opposite the economically more powerful England and strengthen the argument for independence.[48]

Philologists, the discipline of philology and the university as institution in nation-building and nationalism are more intrinsically linked than has been acknowledged in many cases. It was according to linguistic boundaries that nations and the nineteenth-century ideal of the congruent nation-state were constructed. Linguistic and literary proof was applied to substantiate claims in nation-building processes and nationalism. Universities as monopolies of research and the accumulation of knowlege were the core within this phase of the nation-building process. The agitation for a Catholic university in Ireland and the role of the Irish language in intermediate and university education shows the importance attributed to both language and university in the nation-building process at the time. Thus, appointment policy, resourcing, and implications for research results are areas which could highlight the ways in which and to what extent philology and university were intertwined in the nation-building process. Furthermore, foreign influence – in this case the cooperation with German Celticists – in the establishment of language schools and the university structure (hence in the nation-building process) have fallen aside in Irish historiography. It is an area worth investigating as nation-building is never a process that happens in a vacuum but that is determined by outside factors as much as by domestic factors. As the few examples given here indicate, the transnational network of academics prior to the First World War contributed to the establishment of research institutes. Additionally, the experience of Irish students at German universities must have had an impact on the development of universities and the academic discipline on their return to Ireland. The study of the transnational impact on the development of Celtic studies in Ireland and the role of the university within the Irish nation-building process enhances our understanding of Ireland in the late nineteenth and early twentieth centuries.

47 For a similar argument see Svajatoslav Pacholkiv, *Emanzipation durch Bildung. Entwicklung und gesellschaftliche Rolle der ukrainischen Intelligenz im habsburgischen Galizien, 1890–1914* (München: Oldenbourg, 2002).   **48** Crowley, *Language and history*, pp 107–8.

Saxon and Celt on the Rhine?
Race, religion and representation in Irish reactions to the Franco-Prussian war, 1870–1

GARY K. PEATLING

Racialization is a fruitful paradigm of academic analysis, and the explanation of Irish historical experience in terms of this paradigm is acquiring increasing strength within scholarly study. By emphasizing the socially constructed nature of race, the concept of racialization can help to iterate the historical contingency and flexibility of identification and representation. The concept thus has an important relevance to the analysis of representation of 'peripheral' or colonized European peoples such as the Irish.[1] Ironically, however, applications of the concept of racialization to Irish history often involve a closure or metanarrative which, while clearly well adapted to instances of conflict and negative stereotyping, suppresses other aspects of Irish historical experience. To recover moments in nineteenth-century Irish history which do not conform to this typology is thus to highlight the need for more nuanced understandings of historical processes affecting Ireland. Investigations of a neglected range of responses in Ireland to events more usually studied in a European than in an Irish context demonstrate also the limitations of rival or unconnected explanations of aspects of Irish history, challenging, for instance, binary oppositions between Protestants and Catholics, homogenizations of Irish Protestantism, and understandings of the relationship between Irish Presbyterians, unionists and Britishness. Irish responses to the Franco-Prussian War of 1870–1 and its sequels are one such field of study.

Since class lost its lustre as a central category of historical explanation,[2] race, often complimented with gender, would appear to some extent to have taken its place. Study of the process of racialization has convincingly demonstrated that 'races' are socially constructed categories, only conditionally related to biological or genetic signifiers or skin colour.[3] According to a recent and important strand of this work, whiteness as an identity does not transhistorically articulate the equivalence of all white ethnic groups.[4] The white-black binary, which is, according to supposedly

---

1 Vic Satzewich, 'Whiteness limited: racialization and the social construction of "peripheral Europeans"' in *Histoire Sociale-Social History*, 33:66 (2000), 271–89. 2 Patrick Joyce, *Democratic subjects: the self and the social in nineteenth-century England* (Cambridge, 1994). 3 Robert Miles and Malcolm Brown, *Racism* (London, 2003), especially pp 8–9: Colette Guillaumin, *Racism, sexism, power and ideology* (London, 1995), pp 99–107. 4 Ruth Frankenberg (ed.),

common-sense assumptions, the key (or indeed only) racial distinction, is actually a historically specific formation, and failure to recognize its contingency is to reaffirm racist attitudes.[5] Studies of unstable and historically conditional racializations of white, historically victimized, ethnic groups within Europe, such as the Irish, and of the contingent attribution of whiteness to such groups, have an obvious pertinence to this academic paradigm: suggestions, for instance, that the (Catholic) Irish 'became white' at an earlier stage in the United States than in Britain cohere to deconstructions of notions of race by implying that such notions are contextually limited in nature.[6]

The ultimate limitations of the paradigm of racialization within Irish studies have recently been suggested by its susceptibility to two opposing pitfalls. The first, notwithstanding contrary implications of the paradigm, is a continued residual tendency to conceptualize processes of racialization and racism in terms of a typology of white and black. Thus analysts often leap from enunciating the existence of British anti-Irish racism to supposing that Irish historical experience is comparable to that of colonized non-white peoples or indigenous peoples undergoing processes of near-extermination[7] – a comparison in most historical conjunctures devoid of historical relativism.[8] Secondly, and conversely, there is a tendency to regard racism as an inclusive – rather than reductive – category, encompassing experiences and social and cultural formations surely better explained in other ways. The drawback of this process is analogous to the effect of the overuse of the term 'racism', whereby an accusation that should powerfully stigmatize unacceptable attitudes is rendered commonplace or toothless, or even comes to be worn as badge of pride by those who imagine themselves as victimized by a linked anti-racist political discourse.[9] Similarly, if racialization is used by analysts as a master category of historical explanation, it may ironically appear to explain nothing: so many diverse representations would be incorporated under its rubric that those other factors that explain the differences between diverse supposed manifestations of racialization would appear more significant than racialization itself. This does not detract from the point that there are, of course, processes and discourses, in the Irish and in other white European cases, which it is useful to understand or explain as racialization; but other factors may in themselves constitute better, simpler and less counterproductive explanations of further representations.

Displacing whiteness: essays in social and cultural criticism (Durham, NC, 1997); Birgit Brander Rasmussen et al. (eds), *The making and unmaking of whiteness* (Durham, NC, 2001). **5** Bronwen Walter, 'Challenging the black/white binary: the need for an Irish category in the 2001 Census' in *Patterns of Prejudice*, 32:2 (1998), 73. **6** Bronwen Walter, *Outsiders inside: whiteness, place and Irish women* (London, 2001): Noel Ignatiev, *How the Irish became white* (New York, 1995). **7** Robbie McVeigh, *The racialization of Irishness: racism and anti-racism in Ireland* (Belfast, 1996), p. 40: Luke Gibbons, *Transformations in Irish culture* (Cork, 1996), pp 6–13, 150–4. **8** James Livesey and Stuart Murray, 'Review article: post-colonial theory and modern Irish culture' in *Irish Historical Studies*, 30:119 (1997), 452–61. **9** Lawrence Blum, *I'm not a racist, but – ; the moral quandary of race* (Ithaca, 2002).

A specific example is the treatment of Catholicism as little more than one racial signifier and facet of the racial othering of the Irish. This appears for instance in the writings of Anne McClintock, Catherine Hall, and Mary Hickman.[10] Admittedly, there is considerably more to the observations of each of these three writers, including an appreciation of the instability of nineteenth-century racializations of the Irish; but since the key historical significance of Catholicism, especially in that century, was quite other than as a racial signifier, to highlight this dimension is, then, curiously reductive and misleading. Hall argues that 'race [was] deeply rooted in English culture [and] questions of race and ethnicity were also always present in the nineteenth century, foundational to English forms of classification and relations of power'.[11] In her analysis of the parliamentary reform debates of 1867, Hall thus suggests that 'the racialised Irishman' 'stood as a potent "other" to the respectable Englishman, who had proved his worth and deserved a vote'.[12] Hall is not the only writer to suggest that the Irish were a significant racial other to the British.[13] Yet Hall herself seems to recognize the limits of an approach which sees the racialization of white Europeans as critical to British/English identity: identification with the nationalisms of subjugated or incorporated white Europeans became a badge of pride among mid-century English radicals, and the logic of such discourses involved also an increasing recognition even of Irish nationalists.[14] As Hall adds, 'excluding large numbers of the Irish population in England from the franchise through restrictions about stable residence was one thing; simply excluding them from rights of democratic participation because they were Irish would have been quite another'.[15] Hickman meanwhile sees Ireland's representation in Britain as a telling instance of racialization within the '*interior* of Europe'.[16] There are two problems with this description. Firstly, the term '*interior*' of Europe appears to blur distinctions between core and periphery. Secondly, Hickman too seems virtually to normalize racism as 'part of the constitution of the modern national state', endemic to the process of state or national identity formation.[17] While the historical relationship between racism and

10 Catherine Hall, *Civilising subjects: metropole and colony in the English imagination, 1830–1867* (Chicago, 2002), pp 428–30: Anne McClintock, *Imperial leather: race, gender and sexuality in the colonial contest* (New York, 1995), pp 52–61: Mary J. Hickman, *Religion, class and identity: the state, the Catholic Church and the education of the Irish in Britain* (Aldershot, 1995): Mary J. Hickman, 'Incorporating and denationalizing the Irish in England: the role of the Catholic Church', in Patrick O'Sullivan (ed.), *The Irish world-wide: religion and identity* (New York, 1996), pp 196–216.   **11** Catherine Hall, *Civilising subjects*, p. 8.   **12** Catherine Hall, 'The nation within and without', in Catherine Hall, Keith McClelland and Jane Rendall, *Defining the Victorian nation: class, race, gender and the Reform Act of 1867* (Cambridge, 2000), p. 220.   **13** Hickman, *Religion, class and identity*, pp 19, 22, 5; Michael de Nie, '"A medley mob of Irish-American plotters and Irish dupes": the British press and transatlantic Fenianism' in *Journal of British Studies*, 40:2 (2001), 234–5, 214.   **14** Catherine Hall, '"From Greenland's icy mountains . . . to Afric's golden sand": ethnicity, race and nation in mid-nineteenth-century England' in *Gender & History*, 5:2 (1993), 212–30.   **15** Catherine Hall, 'Rethinking imperial histories: the Reform Act of 1867' in *New Left Review*, 208 (1994), 23.   **16** Hickman, *Religion, class and identity*, p. 22.   **17** Ibid., p. 21.

nationalism may have been at times derivative,[18] Hickman's utilization of a formation such as 'English/British racist nationalism'[19] seems to go further than this: to see
racism as such an inevitably central feature of nationalism that the latter has virtually
no separate existence is little more profitable than regarding religious conviction and
practice as acting solely or largely as a racial signifier.

As critics as diverse as Hickman and Jonathan Clark have suggested, there may be
a temptation on the part of predominantly liberal and secular academics to underes-
timate the significance of religion to their historical subjects.[20] Clark however would
argue that, as contrasts with Continental Europe suggest, the central role occupied
by religious belief in national identity in this British-Irish context was far more
significant and positive. While far from denying that religion could also be a cause of
conflict, Clark, amongst others, suggest that a common sense of place within a moral
order underpinned by religious faith was the basis of the long-established coherence
of a Christian Britishness, apparently including the north of Ireland. Secular scholars
such as Linda Colley, who prefer to study religion as a facet or representation of class
or national identity, patronize their subjects, distort their data, and may even actively
contribute to the break-up of this Christian Britishness themselves.[21] Ironically
however, Clark's inadequacies, like those of Colley, are illustrated by the Irish context,
which is not exceptional in the sectarian dynamic in the formation of Britishness.
Indeed, as Patrick Griffin suggests,[22] far from Catholic Europe, Catholic France, or
even Catholic Ireland, being the foil against which an inclusive Protestant Britishness
coalesced, the Presbyterians of Ulster exemplify the potency of tensions and divisions
throughout the British world, tensions not altogether eradicated by the sectarian
violence of 1798. Given that the acceptance of the Britishness of Catholics would
prove a still more intractable problem,[23] religion divided as much as it united those
who sometimes identified themselves with Britain, including in Ireland: if we are to
ask in Gramscian terms when was the moment of Christian or even Protestant
Britishness, the answer must surely lie within relatively recent historical memory. As
will be shown, the context of reactions in Ireland to European events in the 1870s is
illustrative of an earlier state of disunity.

18 Miles and Brown, *Racism*, pp 145–50. **19** Hickman, *Religion, class and identity*, p. 55.
20 Ibid., pp 14–5. **21** Linda Colley, *Britons: forging the nation, 1707–1837* (New Haven,
1992); J.C.D. Clark, *Revolution and rebellion: state and society in England in the seventeenth and
eighteenth centuries* (Cambridge, 1986), pp 104–8, 111; J.C.D. Clark, 'Protestantism,
Nationalism, and national identity, 1660–1832' in *Historical Journal*, 43:1 (2000), 276, 264, 266;
Callum G. Brown, *The death of Christian Britain: understanding secularisation, 1800–2000*
(London, 2001); Maurice Cowling, *Religion and public doctrine in modern England* (Cambridge,
1980–2001). **22** Patrick Griffin, 'Defining the limits of Britishness: the "new" British
history and the meaning of the revolution settlement in Ireland for Ulster's Presbyterians' in
Journal of British Studies, 39:3 (2000), 263–87; Patrick Griffin, *The people with no name: Ireland's
Ulster Scots, America's Scots Irish, and the creation of a British Atlantic world, 1689–1764* (Princeton,
NJ, 2001), pp 171–2. **23** Dermot Quinn, *Patronage and piety: the politics of English Roman
Catholicism, 1850–1900* (Basingstoke, 1993); Steven Fielding, *Class and ethnicity: Irish Catholics
in England, 1880–1939* (Buckingham, 1993).

There is a superficial parallel, and some historical connection, between this historical problem of the tense relationship to Britishness on the part of Ulster Protestants, and especially Ulster Scots and the lack of moral and political legitimacy which world and British opinion accords the current leading political incarnations of such groups. Common explanations for this situation draw upon unflattering but symbiotic stereotypes of both the Catholic Irish and Ulster Protestants, especially Presbyterians – the latter being represented as either devoid of eloquence (and thus little capable of making their case before the world) or as subscribing to political and religious supremacism. Such ahistorical interpretations as these do not of course stand up to serious academic scrutiny, and the task of nurturing a more sophisticated understanding of processes in Irish history is assisted where explanations focusing on racialization, the unity of Christian or Protestant Britain, or unionism's problem of legitimacy are complemented by analysis of neglected historical moments in which these three factors are little in evidence. Interactions between Ireland and Continental Europe can offer such conjunctures.

The effects of the Franco-Prussian conflict of 1870–1 were to unite Germany under Prussian leadership as the most powerful state in western and central Continental Europe for two generations, and to bring down the dictatorship of Napoleon III in France. Secondary consequences included the revolt of the Paris Commune, brought down by conservative French republicans in a repression more bloody than the notorious Terror of 1793–4 in Paris,[24] the ending of the pope's temporal power over Rome, and the revival of Russian military access to the Black Sea, with Britain reluctantly acknowledging Russian renunciation of the clauses of the 1856 Treaty of Paris to this effect.[25] More audacious interpretations indeed see the war as facilitating the germination of the seeds of Nazism and thus of subsequent history of Europe.[26] In an Irish context, what is most interesting is the way in which the conflict and interpretations of the Franco-Prussian War informed, were influenced by, and were refracted through contemporaries' outlooks, self-presentations, language and alignments.

Aspects of the conflict admitted of analysis using the terms of racial stereotyping: it was a conflict of 'Teutones and Celts' fired by 'antagonism of race', as one Belfast newspaper put it,[27] and indeed the war occasioned a debate conducted in the language of race between French and Prussian scientists as to the character of their peoples.[28] The sturdy and disciplined Teuton had apparently worsted the ill-disciplined French Celt in battle, the emotional volatility of the latter being

24 Charles Sowerwine, *France since 1870: culture, politics and society* (Houndmills, 2001), pp 12–26 especially p. 25; Robert Tombs, *The war against Paris, 1871* (Cambridge, 1981).   **25** Werner Eugen Mosse, *The rise and fall of the Crimean system, 1855–71: the story of a peace settlement* (London, 1963), pp 158–83.   **26** J.C.G. Röhl, *From Bismarck to Hitler: the problem of continuity in German history* (London, 1970); Hans-Ulrich Wehler, 'Bismarck and imperialism, 1862–1890', in James J. Sheehan (eds), *Imperial Germany* (New York, 1976), pp 180–222.   **27** *Belfast Weekly News*, 10 September 1870.   **28** Nancy Stepan, *Idea of race in science: Great Britain, 1800–1960* (Hamden, CN, 1982), p. 101.

apparently further demonstrated by the chaos of Paris in the spring of 1871. Discourses surrounding these events also applied such stereotyping to their connections to Ireland. One Belfast Conservative delighted that pro-French sympathizers in Ireland who had gone to participate in the conflict fled chaotic France to return to Ireland and the very 'Saxon and Protestant rule' that they had tried to resist at the hands of Prussia.[29] A few years later the British historian Goldwin Smith, an impassioned if warped observer of Irish affairs, tried to demonstrate the unfitness of Irish Celts for home rule by pointing to French Celts' periodic fits of revolutionary madness. But even for Goldwin Smith, the French and the Irish were separated by history as much as linked by race:

> We know how even the Celt who had undergone Roman and Frankish training behaved in the French Revolution. Nor is it likely that the strongest and most gifted part of the race would be that which in the primeval struggle for existence was thrust away to the remotest part of the West.[30]

Europe's core and Europe's periphery intermeshed less for Smith than for Hickman. Nineteenth-century European observers often spoke of 'race' and 'nation' interchangeably:[31] but care needs to be taken in importing this meaning of 'race' into a modern academic universe of discourse very unlike that of 1870–1: the former has endowed 'race' and 'racism' with powerful resonances which are only sparsely appropriate to the context here under discussion. Even the London *Times*, supported by Ulster newspapers, admitted in the bloodiest Parisian days of 1871 that 'Frenchmen are men, and we shudder for our race'.[32] Equally, the language of Conservative Ulster newspapers at this time in praising the achievements of what they intermittently described as fellow 'Ulstermen' or fellow 'natives of the "Green Isle"' in North America, betrays the significant ambivalence in contemporary conceptions of race: 'Irish settlers of all grades have largely contributed. If forests were to be cleared of their giant pines, the Celt was found wielding the axe with a sturdiness of stroke and a perseverance of action that astonished his fellow-labourers'.[33] Racialization thus has a limited significance to Irish reactions to the European context of 1870–1, much of which is best otherwise understood.

Although many historians suggest that the seeds of north-east Ulster's separateness from the rest of Ireland had been sown earlier in the nineteenth century,[34] there was little evidence of a unified of Christian or even Protestant Britishness which

29 'Ulster Scot's letters to his friends at home and abroad' (hereafter 'Ulster Scot's letters') in *Belfast Weekly News*, 22 October 1870.   **30** Goldwin Smith, *Essays on questions of the day, political and social* (New York, 1893), pp 268, 266.   **31** Miles and Brown, *Racism*, pp 148–9. **32** *Londonderry Standard*, 27 May 1871, 2.   **33** *Belfast Weekly News-letter*, 1 January 1870. **34** S.J. Connolly, 'Ulster Presbyterians: religion, culture, and politics, 1660–1850', in H. Tyler Blethen and Curtis W. Wood, Jr (eds), *Ulster and North America: transatlantic perspectives on the Scotch-Irish* (Tuscaloosa, 1997), p. 40; Christine Kinealy and Gerard Macatasney, *The hidden famine: poverty and sectarianism in Belfast, 1840–50* (London, 2000).

extended to the north of Ireland in the 1870s. The Protestant press in Ulster still found plenty of space in which to identify with 'Ireland' while opposing home rule.[35] Protestant unity, religious identities, and sectarianism within an Irish context appear to offer a more powerful explanatory mechanism. Sections of Irish Catholic opinion did identify with Catholic France in the conflict, a fact which the Protestant press was fond of alluding to once the major issue of the conflict was resolved.[36] The Presbyterian Liberal newspaper the *Londonderry Standard* reported in some distress in September 1870 that two factions calling themselves 'Prussians' and 'Frenchmen' squared up to each other in Enniskillen, under the impression that the two armies fighting on the Continent represented religious factions or causes.[37] Meanwhile the Protestant press occasionally went so far as to connect the outbreak of war with the proclamation of Papal Infallibility. 'Many would say it is not a mere coincidence', insinuated the *Belfast News-letter*, 'which announces almost simultaneously . . . the Dogma of Infallibility, and a proclamation of war on the part of a Power which has done so much to realise that Dogma'.[38] Within a few months the *News-letter* exulted over the unification of the

> Land of the Reformation! . . . It is impossible not to rejoice with Germany, though we certainly do not exult over the misfortunes of the French, for there three centuries ago a solitary monk challenged the world and triumphed; there still are names which are dear to the heart of every lover of civil and religious liberty . . . and in their inhabitants the spirit of Luther still lives. Call these people Hussites, or Lutherans, or Calvinists; call them section-ally as you may, they are Germans, children of the Reformation — Protestants.[39]

Writers in the *Belfast Weekly News* similarly laced commentary on the conflict with a plea for Irish Protestant unity under Tory, Anglican and Orange hegemony: the 'genius of Orangeism' lay in 'banding together to oppose those who would undo all that the Reformation and [Glorious] Revolution had done, and in promoting union among Protestants of all denominations'.[40] Presbyterian radical publications such as the *Standard* were trying, in the view of the *Weekly News* 'to excite the sectarian prejudices of the Presbyterians of Ireland against our Conservative aristoc-racy and landed proprietors'.[41] The fact that one regular correspondent who was particularly insistent in articulating these views adopted the pseudonym 'Ulster Scot' — associated by modern historians with Presbyterianism[42] — is however suggestive of the fluidity of such identifications. So too is the refusal of the *Standard* to swallow

35 *Londonderry Sentinel*, 6 September 1870: *Belfast News-letter*, 12 September 1873.   **36** *Belfast News-letter*, 6 September 1870; 'Ulster Scot's letters' in *Belfast Weekly News*, 3 September 1870.
37 *Londonderry Standard*, 7 September 1870.   **38** *Belfast News-letter*, 19 July 1870, 2; *Belfast Weekly News*, 30 July 1870.   **39** *Belfast News-letter*, 6 September 1870.   **40** *Belfast Weekly News*, 12 November 1870.   **41** 'Ulster Scot's letters' in *Belfast Weekly News*, 13 May 1871.
42 Connolly, 'Ulster Presbyterians', pp 24–40.

this prescription: for this paper, the unification of Catholic Bavaria and Protestant Prussia was an object lesson in bi-sectarian unity,[43] while Orange Order and Apprentice Boys' insistence on divisive and provocative annual processions demonstrated a failure to heed the ominous French warning of the calamity of civil conflict.[44] The *Standard* articulated another variety of Irishness: if it was perturbed by the presumption of home rulers to speak for 'Ireland',[45] the arrogant assumption by the newly disestablished Episcopal Protestant church of the title '*the* Church of Ireland' was also alienating:[46] doctrinal and political issues prevented it from accepting any prospect of unity under an Orange banner.[47] It rejected the idea that the war of 1870–1 comprised a 'struggle between Protestantism and Roman Catholicism, as rival systems of faith; on the contrary, it is the old war of Gallic supremacy in Europe'.[48] Catholic and Fenian support of France in the 1870s was also doubtless strategic as much as sectarian, inspired by the hope that a revived Napoleonic empire would provide Ireland's opportunity once more. It was only at length that certain arguments in the *Standard* cohered to Protestant unity in Ireland. In March 1871, it noted that it was

> a remarkable fact, that what are improperly called the 'Latin races', meaning chiefly the Italians, French and Spaniards, including even the most distant colonial branches of the latter, while passionately ambitious of Republican freedom, are absolutely incapable of self-government by means of republican institutions.

The *Standard* however rejected the possible pseudo-scientific conclusion: 'political infirmities must be traced to influences different altogether from mere blood-affinities'.[49] The *Standard* shortly presented what it regarded as a better explanation, that destructive atheistic doctrines seemed to flourish in nominally Catholic countries:

> France is not the only country now reduced to this woeful plight in spiritual matters, since Italy, Spain, and other Continental countries which, from time immemorial, have enjoyed the unmixed advantages of Infallibilist instruction, are all deeply infected with the leaven alluded to, in common with the people of France! This is a mystery whose solution deserves to be thoughtfully pondered, especially since Germany, sometimes libeled as preeminently the land of European 'Infidelity', is in truth quite free from all the eminently diabolical extravagances of the French system.[50]

43 *Londonderry Standard*, 7 September 1870.   **44** *Londonderry Standard*, 29 March 1871, 2; *Londonderry Journal*, 30 July 1870.   **45** *Londonderry Standard*, 12 November 1873.   **46** *Londonderry Standard*, 1 April 1871.   **47** *Londonderry Standard*, 20 May 1871.   **48** *Londonderry Standard*, 30 July 1871.   **49** *Londonderry Standard*, 29 March 1871.   **50** *Londonderry Standard*, 31 May 1871.

'Ulster Scot' agreed that the course of French history indicated a symbiotic relation-ship between Catholicism and infidelity, as between despotism and revolution.[51] But such claims, even from the Conservative Ulster press, were periodically qualified by a realization that French Catholicism was at least Christian, and therefore preferred to atheism.[52]

Aspects of Protestant responses to the war do resonate with supremacism in the form of the equation of might and right. If Protestant Prussia was a synecdoche for Ulster and Catholic France for southern Ireland, the events of 1870–1 nurtured a pre-existing sense that the Protestant north would more than hold its own in a straight fight. As the *Belfast Weekly News* exulted in the autumn of 1870,

> Protestant nations are winning everywhere, while Roman Catholic nations are retrograding, as is shown in the recent history of Austria, and Italy, and Spain, and France … Are not the three greatest Powers in the world – England, Germany and the United States of America – Protestant Powers, while the fourth great Power, Russia, is anti-Catholic?[53]

This was, the *News-letter* agreed, 'something more than accident'.[54] 'Ulster Scot' suggestively noted that 'King William, like his namesake of memory, is everywhere the conqueror. "The eldest son of the Pope" flees before the Protestant Prussian Sovereign'.[55] In a recent critique of assumptions of the late Victorian prevalence of racist forms of Darwinian ideas, Paul Crook has correctly shown that James Anthony Froude was much more influenced by the Carlylean argument that political order ultimately rested on force than by Darwinian thought.[56] But, in the present context, Crook's approach has its limitations both in underestimating the element of racist paranoia in British responses to Irish political developments (although there is less of this in *The English in Ireland* than one might imagine), and in overlooking ways in which right transcended might in the schemas of Froude and others. Sheer necessity may, to Froude's mind, have justified penal legislation against Catholics in eighteenth-century Ireland; but the victory of Anglican hegemony did not justify English 'cruelty and oppression' towards Ulster's Calvinists – a situation which moved Froude instead to an almost Gladstonian pitch of moral indignation.[57] Goldwin Smith, although in an advanced state of racist paranoia, was no uncritical adulator of Prussian militarism, but influenced by an ill-informed sense that German unity (like the defeat of slavery in the United States and the eclipse of Fenian nationalism)

51 'Ulster Scot's letters' in *Belfast Weekly News*, 3 June 1871.   **52** *Belfast News-Letter*, 28 August 1873.   **53** *Belfast Weekly News*, 10 September 1870.   **54** *Belfast News-letter*, 1 January 1873.   **55** 'Ulster Scot's letters' in *Belfast Weekly News*, 3 September 1870.   **56** Paul Crook, 'Historical monkey business: the myth of a Darwinized British imperial discourse' in *History*, 84:276 (1999), 647–8; James Anthony Froude, *Froude's Lectures on Ireland and Irishmen*, ed. James E. McGee (New York, 1872), pp 23–4, 132; James Anthony Froude, *The English in Ireland in the eighteenth century*, 3 vols (London, 1881), vol. 1, pp 1–11.   **57** Froude, *Froude's Lectures*, p. 159.

would be 'the triumph of a real civilization over a gilded barbarism'.[58] A further problem for those who would match unionism with triumphalism is that the Ulster Protestant press denounced Napoleonic France in 1870 long before the upshot of the conflict was clear – and even in moments when a French victory seemed plausible – on the grounds that French provocation was a major cause of war, and had thus placed France in the wrong, irrespective of its might.[59] Moreover, the fact that Protestantism was 'assuming the government of the world, while its great antagonist is failing everywhere' was imagined to be the result not of military power, but of Protestant nations' orderly progress and concession of 'the right of private judge-ment': the inaccuracy of such analysis did not mean it was any less sincerely held among conservative Ulster Protestants.[60]

Providentialist readings of events in Continental Europe which seemed to support assumptions of Anglo-Saxon Protestant superiority were of course uncon-genial not only to British eccentrics such as Smith and Froude. Napoleon and the Paris Commune found but few apologists in Britain.[61] These assumptions had complex political, religious and cultural roots, not always grounded in 'race', but such an apparent affirmation may have enhanced British identifications with Protestant unionist aspirations in the subsequent home rule debates.

For Irish observers, European events in 1870–1 were pregnant with resonances of hope, anxiety and opportunity. The nature of these resonances was conditioned by an interlocking set of ideologies, largely religious, political, cultural and military. Ideas about race did inform reactions; but those seeking to have their political cake and eat it had to be more flexible than dependence on such a single tool, socially constructed or not, would allow them to be. Contingency was in evidence in other reactions in Ireland in 1870–1: if *some* events could underpin racial theory, Protestant unity was only latterly in evidence, and there was little evidence of a unity of Protestant Britishness. With it came a moment of Irish Protestant legitimacy which challenges superficial interpretations of Irish political history: notwithstanding recent reversals, Protestant confidence was reflected in the view that Protestant ascendancy – whether under the Union or home rule[62] – actively enhanced civil and religious liberty. This was not mere supremacism, but a more subtle ideology in which might and right were codependent. The contingency of political identification in Ireland in 1870–1 was best reflected in northern Presbyterianism, drawn alternately to Irish Protestant unity, notwithstanding its Tory facets, or to Irish radicalism, notwithstanding Fenianism and 'Popery'. Only analysts in search of convenient explanations or alibis for present concerns tend to deny the potency of such possibilities and assert the timelessness of single narratives and explanations.

58 Goldwin Smith papers (Bodleian Library, Oxford, microfilm copies), MS Film 971, Smith to Max Müller, 8 August 1870.   **59** *Londonderry Sentinel*, 19 July 1870; *Belfast News-letter*, 18 July 1870.   **60** *Belfast Weekly News*, 22 October 1870, 4; *Belfast News-letter*, 16 May 1873.   **61** Royden Harrison (ed.), *The English defence of the Commune, 1871* (London, 1971). **62** *Dublin Evening Mail*, 12 August 1870.

Continental art and the 'Cockneyfied Corkonian': German and French influences on Daniel Maclise

LEON LITVACK

Daniel Maclise (1806–70) is best known in an English context for his illustrations for Charles Dickens's Christmas Books in the 1840s, and for his frescoes in the Palace of Westminster in London. In an Irish context he is famous for his illustrated edition of Thomas Moore's *Irish melodies* (1845), and such large and important works as *The Marriage of Strongbow and Aoife* (1854), which hangs in the National Gallery of Ireland. The influences on his art are various, including classical and Renaissance models, as well as more contemporary English and Continental European sources. Given that his mature work was executed while he was resident in London, it is understandable that critics have tended to compare his output to that of his English contemporaries; however, owing to the scope of his travels and the range of his stimuli, it may be argued that he is more properly situated in a larger context of nineteenth-century European artistic endeavour, including book illustration, monumental painting, and frescoes. Maclise's upbringing and early training in Cork also, of course, qualify him in certain ways as an Irish artist, who maintained an interest in the island's history, culture, and fortunes throughout his career; thus he may usefully serve as a point of inquiry for the artistic linking of Ireland and Europe in the nineteenth century.

Maclise was born in Cork in 1806, and learned Italian and French as part of his early education.[1] From 1822–26 he attended the Cork Academy of Arts, together with the Irish sculptor John Hogan (1800–58), where much of the institution's curriculum revolved around classical models.[2] He also attended anatomy lectures and participated in dissections – an aspect of training that was not stressed in English art schools.[3] Maclise established a studio in 1825, and familiarised himself with local

<hr />

1 W. Justin O'Driscoll, *A memoir of Daniel Maclise, R.A.* (London, 1871), p. 25.   **2** In particular Maclise appreciated the strong monumental, symmetrical, and static elements in classical art. See ibid., pp 10–11, and Daniel Maclise, MS autobiography in the Royal Academy Archives, London, catalogue no. MIS/MAC/1, pp 16–18 (hereafter 'MS autobiography'). The record, which features an account of Maclise's family background, early training in Cork, and period at the Royal Academy, was used by Edward Kenealy to compile his portrait of the artist ('Our Portrait Gallery – No. XLV') in the *Dublin University Magazine*, 29:173 (May 1847), 594–607. In particular Maclise appreciated the strong monumental, symmetrical, and static elements in classical art.   **3** MS autobiography, p. 34. The fact that Maclise was schooled in anatomy in Ireland, under Dr Philip Woodroffe (surgeon at Dublin's foundling hospital and Dr Stevens's Hospital), might account for the collections of pictures, including prints of works by Raphael and Michelangelo.[4] A patron, Richard Sainthill (1787–1870), who was an antiquary and coin collector, encouraged his interest in heraldry and medieval lore; it was through Sainthill that the artist met the antiquary Thomas Crofton Croker (1798–1854), author of *Fairy legends and traditions of the south of Ireland*.[5] This pioneering study of Irish folklore appeared in the wake of the fairy tales published by Jacob and Wilhelm Grimm in 1825, and served as a romantic reaction against an exclusively classical tradition.[6] Maclise illustrated the second edition of Croker's work in 1826. He also undertook sketching tours of Tipperary and Wicklow, though he never developed an interest in or sensitivity for landscape.

In a letter to Croker of 1825, he relates an amusing anecdote concerning a dinner he attended in the company of three Frenchmen:

> I dined with Mr Marcel yesterday, and as there were three genuine Français chez lui, of course I was exerted to make out their prattle, they railed at everything Anglais, because I suppose there was nothing English at the table, they made faces at roast beef, looked with contempt on Potatoes, despised the fashion of drinking health to each other and in laughter at it, when one took up the decanter he pressed its mouth to the water glass and was on the point of pouring 'till he saw his more modest English neighbours, however he declared it très bon, but speaking of whisky they were quite possessed, one would think, C'est le diable C'est this & C'est that followed each other in quick succession, nor could they prevail on themselves to make any Punch – at the same time they gulped down a horrid Italian dish called Tagliarini and another called Pulpetti.

Despite his dislike of such samples of Continental cuisine, it seems Maclise enjoyed the company of his visitors.[7]

In July 1827 Maclise arrived in London, and attended the Royal Academy schools from 1828–31. He was introduced by Croker to a wide literary circle, including Samuel Carter Hall (1800–89), who later became editor of the *Art-Union*,[8] and the

detailed anatomical knowledge the artist displayed. His interest in anatomy might also have been inspired by the work of his brother, Dr Joseph Maclise, author of *Comparative osteology* (1847), *Surgical anatomy* (1851) and *On dislocations and fractures* (1859). **4** Maclise copied well known prints owned by the Penrose family, including Raphael's *Transfiguration* and Michelangelo's *Last judgement*. **5** MS autobiography, p. 29. Croker also published *Legends of the lakes* (1829), and *Popular songs of Ireland* (1837). **6** Interestingly, the Grimm brothers speedily translated and published Croker's book as *Irische Elfenmärchen* (Leipzig, 1826). **7** Daniel Maclise, letter to Thomas Crofton Croker, 1825, in *Catalogues of the Royal Academy of Arts, illustrated with original drawings, autograph letters, & portraits*, vol. 15 (1828–9, in the possession of Edward Basil Jupp, F.S.A.), item no. 229. Tagliarini are long, ribbon-like noodles; polpette are meatballs. Kenealy confirms that by 1847 Maclise spoke both Italian and French well ('Our Portrait Gallery', p. 607). **8** Hall was a writer and journalist, who claimed to have known almost every distinguished artist and writer of his day. See his

Corkonian William Maginn (1793–1842), co-founder of *Fraser's Magazine*,[9] to which Maclise contributed eighty caricatures of 'Illustrious Literary Characters' between 1830 and 1838, under the pseudonym 'Alfred Croquis'.[10] In July 1830, shortly after the Orléanist revolution which brought Louis-Philippe to the throne, Maclise made his first visit to France, where he studied works at the Louvre and Versailles.[11] According to the artist's biographer, Paris 'bore all the traces of the sanguinary conflict that had just ended and he was deeply impressed by the horrors of the scene'.[12] Among contemporary French works he saw was Théodore Géricault's *The Raft of the Medusa* (1819, now in the Louvre; fig. 1), depicting a small group of survivors of a French shipwreck near Senegal in 1816. The historical event on which the painting was based was an extremely emotive – and politically sensitive – one because of mismanagement, inexperience, and the delay in rescuing the survivors on the raft: by the time they were found only fifteen of the original 149 were still alive.[13] The depleted group depicted by Géricault was stranded for nearly two weeks, and experienced terrible agony and deprivation. The emphasis in the seven-metre-wide canvas, which features twisting survivors and corpses, as well as tilting diagonals, is on human suffering, terror, anguish, and tension; the poses of the figures were drawn from such antecedents as Raphael and Michelangelo. It had an influence on such French artists as Eugène Delacroix (1798–1863), and also had a lasting influence on Maclise.

Maclise's appreciation of such weighty subjects as Géricault's encouraged him to

Retrospect of a long life: from 1815 to 1883 (2 vols, London, 1883). The *Art Union Monthly Journal*, founded in 1839, was the first magazine devoted entirely to the fine and applied arts. In 1849 Hall renamed it the *Art Journal*.   **9** *Fraser's*, the general and literary Tory journal, counted among its contributors Samuel Taylor Coleridge, Robert Southey, Thomas Carlyle, William Makepeace Thackeray, and Father Prout (Francis Mahony).   **10** The series was republished in 1874, edited by William Bates, as *A gallery of illustrious literary characters*.   **11** See MS autobiography, p. 35.   **12** O'Driscoll p. 44.   **13** After the battle of Waterloo and the restoration of the French monarchy, the British offered the French the port of St Louis on the African coast, to serve as a trading base. A squadron of four ships, including the *Medusa*, was sent in 1816, under the command of Captain Hugues Duroy de Chaumereys, to install the French governor, Colonel Julien Désiré Schmaltz. Schmaltz prevailed upon de Chaumereys to sail the *Medusa* dangerously close to the African coast, in an effort to reach St Louis more quickly. On 2 July the ship ran aground; a plan was conceived to place the more important passengers in lifeboats, while some 150 soldiers and crew would take their chances on a raft (measuring 20 m by 7 m) constructed of ship's timbers, which would be towed to safety by the lifeboats. The raft was hopelessly overcrowded; in order to reduce the risk of the lifeboats' being overwhelmed, de Chaumereys gave the order for the undersupplied raft to be cast adrift. The decision was catastrophic: rations were lost, quarrels were constant, and, with the hope of rescue fading, some resorted to cannibalism. The fifteen remaining survivors were found after nearly two weeks; five of them died shortly after their rescue. De Chaumereys was court-martialled, but found not guilty. See Alexander McKee, *Death raft: the human drama of the Medusa shipwreck* (1975); Lorenz Eitner, *Géricault's 'Raft of the Medusa'* (London, 1972) and Albert Alhadeff, *The raft of the Medusa: Gericault, art, and race* (Munich, 2002).

1 Théodore Géricault, *Le Radeau de la Méduse (The Raft of the Medusa)* (1819). By kind permission of the Réunion des musées nationaux, Paris. The aim of Géricault (1791–1824) was to transform a controversial contemporary tragedy into something monumental and heroic. The painting depicts the remaining fifteen of raft's original 150 occupants (who drifted for nearly two weeks) at the moment they catch sight of the *Argus* (which, ironically, had been sent to look for lifeboat survivors who might have put ashore) on the horizon. Interestingly, Géricault stylizes his figures, implausibly endowing them with athleticism and vigour. The artist made an intensive study of the disaster, and interviewed some of the survivors; he even had the carpenter of the *Medusa* build a model of the raft in his studio. The work, originally entitled *Shipwreck*, was shown at the Paris Salon in 1819. In 1820 the huge canvas was exhibited in London, where it met with considerable success in exhibitions. Reception among the French critics was, however, more mixed, owing to the political ramifications of the Medusa disaster. The painting was eventually offered for sale; potential buyers included a consortium of French nobility, who wished to cut up the canvas for sale in smaller pieces. Ironically the picture was purchased by Louis XVIII, who donated it to the Louvre, where it hangs today. *The Raft of the Medusa* made a lasting impression on Maclise, who, like Géricault, studied cadavers in an attempt to acquire an intimate understanding of the human form.

2 Friedrich August Moritz Retzsch, 'Hamlet: Act III, scene 2', from *Umrisse zu Hamlet* (Leipzig and London, 1828). Retzsch's series of illustrations from Shakespeare was one manifestation of the growing interchange between England and Germany in the fields of literature and the fine arts in the early nineteenth century. Maclise owned a copy of Retzsch's work.

endow his painting with new authority and seriousness. Contemporary German art also played a part in this process. The self-confessed 'Cockneyfied Corkonian'[14] clearly felt the growing intellectual and cultural affinity and interchange that developed between England and Germany in the early part of the nineteenth century – especially in literature, music, and the fine arts.[15] In the 1820s and 1830s, for example, Shakespeare became a favourite subject for German illustrators, including Friedrich August Moritz Retzsch (1779–1857), whose outline engravings were very popular in England. In 1828 he published his series of engravings, *Umrisse zu Hamlet*, drawn from Shakespeare's play (fig. 2).[16] Maclise owned a copy of this work, along with the German artist's outlines to Goethe and Schiller,[17] and drew from them freely. He

14 See *The letters of Charles Dickens*, Pilgrim edition, ed. Graham Storey and K.J. Fielding (Oxford, 1981), 5, p. 606, note 2. This self-description appeared in a letter of introduction which Maclise had sent to Dickens, on behalf of John Francis Oliffe (1808–69).   **15** Turpin speculates that Maclise might have become curious about German culture at the time he executed his illustrations for *Fraser's Magazine* (John Turpin, 'German influence on Daniel Maclise', *Apollo* [February 1973], 169).   **16** See William Vaughan's chapter on 'F.A.M. Retzsch and the Outline Style', in *German Romanticism and English art* (New Haven, 1979), pp 123–54.   **17** See ibid., p. 281, note 101. Vaughan observes that the connection with Retzsch was noted in the *Athenaeum* (7 May 1842), pp 409–10; he also recalls that copies of

3 Daniel Maclise, *The Play Scene from Hamlet* (1842); anonymous engraving, by kind permission of the Courtauld Institute of Art, London. From Retzsch's outline (Fig 2) Maclise borrowed compositional devices like symmetry: the figures are compressed into a rigidly proportioned composition, like a triptych, with two balancing groups in the foreground framing a central recess. He also adopted the elaborate allegorical symbolism of Retzsch, as for example in the use of statuary: on the left of Maclise's picture is a statue of Prayer, standing with clasped hands in a niche above Ophelia. In the wall tapestry to the left two biblical scenes are depicted: the 'Temptation in the Garden of Eden' and the 'Expulsion'. Complementing these on the other side are a statue of justice and tapestries of the 'Sacrifice of Abel' and 'Cain Murdering Abel'. These biblical subjects form an allegorical counterpoint to the action of the play. Maclise painted two versions of this subject: one is in the Tate Gallery, London; the other is in the Forbes Magazine collection, New York.

painted *The Banquet Scene from Macbeth* (1840), based on Retzsch, as well as *The Play Scene from Hamlet* (fig. 3), which took the Royal Academy by storm in 1842, and is a clear, unashamed pastiche of the German artist's outline.[18] It drew praise from the likes of Thackeray, who called it one of the 'most startling, wonderful pictures that the English school has ever produced';[19] Samuel Carter Hall, writing in the *Art-Union*, pronounced that it was 'in all respects, a *chef-d'oeuvre* of the British school', and

Retzsch's Shakespeare outlines were in Maclise's sale (*Remaining works of . . . D. Maclise, RA*, Christie, Manson & Woods, 24 June 1870, lot 117). **18** 'The Play Scene from *Hamlet*', in *Umrisse zu Hamlet* (Leipzig and London, 1828). **19** Michael Angelo Titmarsh [W.M. Thackeray], 'An exhibition gossip', *Ainsworth's Magazine*, 1 (1842), 321. The piece, cast in the form of a letter to a French painter ('Monsieur Guillaume'), compares the exhibitions at the Royal Academy and the salon for 1842.

'worthy of association' with Shakespeare's 'more magnificent creations'.[20] Maclise borrowed such compositional devices as symmetry, as well as the elaborate allegorical symbolism, from Retzsch.

There were other aspects of book German illustration which fascinated Maclise. One example is his collection of images from Gottfried Bürger's *Leonora*,[21] a popular eighteenth-century German poem, which had been illustrated, among others, by William Blake.[22] Maclise's source was Retzsch's outlines to *Leonora*, published in 1840.[23] Although Retzsch shows his figures in eighteenth-century dress (fig. 4), Maclise places the story in a medieval setting (fig. 5), because he was more concerned with a symbolic than a realistic interpretation; interestingly, he chose to depict the same scenes as Retzsch. With the careful integration of Gothic letterpress, illustrations and decorated borders, Maclise's work is unmistakably Germanic in style and mood. This important characteristic of his style is confirmed in *The Athenaeum*:

> In style, we know of no German work that surpasses this – essentially German in character – in the fancy and vigour of design, – or equals it in the beautiful execution of the wood-engraving. Maclise is as German as the Germans themselves: – and though we do not object to find in such a work Maclise winning the race of ornamental decoration, yet we would rather see him taking an original course of his own than following that of his Continental brethren.[24]

As Maclise's career progressed, such observations on his Germanic bent were increasingly associated with his output.

The Germanic characteristics of Maclise's book illustration extended beyond Bürger's poem, to his illustrations for a new edition of Thomas Moore's *Irish Melodies*,[25] which used as their model the edition of *Das Nibelungenlied* by Julius Hübner, Eduard Bendemann, and Alfred Rethel, published in 1828. Maclise's 160 designs represent his finest achievement as a book illustrator, and drew praise from Moore himself, to whom many of the drawings were submitted before publication.[26]

20 [Samuel Carter Hall], 'The Royal Academy: seventy-fourth exhibition – 1842', *Art-Union* 4 (1842), 120.   21 Trans. Julia Cameron (London, 1847). The poem tells the story of Leonora, whose lover, William, departs for the wars and does not return. Distraught with grief, she pleads for death. Eventually William returns late one night, a strange unearthly figure, and bids her ride a hundred miles with him to the bridal bed. They set off on a strange demon ride, reminiscent of Goethe's *Ride of the erl king*, surrounded by the figures of the dead carrying a coffin, and the poem culminates with Leonora's own death at the end of the ride. See Richard Ormond, *Daniel Maclise, 1806–1870* (London, 1972), p. 80.   22 *Leonora: a tale, translated and altered from the German . . . by J.T. Stanley* (London, 1796).   23 *Retzsch's outlines to Burger's ballads: Leonora, the Song of the brave man, and the Parson's daughter of Taubenhayn* (Leipzig, 1840).   24 'Fine arts', *Athenaeum* (9 January 1847), 49. The *Art-Journal* noted: 'the genius of Maclise has been almost of necessity led to adopt the style of Germany in this effort at illustrating a German ballad'.   25 The designs are described in O'Driscoll's biography, pp 125–9.   26 Moore declared in his preface: 'I deem it most

4 Friedrich August Moritz Retzsch, illustration to Bürger's *Leonora*, from *Retzsch's outlines to Burger's ballads: Leonora, the song of the brave man, and the parson's daughter of Taubenhayn* (Leipzig, 1840).

The text and illustrations are carefully dovetailed; the use of trellises, decorative borders and heroic figures is very much in the German iconographic mode. Maclise venerated the *Irish Melodies*, and, together with his friend Charles Dickens, would, of an evening, 'hum or sing over the Irish Melodies together'.[27] Maclise's illustrations reflect the various subjects of Moore's poems: allegory, religion, chivalry, revelry, love, fairy tale, dream, and death. In 'The Minstrel Boy' (fig. 6) the artist presents a scene of love on the left; but on the right he depicts the dying hero destroying his harp. Maclise's interpretation avoids realistic scenes; instead the images concentrate on the dreamy, somewhat melancholy quality of the verses. The picture and poem have been interpreted by scholars as a lament for a vanished Celtic past, and the finding of a refuge in sensuality and imagination.[28]

fortunate for this new Edition that the rich, imaginative powers of Mr MACLISE have been employed in its adornment; and that, to complete its national character, an Irish pencil has lent its aid to an Irish pen in rendering due honour and homage to our country's ancient harp' (*Moore's Irish melodies* [London, 1845], p. iv). **27** This was recalled by Dickens' daughter, Kate Perugini, in 'Charles Dickens as a lover of art and artists', *The Magazine of Art*, ns 1 (1903), 127. For more information on Dickens and Maclise see Leon Litvack, 'Dickens, Ireland, and the Irish', *Dickensian*, 99:2 (2003), 137–52. **28** See Ormond, p. 80, and Turpin, 'German influence on Daniel Maclise', 171.

r.

The mother to her comfort flies:
"Oh! why this grief so wild?"
She clasps her daughter in her arms,
And cries "God calm my child!"

5 Daniel Maclise, illustration for *Leonora*, trans. Julia M. Cameron (London, 1847). The artist's placement of his figures in a medieval setting demonstrates his concern with symbolic – rather than realistic – representation. The scenes he chose to depict are the same as those selected by Retzsch.

Samuel Carter Hall explained the terms of the public's attraction to German prototypes in an article in the *Art-Union* in 1839:

> To describe this [modern German] taste, we must seek to evoke that calm and majestic form of art which belongs to early times, and first issued from the quiet sanctuary of monastic retirement. There is in it the solemnity which springs from a deep religious feeling, half materialising the objects of its worship, and the simplicity natural to those who live detached from the world, and debarred from all part in its varied interests and pursuits. We must follow the solitary to his cell, and see him undisturbed by the attractions that occupy and interest other men, giving his whole soul to realize the one class of ideas with which his mind is filled – imbued himself with solemn and religious fervour, it is stamped on his works ... [The public] will find in [German] works the mystic spirit that hovers over so many German minds, and tinges so many of their productions in literature and art.[29]

The emphasis here is on the moral and meditative aspects of German art, particularly as they contribute to a budding nationalism. The Germans – particularly in the south of the country, in regions such as Bavaria – harkened back to folk tales, the fairy tales of the Grimm brothers, and, as mentioned above, the *Niebelungenlied*, in an attempt to reinvent themselves.

The article by Hall was inspired by the work of a German group whose efforts were becoming known in England in the 1830s and 40s. They were known as the Nazarenes: a group of like-minded artists, including Peter Cornelius (1783–1867, about whom Hall wrote the article) and Friedrich Overbeck (1789–1869), who worked in Rome, and later northern Europe, from 1818 to the 1840s.[30] The label *Die Nazarener* was at first applied mockingly, because of the group's heavy concentration on biblical subjects, the strict monastic life they lived at San Isidoro (a sixteenth-century Irish Franciscan monastery in Rome) and their physical appearance, which included the wearing of wide, trailing cloaks, and long, flowing hair. The Nazarene group shared a leaning towards spiritually ponderous subjects, a commitment to crystalline linearity and local colour, and a fascination with Renaissance art of the fifteenth and early sixteenth centuries, including the work of Dürer, Michelangelo, and Raphael. They enjoyed a favourable European reputation, particularly in Christian revivalist milieux, such as that of Jean-Auguste-Dominique Ingres (1780–1867) and his followers, who were attempting to revive religious inspiration of art in France. English visitors to their studios included members of the Pre-Raphaelite brotherhood, and the novelist George Eliot.

29 [Samuel Carter Hall], 'The German school: Pierre Cornelius', *Art-Union*, November 1839, p. 168. Most of the article talks about Cornelius' work in Munich's Lugwigskirche, where he painted a fresco of the Last Judgment. **30** The definitive history of the movement is Keith Andrew's *The Nazarenes* (Oxford, 1964).

6 Daniel Maclise, 'The Minstrel Boy', in *Moore's Irish melodies* (London, 1845). The model for these plates was the German edition of *Das Nibelungenlied* by Hübner, Bendemann, and Rethel (1828). The use of trellises, decorative borders and heroic figures is characteristic of the German iconographic mode.

In Britain the chief proponents of German art in the 1840s included the painter Charles Eastlake (1793–1865),[31] who controlled the decoration schemes for the Palace of Westminster, and Prince Albert. Like Germany, England was trying to inculcate or invent high art for a noble, national purpose. In 1841 a body of Commissioners for the new Houses of Parliament was formed, with Albert (recently arrived in England) as president, and Eastlake as secretary. The design competition they promoted stipulated that the new Palace should be built in a 'national' style (which in England's case meant either Gothic or Elizabethan) and both Albert and Eastlake favoured the employment of German artists.[32] The Commissioners were well acquainted with the didactic vein of German monumental art, and looked principally to the schools of Munich, Düsseldorf, and Berlin for inspiration; the Nazarene tradition, especially as represented by Cornelius (who visited London to advise Eastlake in 1841) was their ideal.[33] These German painters intended art to become part of the fabric of daily life, inseparable from its context; for this reason they accepted many commissions – particularly from Ludwig I of Bavaria – for decorating public buildings, such as churches, town halls, and palaces. This strategy suited the Westminster commissioners, who saw fresco (which, by its nature, involved the pictorial decoration of architecture) as a key genre. When the artist William Dyce (1806–64), who had visited Germany and was heavily influenced by the Nazarenes, was questioned by the Select Committee on Fine Arts in 1841, he was asked how painting and sculpture were used to adorn German architecture, he replied: 'It seems to me that the manner in which the three arts of architecture and painting and sculpture are combined, is greatly advantageous to the progress of all three'.[34] He went on to describe how at Munich the painting of figures on buildings had produced pleasing effects; he singled out for special praise the work of Cornelius at the Glyptothek (fig. 7, where inspiration was drawn from classical subjects, such as Zeus and Apollo); the efforts of Wilhelm von Kaulbach (1805–74) at the Pinakothek (depicting the history of modern German art); and the images of Julius Schnorr von Carolsfeld (1794–1872) at the Munich Residenz (largely drawn from *Das Nibelungenlied*). On further questioning, Dyce confirmed that the principles of German 'improvement', which allowed them to create national works derived from

31 Eastlake was knighted in 1850. In that year he became president of the Royal Academy, and in 1855 he was appointed the first director of the National Gallery in London. **32** See Vaughan, *German Romanticism and English art*, p. 7. **33** See T.S.R. Boase, 'The decoration of the new palace of Westminster 1841–1863', in *Journal of the Warburg and Courtauld Institutes*, 17 (1954), 323. See also Gunther Metken, 'Ein nationaler Stil? England und des nazarenische Bespiel', in *Die Nazarener: romantischer Geist und christliche Kunst im 19. Jahrhundert* (Regensburg, 1982), pp 355–64. Interestingly Augustus Pugin (1812–52), who was the inspiration behind the decoration of the palace, judged Friedrich Overbeck (who had influenced the architect's own drawing and decoration) to be the 'prince of Christian painters' (*Contrasts, or a parallel between the noble edifices of the middle ages and corresponding buildings of the present day, shewing the present decay of taste* [London, 1841], p. 18. **34** *First report from the select committee on fine arts* (London, 1841), p. 23.

7 Peter Cornelius, fresco of Apollo on the ceiling of the Göttersaal (Hall of the Gods) in the Glyptotek, Munich, 1825–6. By kind permission of the Courtauld Institute of Art, London. The Glyptothek (destroyed in World War II) was part of a programme of building commissioned by the emperor Ludwig, who employed Cornelius and his followers to paint historical, allegorical, and religious subjects on the walls of public buildings. In the Göttersaal the focus was classical: Zeus as ruler of Olympus appeared above the door, and was flanked by stories from the life of Apollo. These frescoes served as prototypes for Prince Albert's Buckingham Palace Garden Pavilion (Fig. 8).

serious, weighty, or grand subjects, were guided by contemplation of religion, as well as ancient Greek poetry. He also noted a shift in German style towards the Italianate, and an increasing naturalism, accompanied by more dramatic display. Dyce concluded by confirming that the arts would be very much improved in Britain if the new houses of parliament were to be decorated with painting and sculpture; he cautioned, however, that while there were many indigenous artists who had sufficient talent to effect the decoration, there were, at that time, no fresco painters.[35]

The committee concluded that further study and assessment were required. To this end, a competition was announced in 1842, and Maclise set himself to the task. By way of preparation, in 1843 he participated in a trial commissioned by Albert, to decorate the newly built Buckingham Palace Garden Pavilion[36] with frescoes, based on Milton's *Comus*, of which the Prince had seen a performance in Covent Garden

35 Ibid., p. 25.   **36** The building eventually fell into disrepair, and was dismantled in 1928.

8 Daniel Maclise, fresco of a scene from Milton's *Comus*, in the Buckingham Palace Garden Pavilion (1843); from *The decorations of the garden-pavilion in the grounds of Buckingham Palace, engraved under the superintendence of L. Gruner* (London, 1846), plate 4. The Lady of the poem is seated in the marble chair where she has been imprisoned; over her stands Sabrina, goddess of the river Severn, who is about to sprinkle her with water and release her from the enchanted chair. The fresco owes a debt to Raphael's *Parnassus* (1509–10), while the figure of Thyrsis on the right is reminiscent of the work of Overbeck. Other artists who decorated the principal space (in the shape of an octagon) included Clarkson Stanfield, Thomas Unwins, Charles Robert Leslie, William Ross, Edwin Landseer, William Dyce, and Charles Eastlake.

in March 1842 (fig. 8).[37] The structure (selected because of its exemplification of Italian decorative art) may have owed a debt to the frescoed room in honour of Goethe and Schiller in the Schloss at Weimar, decorated in 1836–44 by a pupil of Cornelius.[38] In her introduction to a volume of lithographs from the pavilion, Anna Brownwell Jameson confirmed the importance of the experiment: 'The introduction ... of Fresco Painting in this country has become, in connexion with a great national monument [the Palace of Westminster], a topic of general interest, an affair of national importance'. *Comus* was chosen because the work embodied 'classical, romantic, and

37 For a full description, and hand-coloured lithograph illustrations, see *The decorations of the garden-pavilion in the grounds of Buckingham Palace, engraved under the superintendence of L. Gruner ... with an introduction by Mrs [Anna Brownell] Jameson* (London, 1846).   38 Winslow Ames, *Prince Albert and Victorian taste* (London, 1967), p. 53.

pastoral' elements, and allowed for a parallel to be drawn between the unnamed lady of the poem and Queen Victoria.[39] This concentration on a central female figure, whether sitting or on a pedestal, was something to which Maclise would return in later work.

He undertook further preparation by going to Paris for a second time in September–October 1844, with the specific object of studying French monumental painting. He noted, in a letter to his friend John Forster:

> It has taken me three days continually walking to see the miles of canvasses at Versailles. I have gone into all the churches hunting after dim old frescoes . . . My belief is that we in London are the smallest, & most wretched set of snivellers that ever took pencil in hand – and I feel that I could not mention a single name, with full confidence, were I called upon to name one of our artists in comparison with one of theirs.

He particularly appreciated the work of Paul Delaroche, of whose *Hemicycle* in L'école des Beaux-Arts Maclise said, 'I cannot say a word – It is impossible for me ever to convey to you my admiration for that splendid work – I go to see it every day almost, and the guardian who shows it welcomes me, and smiles at my enthusiastic admiration of it'.[40] Completed in 1841, it is done in oil paint mixed with wax, and constitutes an encyclopaedic assembly of the most renowned artists of the past, from the age of Pericles to the time of Louis XIV. The semicircular format, and the positioning of the work within the architectural space, combine to make a particular address to the spectator, who can easily make eye contact with the individual figures. It also makes a point about the importance of French art in the context of education and spectacle: the painting is located in the Amphithéâtre d'honneur, which is used on ceremonial occasions for the distribution of prizes to the students of the Beaux-Arts, where Delaroche was professor.

One other noteworthy point about the relevance of early nineteenth-century French painting for Maclise concerns the presentation of events from history. Marrinan makes the point that under Louis-Philippe's July Monarchy (1830–48) there was an explosion in the visual arts in France. Painters were commissioned to fill the galleries at Versailles, and three to four thousand pictures a year were presented to the jury in the Salon. History painting was particularly encouraged by means of commissions, so as to cast the events of French history after the Great Revolution in such a way as to explain and legitimize the ideology of the July monarchy. Thus retrospection became a national pastime and history a public passion.[41] The most

---

39 *Decorations of the garden-pavilion*, pp 5–6. Jameson had given an extensive account of modern German art in an earlier work: *Visits and sketches at home and abroad* (1834). **40** 'Daniel Maclise: letters, notes and papers', item no. 17, dated 23 September 1844 in the National Art Library, Victoria and Albert Museum, cat. no. Forster 48.E.19. **41** Michael Marrinan, *Painting politics for Louis-Philippe: art and ideology in Orléanist France, 1830–1848* (New Haven, 1988) 23.

interesting case of the influence which history painting exercised is Eugène Delacroix' *The 28th of July: Liberty Leading the People* (fig. 9; 1830). The picture, now in the Louvre, presents a standard iconographic image, encompassing a barricade, the tricolour, and a charging figure. It was presented at the Salon in 1831, and was, curiously, bought by the Interior ministry, rather than by the crown. It was then shown in the Luxembourg Museum in 1832, but then removed, because of the growing political strife and a hardening of the government's conservatism, and its desire to suppress all potentially seditious images. Liberty, as a powerful woman, strides forward, bearing the flag which was a standard image of the Empire, Bonaparte, and unfettered nationalism. The picture's plane, however, presupposes an eye level near Liberty's foot, so that the viewer is forced to take his or her place among the dead, on the verge of being run over by the gigantic barricade fighters. It thus becomes an aggressive picture, refusing to yield up a space or a viewer or witness; instead the audience run the risk of becoming the next victims. The tightly framed image exaggerates the scale and energy of these revolutionaries, who seem to burst through the boundaries of the canvas, thus engaging the viewer in the drama. The foreground is strewn with both rubble and victims, generating a dynamic relationship among combatants, cadavers, and spectators. The illuminated figure of the corpse in the lower left is also interesting, because it recalls the work of Géricault in *Raft of the Medusa*: he is stripped of shoes and trousers, thus introducing a rather shocking nudity into this street scene; such touches, emphasising the human tragedy of the event,[42] are also found in the large-scale history paintings by Maclise.

For the technical aspects of the Westminster frescoes Maclise owed an important – though, as it turned out, ill-advised – debt to the Germans. By 1855 (only one year after the building was completed) signs of decay began to appear in all the paintings: they deteriorated and darkened, owing to damp in the plaster, the adverse effects of gas lighting, and the dry paint technique used to achieve the desired quality of finish.[43] The problem was considered by the Commissioners on the Fine Arts, who in 1859 sanctioned an exploratory visit by Maclise to Germany, where he examined contemporary fresco techniques.[44] In Berlin he inspected large subjects by Kaulbach,[45] and by his pupils Michael Echter (1812–79)[46] and Julius Muhr (1819–65).

42 See ibid., p. 71.   43 See Malcolm A. C. Hay, 'The Westminster frescoes: the restoration of the Victorian murals', *Apollo*, ns, 135 (May 1992), 307–9. The problem affected the work of such artists as Charles West Cope, Sir John Tenniel, Edward Armitage, John Rogers Herbert, George Frederick Watts, and John Callcott Horsley. The dry paint medium was easily affected by damp, which emanated from the wet plaster, and by condensation, which ran down the frescoes from the stained glass windows above, owing to the heat generated by the gasoliers and large fireplaces.   44 Maclise did not speak German, and so used Eastlake (who was in the country at the same time) as his interpreter. The fact that these two travelled together must have affected whom Maclise met, what he did, and what he saw.   45 Kaulbach executed an interesting series of paintings in 1848 celebrating the flowering of art and architecture under Ludwig I; the works included portraits of a host of contemporary figures. He succeeded Cornelius as chief artist at Munich.   46 Echter painted a number of

9 Eugène Delacroix, *Le 28 Juilliet, la Liberté guidant les peoples* (*The 28th of July: Liberty Leading the People,* 1830). By kind permission of the Réunion des musées nationaux, Paris. This modern allegory celebrated the July Revolution of 1830, which saw the overthrow of Charles X and the ascension of Louis-Philippe. Its presentation of historical events had relevance for Maclise.

He visited the new Pinakothek in Munich, and noted of the frescoes he saw: 'Of these works it may indeed safely be said that they form a series of the noblest embellishment of one of the grandest halls which architecture has yet dedicated to the

frescoes in the Altes Bayerisches Nationalmuseum, depicting such historical scenes as the triumph of Kaiser Heinrich II in the battle of Mellrichstadt in 1078, and the marriage of Friedrich I (Barbarossa) to Beatrice of Burgundy in 1157. There is also an interesting fresco of Wolfram of Eschenbach (holding a harp) triumphing in a song contest at Wartburg in 1207.   **47** *Twelfth report of the commissioners on the fine arts, with appendix* (London, 1861), p.

development of a kindred art'.[47] He particularly admired the frescoes executed by Kaulbach, as well as those done under the direction of Cornelius. For technical advice Maclise consulted with the theoretical and applied chemist Max Josef von Pettenkofer (1818–1901), an expert in the preservation of oil painting,[48] and a student of the mineralogist Johann Nepomuk von Fuchs (1774–1856), who perfected the use of alkali silicates as bonding agents in paints. These men stimulated Maclise's enthusiasm for the *Eisenglass* (waterglass) wall painting technique, also called 'stereochromy'; it involved spraying a solution of liquid silica onto the wall, thus fixing the paint to the plaster. Indeed once the waterless paint was applied, it was permanent. The interest in Fuchs's work was such that in 1859 Prince Albert directed the translation and private circulation of the chemist's work on stereochromic painting.[49] The benefits of this medium for the rendering of fine detail were such that two of the Westminster artists, Charles West Cope and Edward Matthew Ward, converted to the waterglass method mid-way through their commissions.

In the long run, however, the waterglass method proved disastrous for Maclise and others at Westminster. While it had the advantages of longevity and of facilitating the display of detail, the contrasts between light and dark areas began to fade only a few years after completion of the works. Repairs and repainting were carried out from the 1860s onward; indeed some of these early conservation efforts (including the application of wax) inflicted additional damage on the paintings. One of Maclise's frescoes that has suffered over time is his first effort, *The Spirit of Chivalry* (fig. 10; 1847).[50] The Royal Commission on Fine Arts invited artists to submit cartoons for frescoes which would occupy the six arched compartments in the new House of Lords, and would be illustrative of the chamber's function and its relation to the sovereign. Maclise first submitted a cartoon, a coloured sketch, and a specimen of fresco painting. Like the *Comus* fresco, this symmetrical composition features a central female allegorical figure on a podium, and owes debts to contemporary French and German art. Maclise intimated to his friend John Forster that the principal figure was meant to be a type of Queen Victoria.[51] The other figures represent the intellectual influence of chivalry; they include a bard with his harp (a symbolic figure often found in Maclise's work), who inspires youth. Scholars are divided over the significance in Maclise's paintings of the harp. Boydell has demonstrated that in *Irish Melodies* and in *The Origin of the Harp* (1845, inspired by Moore's work) Maclise

16. Maclise's appendix is dated 27 March 1861. **48** Von Pettenkofer is, however, most famous for his work on practical hygiene. **49** *On the manufacture, properties, and application of water-glass, soluble alkaline silicate, including a process of stereochromic painting* (London, 1859). Albert personally recommended this work to Maclise. **50** In 1871 *The Spirit of Chivalry* was reported to be decaying rapidly and very much injured; it was repaired in 1874, 1894, 1895 (with no attempt made to repaint or redraw the damaged parts), 1937, 1951, and 1997. See R.J.B. Walker, *A catalogue of paintings, drawings, engravings and sculpture in the palace of Westminster, compiled during 1959–77*, vol. 3 (Croydon, 1988), p. 102. **51** Letter in the Forster Collection, National Art Library, Victoria & Albert Museum, MS no. 48.E.19, item no. 232

produced images that attested to an evolving iconography of the instrument:[52] whereas in the late eighteenth century it had served as an important political symbol for the likes of the United Irishmen,[53] by the 1840s the harp had become a pictorial evocation of sentimental romantic mythology. The versatility of the harp for Maclise is attested to in such pictures as *Robin Hood* (1839). Despite this metamorphosis of function and its appearance in a host of contexts, Weston's recent study belabours the point that Maclise – who was born in Cork but lived in London for most of his working life – felt uneasy about his Irish identity, and that he used his art to strike back at metropolitan institutions that constantly reinforced his isolation and cultural inferiority. Weston reads the harp as an 'Irish subtext'[54] – a view difficult to sustain, especially since the harp, in the context of a fresco at Westminster designed to praise chivalry, is not necessarily an indication of Irishness. Interestingly, though, when *Punch* responded to Maclise's design in 1845 (fig. 11), it clearly saw the bard or harpist as Irish, in the person of Daniel O'Connell, 'inspiring Youth – that is to say, D'IS-RAELI, commonly called Young England Ben – by a series of recitals, in which he is playing as usual the "precious lyre"'.[55]

   The Spirit of Chivalry is an abstract allegory with an underlying social significance. It evoked a spirit of patriotic idealism, inspired by German prototypes, including Friedrich Overbeck's *The Triumph of Religion in the Arts* (1832–40), and French ones, particularly Delaroche's *Hemicycle* (itself influenced by the Nazarenes), from which Maclise copied the figure of an architect holding a model of a church. *Chivalry* blended nineteenth-century historicism with Renaissance allegory; it revealed Maclise's deepening conception of epic art, and confirmed his natural bent towards monumental painting. It also confirmed the extent to which he emulated the Germans long before he visited their country.[56] From the Germans he learned to strengthen his sense of composition and powers of draughtsmanship; yet he was not a 'Germanist' in that he (unlike William Dyce) did not share the religious ideals of the Nazarenes.

   It is difficult to summarize the extent to which Continental art influenced Maclise when he is scrutinized particularly as an Irish artist. The contribution of German art to the conception of the illustrations for Moore's *Irish Melodies* has been noted above. The perceived lament for a Celtic past does, of course, have political overtones; but the potential of book illustration for political critique is, perhaps,

52 Barra Boydell, 'The female harp: the Irish harp in 18th- and early 19th-century romantic nationalism', in *RIdIM/RCMI Newsletter*, 20:1 (1995), 10–17. **53** The United Irishmen had used the figure of Liberty or Hibernia/Erin together with a winged-maiden harp in such songbooks as *Tun'd to freedom* (1795). **54** *Daniel Maclise: Irish artist in Victorian London* (Dublin, 2001), p. 96. **55** *Punch*, 8 (1845), 88. **56** William Vaughan characterizes Maclise as a 'convert' to a 'severe and idealistic form' of Germanic medievalism; he confirms that *The Spirit of Chivalry* contained 'what was seen as a *Germanic* thoroughness and regularity of design' ('The Pre-Raphaelites and contemporary German art', in Franz Bosback and Frank Büttner (eds), *Künstlerische Beziehungen zwischen England und Deutschland in der viktorianischen Epoche* (Munich, 1998), p. 78).

10 Daniel Maclise, *The Spirit of Chivalry* (1846–7); by kind permission of the Palace of Westminster. Influences on this painting include Raphael's *School of Athens*,1483–1520 (which in turn inspired Delaroche's *Hemicycle*), and Raphael's *Disputa* (1510–1511). Maclise's iconography is clearly enunciated. In the centre of the fresco the Spirit of Chivalry, represented by an idealized Madonna-like figure robed in white and holding a laurel wreath, stands at an altar supported by carved angels, the centre of chivalric devotion. On either side of her are figures personifying the military, religious, and civil powers: a warrior king with his crusader knights on the left, an archbishop and two scholars on the right. They represent, as by an upper court or house, the final acquisition of Chivalry's honours and rewards. Beneath, as not having obtained, but within the reach of, the crown, a young knight in armour, kneeling, vows himself to chivalric services, attended by his page, and invited by his lady's favour. His sword is dedicated 'à Dieu et aux Dames'. The other figures represent the intellectual influence of chivalry: there is a musician, painter, sculptor, philosopher, architect, poet, and a bard with his harp (a symbolic figure often found in Maclise's work). Maclise intimated to John Forster that the upper part of the fresco was intended 'to be a type of the House of Lords . . . as the principal figure is meant to be typical of the Queen herself' (letters from Maclise to John Forster, in the Forster Collection, National Art Library,Victoria & Albert Museum, MS no. 48.E.19, item no. 232). It is interesting to compare the figure of the bard in this picture with that found in *The Marriage of Strongbow and Aoife* (1854; Fig, 12).

11 [John Tenniel], 'The spirit of chivalry of the house of commons', in *Punch* 8 (1845): 88. Maclise is berated by *Punch* for rendering his figures as ideal, rather than real personages. Here the Speaker represents Chivalry, and is flanked by Wellington in spectacles on the right, and Peel as a chivalrous knight on the left. O'Connell appears at the bottom as the bard, holding the harp, while Disraeli kneels beside him, playing the lyre. These cartoons were conceived as a satirical response to their more high-minded originals, which artists were asked to submit by the Fine Art Commissioners.

dwarfed by the visual impact made by such monumental works as frescoes, executed on a large scale, and intended for the adornment of public buildings. By the 1850s Maclise had demonstrated that he could endow his work with drama, was able to chiaroscuro and the positioning of contrasting figures to good effect, and could develop elaborate allegorical symbolism to convey the desired message. He could emulate the monumentalism of the Germans, and was sensitive to their romantic medievalism; he was equally amenable to developing pursuits similar to the French in terms of education and spectacle. All of these elements come together in one of his best pictures, which testifies to his achievement as an Irish artist: *The Marriage of Strongbow and Aoife* (1854; fig. 12).

The picture was originally intended as a fresco: the subject was originally one of those set by the Fine Arts Commissioners for the Painted Chamber at the Palace of Westminster, in order to depict the acquisition of territory constituting the British empire;[57] Maclise, however, declined the commission. Insufficient remuneration was, no doubt, a contributing factor, but another issue might have been the proscriptive nature of the Commissioners' agenda; as Dickens noted disparagingly, in relation to *The Spirit of Chivalry*, 'It is so many feet and inches high, by order of the Commissioners; and so many feet and inches broad, by order of the Commissioners. Its proportions are exceedingly difficult of management, by order of the Commissioners; and its subject and title were an order of the Commissioners'.[58] Instead of painting a fresco, Maclise rendered his subject in oil (a more rich and fluid medium) on an immense canvas measuring three meters high and five meters wide. While the tone of this sacrificial event is unmistakable, its social or political thrust is more open to question. It depicts a crucial moment in Ireland's political history.[59]

Maclise himself described the scene, in a note to his friend John Forster:

> The marriage is celebrated on the field of battle – amid its scenes of desolation – The Triumphant Banners of the Conquerors are displayed. Submission of the Irish Chieftains – mourning over the fallen Burial of the Dead.
>
> The historic circumstances of a marriage celebrated on a battle field afforded an opportunity of exhibiting those contrasts of cheerfulness and gloom characteristic of Irish Temperament and Irish Music.[60]

---

57 *Tenth report of the commissioners on the fine arts* (London, 1854), p. 441. 58 [Charles Dickens], 'The Spirit of Chivalry in Westminster Hall', in *Dickens' journalism, volume 2: the amusements of the people and other papers*, ed. Michael Slater (London, 1996), p. 75. The essay was originally published in *Douglas Jerrold's Shilling Magazine* in August 1845. 59 The most comprehensive account of the marriage and the events surrounding it is found in Giraldus Cambrensis' 12th-century work, *Expugnatio Hibernica*. It is briefly recounted by Pamela Berger in her essay 'The historical, the sacred, the romantic: medieval texts into Irish watercolours', in *Visualizing Ireland: national identity and the pictorial form*, ed. Adele M. Dalsimer (Boston, 1993), pp 71, 74–5. 60 Maclise: Letters, Notes and Papers', item no. 126. This was written on the back of an envelope, and enclosed with a letter to Forster (item no. 125), dated 6 April 1854.

12 Daniel Maclise, *The Marriage of Strongbow and Aoife* (1854); by kind permission of the
National Gallery of Ireland. In the centre the Anglo-Norman Richard de Clare, Earl of
Pembroke (known as 'Strongbow'), garlanded like a Roman general, tramples a cross under
foot, after his successful siege of Waterford (the sacked town visible in the background). He
is united with Eva or Aoife, daughter of Dermot MacMurrough, King of Leinster, who gives
her away as part of a pact. Maidens in white attend Aoife, while behind Dermot stand several
of his chained Irish enemies. In the foreground are several strongly lit and dominant groups
of Irish, including warriors kneeling in submission on the right, and a woman, left of centre,
with arms raised and a dead child in her lap; she gives voice to her grief in a pose usually
reserved in Renaissance painting for the massacre of the innocents. Bodies are being lifted
into a grave on the left. Among the dead and grieving there is the kneeling figure of the
bard, who is unable to play his harp because the strings are broken. The painting demonstrates an indebtedness to sixteenth-century Italian art by way of the Nazarenes, and to the
work of contemporary French artists like Géricault and Delacroix.

The brevity of these comments is interesting, because they confirm the simplicity in
which Maclise conceived the picture. Such minimalism is a necessary characteristic
of fresco: while it is conceived on a large scale, it demands a certain singularity of
purpose in order to have maximum impact. Yet Maclise's composition features a
several areas of interest, and large number of figures and accessories (particularly
jewellery), which are more appropriate to an oil painting. He did a great deal of
research for the picture, filling his sketchbooks with drawings of ancient weapons and

costume, as well as croziers and crosses.[61] He also did drawings of Irish antiquities, thus recalling his early years in Ireland, under the direction of Sainthill and Croker.[62] Yet historical painting, like historical fiction, takes liberties with its subject matter. The *Art-Journal* pointed out chronological errors, such as Strongbow's wearing a helmet and a rich suit of mixed armour (elements demonstrating the influence of Kaulbach); these details, the publication confirms, were innovations dating from the time of Henry IV and Edward I respectively, rather than the period of Henry II, which is when the marriage took place.[63] The journal was, nevertheless, mightily impressed with the work, calling it 'one of the best productions of the modern schools'.[64] Maclise had an idealistic and generally sympathetic approach to history in this picture; this can be seen in the Christian iconography he transposes onto key figures. The woman with the dead child recalls not only the massacre of the innocents, but adopts the same pose as in Ingres' *Martyrdom of St Symphorien* (1834), which in turn draws on Titian. Also, in the earlier water-colour version of this painting (where the keening woman appears with bared breasts), Aoife and her companions carry palms, demonstrating that Maclise conceived of them as virgin martyrs. The body being lifted into the grave in the lower left (and indeed the other semi-nude victims) recalls Géricault's *Raft of the Medusa*, as well as a series of classic entombment scenes. Against the skyline on the brow of the hill to the left, a body is lowered, in a scene reminiscent of Raphael's *Deposition* (1507), as well as Cornelius' *The Entombment* (1813–9, also drawn from Raphael). To heighten the sense of pathos Maclise uses a strong chiaroscuro, playing light against shade: for example, the Norman knights are all shrouded in darkness, while Aoife and her entourage are brightly lit. Light and dark are part of a religious theme: the decline of the evening declines behind a hill suggests Golgotha. The pinks, yellows, oranges, cobalt blues and smoky greys in the colour of the sky confirm Maclise's debt to sixteenth-century Italian art.

Ormond confirms that the painting was 'consciously intended to rival Continental achievements', and thus remains somewhat alien to English taste.[65] This foreignness is also emphasised by the pessimistic vein which seems to run through the painting: the viewer is constantly challenged by the artist's political and cultural stance in a painting of a marriage that has been accepted as a symbol of the union between Britain and Ireland. Because of his long residence in London and his extraordinary devotion to his work in the Palace of Westminster, Maclise has always been considered a metropolitan artist. Yet it is interesting to recall that at the time of *Strongbow and Aoife*, his interest in pre-Norman civilization was most pronounced; it found its most sustained expression in the *Norman Conquest* series (1857; now in the

61 See Maclise's sketchbooks, National Art Library, cat. nos. 48.F.60 and 48.F.59. **62** See National Library of Ireland, MS no. 4458. The descriptions to the drawings were appended by Thomas Crofton Croker and others. **63** Maclise also took liberties in his interpretations of *The meeting of Wellington and Blucher* (1861) and *The death of Nelson* (1865). **64** 'The Royal Academy: The Exhibition, 1854' in *Art-Journal*, 1 June 1854, 166. **65** 'Daniel Maclise' in *Burlington Magazine*, 110 (1968), 691

Whitworth Art Gallery, Manchester).[66] These pencil drawings (which resemble a scheme for fresco in their simplicity) depict the destruction of humane and civilized society in the face of military aggression. The Saxons are presented as simple, peaceable people, while the Normans are likened to the Romans, with Duke William interpreted in the role of Caesar. A similar contrast is developed in *Strongbow and Aoife*, where it is permitted heightened emphasis by the profusion of detail. For example, in order to highlight the Irish romanticism of the picture, Maclise introduces such details as the flagstone in the centre foreground, with its interlaced Celtic pattern, as well as the round tower and the plumes of smoke rising from the ruins of Waterford, thus heightening the spectacle of destruction. It is also interesting to note that while the marriage (for which Maclise has cleared a central oval space) constitutes the ostensible event of the painting, the way the foreground is lit, and the level of detail included in this area, points to this as the outstanding field of interest for the painter and viewer.

The presence of the bard (dressed in green cloak) and his harp inevitably leads some critics to claim that this leitmotif is a peculiarly Irish element in Maclise's painting;[67] but as has been demonstrated above, in the discussion of *The Spirit of Chivalry*, this is not necessarily so. It is clear, however, that *Strongbow and Aoife* features a plethora of Celtic elements, many imbued with pathos, in order to heighten the emotional effect. Yet scholars are divided over what the painting infers. Ormond identifies the subject of *Strongbow and Aoife* as 'the downfall of Celtic civilization';[68] Brian Kennedy highlights the old harper's broken strings, and the chronological proximity of the Young Irelanders' rebellion to a painting emphasising that 'the history of foreign domination was a long one'.[69] Boydell concurs about the broken strings, and points out that the harp in the painting (noted for its 'photographic reality') is clearly modelled on the 'Brian Boru' instrument in Trinity College harp; Boydell believes that because it was inspired by an actual example of an early Irish harp, it has the potential to serve as a powerful allegory of Ireland's lost independence.[70] Turpin adds that a feeling of 'tragedy and sacrifice' are engendered in the spectator.[71] Berger believes the painting presents Strongbow's victory as a 'tragic defeat' for the Irish, who 'vainly fought to preserve their traditional way of life' in the wake of Norman aggression. She comments on how Strongbow, the bishop, and Diarmuid constitute the 'triadic forces of subjugation' operating on Aoife, and on how the red in Diarmuid's cloak might mark him out as a traitor. Berger too comments on the bard, highlighting his 'Brian Boru' harp, his bowed head conveying

---

66 These forty-two drawings demonstrated how the Norman occupation of England contributed to the downfall of a humane, art-loving society. An important source was the Bayeux Tapestry; they relate artistically to the work of Cornelius, Schnorr, and others. 67 Weston, p. 96. 68 Richard Ormond, 'Daniel Maclise', p. 691. 69 *Irish painting* (Dublin, 1993), p. 21. 70 'The female harp', 16. 71 John Turpin, 'The Irish background of Daniel Maclise 1806–1870' in *Capuchin Annual* (1970), 192. See also Turpin's 'The lure of the Celtic past in the art of Daniel Maclise' in *Ireland of the Welcomes*, 21:1 (1972), 32–6.

interior lament, and the fact that he is the only figure in the painting dressed in green.[72] Such views are not without their detractors; Cullen asserts that the presence of Celtic ornament and the 'inevitable harp' do not make *Strongbow and Aoife* a nationalist image. Instead this critic emphasises the metropolitan interest in anthropological detail, and the symbolic link between a domestic union – that is, marriage – and political union. Cullen believes that the employment of a Cork artist, who became a Royal Academician, to paint the House of Lords frescoes confirms the role of the Irish artist as 'not one of being an outsider and a malcontent, but one who pleases the centre and thus by extension strengthens the Union'.[73] There are, perhaps, merits to both arguments, and Maclise was aware of the subtleties involved. *Strongbow and Aoife* would probably not have been accepted as a fresco design for Westminster, because of its potentially seditious nature – in the vein of Delacroix' *Liberty Leading the People*.[74] If it was intended as a challenge, presenting – particularly in its attention to detail – a peculiarly Irish view of history and civilisation, then it is entirely appropriate that it hangs in the National Gallery in Dublin, where it serves as a reminder of how this artist, who worked so faithfully in the metropolitan centre, was, when freed from the constraints imposed by commissioners and patrons, able to produce original works that served as a historical and visual challenge, as well as a precursor of the Celtic revival of the late nineteenth century. He could not have roused such sentiments without engaging in an extended dialogue with Continental art, which enhanced those skills necessary for such monumental painting in the grand romantic manner.

Arguments continue to rage about whether Maclise may be described as an Irish romanticist, Irish nationalist, Nazarene imitator, romantic medievalist, 'cockneyfied Corkonian', or, as his friend Dickens considered him, a gifted individual dedicated to the 'exaltation of English art'.[75] The inspiration he drew from contemporary German and French art is clear; yet he did not slavishly emulate his predecessors, and indeed developed an independent style that is unmistakable. As he developed his craft, his oeuvre – and that of his contemporaries in these islands – took on a new grandeur, aided by political, ideological, and artistic trends on the European Continent. Maclise tried to match the Continentals in the increasing ambition of his projects. Thus he was part of the movement to inculcate or invent high art; his attainment of this goal allowed him to achieve the reputation he enjoys today in these islands.

72 'The historical, the sacred, the romantic', pp 75, 76.   **73** Fintan Cullen, *Visual politics: the representation of Ireland, 1750–1950* (Cork, 1997), pp 48, 21.   **74** Interestingly, the *Art-Journal* hoped that the painting would hang in the new Palace of Westminster ('The Royal Academy: The Exhibition, 1854', p. 166). It is also useful to note that while the Westminster frescoes displayed a Gothic influence (adopted as the national style in England), *Strongbow and Aoife* evokes a more Romanesque approach, as in, for example, the rounded central arch behind the principal figures.   **75** 'The Spirit of Chivalry in Westminster Hall', pp 79–80.

Fenianism as a global phenomenon: Thomas O'Malley Baines, papal soldier and Fenian convict

PATRICK MAUME

The nineteenth century was an age of globalization. Developments in transport and communications technology brought the Continents closer together; European peasantries were faced with new forms of competition and upheavals in customary social relations as well as with traditional subsistence crises. Millions of European emigrants sought opportunities in the new worlds of the Americas and Australasia. The spread of mass literacy and the popular press enabled the construction of new forms of political and cultural identity (some of which presented themselves in neo-traditionalist terms). One by-product of this globalising process was the Fenian movement, which to an unprecedented extent tried to coordinate a revolutionary organization in Ireland with a support network in America; hostile loyalists stereotyped Fenianism as the product of rootless American adventurers exploiting an easily-led peasantry. Another by-product was the role of new forms of mass devotional literature and improved communications in popularizing Ultramontane Catholicism; for the first time the pope as an individual (as distinct from his office) became the subject of devotion for a worldwide Catholic audience, many of whom saw Pius IX's struggle against Italian nationalism in eschatological terms.[1] This essay is an exercise in microhistory; it explores the impact of these trends on the life of a single individual, Thomas O'Malley Baines, born in 1844, evicted as a child from a smallholding on the marquess of Sligo's estate near Louisburgh, County Mayo,[2] a Papal soldier in 1860–2, a Fenian recruiter among British soldiers in the years before the Rising, a convict in Australia 1868–72, and finally an Irish nationalist, anti-Chinese agitator, saloonkeeper, and book peddler in California until his death in 1899.

The principal source for Baines' life is his autobiography, *My life in two hemispheres*

---

1 For Cardinal Manning's widely publicized view of the attack on the Papal States as a sign of the imminence of Antichrist see Robert Gray, *Cardinal Manning: a biography* (London, 1985), pp 175–6. Such views could have the awkward side-effect of precipitating millennarian movements which predicted the end or transformation of the papacy (for example, the Italian prophet described in Eric Hobsbawm, *Primitive rebels* [London, 1959], pp 68–71; the Canadian Métis leader Louis Riel expressed similar views in 1884). 2 Baines' origins on the Sligo estate are probably responsible for the mistaken view that he came from Sligo, propounded by William O'Brien and Desmond Ryan, the editors of *Devoy's postbag* (Dublin, 1948–53), vol. 2, p. 154; the views are repeated by Keith Amos in *The Fenians in Australia* (Kensington, NSW, 1988), p. 87.

(3rd ed., San Francisco, 1889); this is a slight and badly written production, which does not deserve to rank with the major Fenian autobiographies. After a brief account of his life (saying almost nothing about his family and childhood) it becomes a rambling account of Baines' travels in California and Australia, full of vague laudations of distinguished Irishmen whom he encountered (obviously he hoped they would buy the book), and finally tailing off amidst advertisements and reprints of Young Ireland ballads. Its principal interest lies in the author's attempts to make sense of his troubled life, and to address some of the tensions between his support for the ancien régime in Italy, his membership of a revolutionary Irish secret society, and his denunciations of 'monarchical institutions' as a threat to America.[3]

Baines opens his account by describing the widespread shock among Irish Catholics early in 1860 at the realization that the Papal States faced an impending threat from the forces of Garibaldi. He equates the threat to the pope with the formative experience of his own childhood:

> It dwells in my mind side by side with another picture, that of a family evicted in the famine days of '48, when the landlord, with ruthless hand, tore the roof from off an humble cottage and thrust into bleak winter a mother and her children, to battle with the blast and hunger fever as best she might. Yes, the two pictures are in my mind to-day, and in both was I an actor.[4]

The Baines family remained in Mayo after their eviction; the 1899 *Mayo News* obituary of Baines states that in 1874 his mother and a sister (Bridget) were living in Westport and that both were buried at Oughavale.[5] Baines says nothing about his family circumstances or his whereabouts at the time he decided to join the Papal Brigade: 'As the reports of [Victor Emmanuel's] doings reached me through the medium of the press,[6] I, with hundreds of others, enthusiastic for the welfare of the Church, and only anxious to lend a helping hand in her need, volunteered for the front.'[7]

Baines and other recruits made their way clandestinely to Dublin and then to Liverpool, where they met a papal agent. They travelled by rail to Hull, and sailed to Antwerp; the recruits gathered at Malines, where they signed enlistment forms and waited for a fortnight before proceeding to Vienna, and thence to the Papal States.

---

3 *My life in two hemispheres* (hereafter *LTH*) is available on microfilm at the University of California and the British Library. I wish to thank Donald Jordan of Menlo College for supplying me with a copy of the microfilm, and acknowledge the comments of Patrick O'Sullivan on the British Library copy. I also wish to acknowledge my use of the article on Baines in the Royal Irish Academy *Dictionary of national biography* (2005). 4 *LTH*, p. 8. 5 *Mayo News*, 24 June 1899. 6 Nationalist papers played a significant role in recruiting for the Papal Brigade: after making contact with an Austrian recruiter, A.M. Sullivan published elaborate advice for fellow-countrymen considering 'emigration to Italy', and the office of his paper, *The Nation*, became the centre of the recruiting effort. See A.M. Sullivan, *New Ireland* (London, 1877). 7 *LTH*, p. 7.

Secrecy was necessary since their passage could have been prevented under the
Foreign Enlistment Act. Baines observes:

> Out of this very secrecy I learned much that was useful to me, and it taught
> me, young as I was, to keep my eyes open and my mouth shut, and the lesson
> I learned was turned to good use for the old land.[8]

Rome and the surrounding territory ('the Patrimony of St Peter') was protected by
a detachment of French regular soldiers, instructed by their government not to intervene elsewhere; the papal government therefore placed its forces (including French,
Belgian and Irish volunteers) in fortresses throughout its other provinces: Umbria,
the Marches, and Romagna. Baines served in the Adriatic port of Ancona, located in
the most discontented part of the papal states; the French and Irish garrison stationed
there hoped to prevent a juncture between the Piedmontese regulars coming down
from the North and the Garibaldians marching up from Neapolitan territories.[9]
Baines thought that the Irish Battalion was militarily weakened because the militia
officer (and future MP) Major Miles O'Reilly was given the command due to 'local
political pressure being brought to bear from Ireland in O'Reilly's favour'. Baines
would have preferred the command to be given to Major Fitzgerald, an officer
seconded from the Austrian Army, 'a strict disciplinarian and idolized by his men . . .
a native born Irishman and had nineteen years practical service in Austria in war and
peace, as against the peaceable militia periodical drills of Major O'Reilly'. Baines
laments that Fitzgerald was lost to the force 'because he could not and would not
become a subordinate to a militia officer of one of the counties of Ireland'.[10] He
complains that the English consul at Ancona and the officers of an English mail
steamer in the harbour encouraged discontent among the brigade and offered
deserters free transportation back to Ireland; Baines writes: 'It is true there was
considerable discontent among the most faithful of the Irish troops for the reason
that the amount of food, consisting in a great part of macaroni, with which the race
was not very familiar, as well as the almost total absence of potatoes . . . and the
severity of the drills and the preparations for war naturally made a few malcontents'.[11]
He also complains that they had no surgeons, and that the Italian physicians were
'charlatans' who practised 'an injudicious mixture of bleeding and starvation'. He
praises an Irish interpreter ('the only one of us, barring the sergeant–major, who had
a smattering of Italian') who accompanied the Italian doctors on their rounds and
surreptitiously increased the diet prescribed for the invalids ('they must not expect
Irish boys to live on soap suds and pipe-stoppers like themselves . . . they won't
perish of hunger if I can help it').[12]

8 *LTH*, p. 8. **9** George Berkeley, *The Irish battalion in the papal army of 1860* (Dublin, 1929).
10 *LTH*, p. 15. Berkeley attributes O'Reilly's appointment to fear that placing an Austrian
officer in command would encourage the view that the Austrians were inciting the papal
resistance and his resignation as commander of Ancona and return to Austria to a
disturbance by soldiers who had been recruited by exaggerated promises with regard to pay
and conditions. (pp. 23, 69–70). **11** *LTH*, p. 15. **12** *LTH*, p. 17.

Ancona surrendered in September 1860, after being besieged from sea and land by Sardinian forces. The prisoners were kept under guard in a field for three days, then marched to Genoa, 'the march lasting thirteen days, on only one of which we were allowed any rest'; after a brief imprisonment they sailed to Marseilles. Baines shows himself particularly concerned to defend the Irish volunteers against the accusations made by the British press at the time that they were 'cowards'and 'mercenaries'. He quotes the Italian general who commanded the siege of Ancona and the report of the French General Lamoricière (commander-in-chief of the papal forces) as proof of their prowess in battle:

> From the English point of view, they were fanatics, but certainly not mercenaries. They left country, home and friends to fight for a cause, in which, rightly or wrongly as Englishmen might judge, they deemed it honourable and holy to die . . . Mercenary considerations could have no place in their motives; for the pay of a Papal soldier was merely nominal, and his rations were poor indeed.[13]

After the surrender most of the Irish troops returned to Ireland (their expenses being paid by public subscription). Baines was among a group of thirty-six or thirty-seven who turned back at Naples and went to Rome, where they formed a small unit called the Company of St Patrick within the papal army, defending the remaining papal territory (the Patrimony of St Peter). As a mark of special honour Pius IX invited them to receive 'the Sacrament of the Eucharist . . . from his own hand on Christmas morning, 1860 . . . in the sisters' chapel of the Vatican'. It appears that this involved the distribution of preconsecrated Hosts rather than a full celebration of Mass. After communion, Baines continues,

> His Holiness, Pius the Ninth, then held up the fisherman's ring which was reverently saluted by each communicant with a fervent kiss. After which, we, with the Franco-Belgian troops, our late comrades in the war, were marched to the Royal Salon of the Vatican, where we were supplied with refreshments, consisting of chocolate, coffee, and ice cream, we being waited upon, not by the household servants, but by the princes and peers of the church, namely, the cardinals and bishops, who vied with each other to honour us by waiting on us, and to show us the most marked attentions and courtesies.[14]

It was a remarkable experience for a sixteen-year-old from Louisburgh.

Baines remained in the papal forces until 1862, participating in several border skirmishes with Italian nationalist forces (he mentions specifically battles at 'Point Carriga' and 'Torrieto on the Tiber'). His comrades included Myles Keogh, later killed with Custer at the Little Big Horn.[15] With the termination of hostilities, Baines left Rome for Ireland, arriving in Dublin in November 1862. He notes:

13 *LTH*, pp 9–11.   **14** *LTH*, p. 12.   **15** *LTH*, pp 17–18.

At that time, in Dublin, they were organizing a new Fire Department. [Sir John Gray] who was chairman of the Water Works Committee of the Corporation, was the leading figure in the enterprise. As almost all the new members were Papal soldiers, I resolved to join.[16]

Possibly we see here an exercise of Corporation patronage in favour of the former papal soldiers. Baines spent the next two years as a fireman.

Shortly after his return to Ireland Baines came into contact with the IRB. 'Of course', he said, 'the cause was to me a dear one and I readily joined.' From 1864 he worked (overseen by John Devoy) full-time as one of the IRB agents who mingled with Irish soldiers, trying to recruit them to the Fenian cause. He recalls swearing in thirty-nine soldiers in one day on the Curragh Camp in April 1865, narrowly escaping arrest through a warning from a friend.[17] He writes: 'I enrolled many thousand men in the good cause, besides the number enrolled by those having authority from me.'

Baines was also a member of a 'Committee of Safety', led by John Cody and linked to Devoy, which assassinated informers despite the IRB leadership's disapproval of such tactics.[18] He recounts one such incident:

> There was one of those named George Clark who was detected disseminating treason among the [papal] Brigade [at Ancona] and encouraging them to desert and avail themselves of the protection offered by the English emissaries . . . he subsequently became a traitor after returning to Ireland at the expense of the English Government. He joined the revolutionary organization then existing and became a loud-mouthed advocate of the organization, but while pretending to be truthful he was found making visits to the detective office in the lower castle yard and betrayed his country and his companions. Detectives from the organization, however, were on his track, and after being fully satisfied as to his treachery he received a trial by a court-martial composed of those in authority, and [was] sentenced to death. It is needless for me to say that he was found shot on the banks of the Royal Canal in a dying condition, but was unable to furnish the names of those who gave him free transportation to his last home.[19]

Here Baines' narrative is like some War of Independence reminiscences, where a speaker describes an incident in a context implying his personal involvement, but does not specifically acknowledge this because of a residual inhibition against openly admitting to having taken life. It is also relevant that when Baines wrote this he still hoped to revisit Ireland.[20]

16 *LTH*, p. 18.   **17** *LTH*, p. 70.   **18** Amos, pp 84–5.   **19** *LTH*, pp 15–16. According to Berkeley (p. 70) Clark, a veteran of a Highland regiment, was one of two leaders of a mutiny at Ancona; when questioned he claimed the British Government had paid him £20 to enlist in the Brigade and stir up dissension.   **20** I owe this point to Peter Hart; for an example

In 1865–6 Baines worked with Michael O'Brien, the future Manchester martyr, on the organization in Britain.[21] He was arrested at Liverpool on 16 August 1866 and returned to Ireland.[22] A particular source of grief was the confiscation of his papal service medal; in later life he sought to obtain a replacement from the Vatican.[23] Baines was kept on remand until his trial on 12 February 1867, when he was sentenced to ten years' penal servitude. He writes of his incarceration:

> My prison life was a daily torture . . . Throughout the winter I was kept in a miserable cell, pierced through with cold and often famished with hunger. One hour was given for exercise in the ice-covered yard. No reading was allowed but such as was given out by the wardens; and you may be sure it did not inform me of what was going on in the outside world. No communication was allowed and the use of tobacco was forbidden . . . had it not been for a strong constitution I certainly would not have survived the terrors of that winter.[24]

Baines' account of his experiences in Millbank Penitentiary and on board the *Hougomont* (the last convict transport sent to Australia) is remarkably cursory; there is nothing like the detail contained in O'Donovan Rossa's prison memoirs or the recently published diary/memoirs of the voyage by Fennell, Cashman and Casey.[25] He does mention the Fenians' disgust and humiliation at being strip-searched on arrival in Millbank and their annoyance at having to share the ship with non-political convicts ('a contingent of the vilest cut-throats in England') between London and Portland.[26]

of a memoir displaying this verbal pattern see Michael Flannery, *Accepting the challenge: the memoirs of Michael Flannery* (Dublin, 2001), pp 70–1. Note also Baines' sarcastic repetition of the references to free passage and detectives – the latter serving to emphasize that Clark's killers saw themselves as acting on behalf of a constituted authority. **21** *LTH*, pp 19, 53. **22** The statement by Terence Dooley that Baines was arrested in February 1867 seems to confuse trial and arrest (*The greatest of the Fenians: John Devoy and Ireland* [Dublin, 2003] p. 59). **23** *LTH*, p. 80. **24** *LTH*, p. 20. **25** Jeremiah O'Donovan Rossa, *O'Donovan Rossa's prison life: six years in English prisons* (New York, 1874); C.W. Sullivan III (ed.), *Fenian diary: Denis Cashman on board the Hougoumont 1867–1868* (Dublin, 2001); Thomas McCarthy Fennell, *Voyage of the Hougoumont and life at Fremantle: the story of an Irish rebel*, ed. Philip Fennell and Marie King (Philadelphia, 2000); John Sarsfield Casey, *Journal of a voyage from Portland to Fremantle on board the convict ship 'Hougoumont' Cap Cozens commander October 12th 1867*, ed. Martin Kevin Cusack (Bryn Mawr, 1988). Baines is mentioned in the Cashman diary, pp 73, 137 (they were in adjoining bunks; see Amos, p. 107). Recent secondary accounts of the voyage may be found in Thomas Kenneally, *The great shame* (London, 1998), and Peter Stevens, *The voyage of the Catalpa* (London, 2002). **26** *LTH*, pp 21, 47; compare Fennell, pp 61–2, and Cashman, pp 136–7. When visiting San Quentin prison during his later career as a bookseller, he told the warden that in his opinion the difference between English and American prisons was as great as that between heaven and hell. He promised to enlarge on his observations of American prisons in a subsequent edition which he intended to produce for sale in Ireland. See *LTH*, pp 35–6.

On 9 January 1868 they arrived off Fremantle in Western Australia. Baines observed: 'It seemed as if the whole police force of the colony had been sent to meet us . . . from terror of the Fenians'. They were set to work quarrying and roadmaking. Again he recalls only scattered details: the first march under the burning sun of Australia, after which they drank themselves sick from a stream; sleeping in 'the buggy church' (an insect-infested building used by all denominations); and hiding coins in a tin of paint, from which they were retrieved with his bare hands on release. When most of the civilian Fenians were released in May 1869, Baines and eight others were detained in prison as particularly dangerous characters.

On 11 March 1871 Baines and the remaining civilian Fenian prisoners received conditional pardons, which bound them not to return to Britain or Ireland during the unexpired portion of their sentence. They travelled to New Zealand (from whence they were promptly deported), and then to Sydney. After spending some fruitless months in the Queensland goldfields, Baines sailed for America, arriving on 1 March 1872.[27]

Soon after his arrival in San Francisco Baines became a saloonkeeper 'on the southeast corner of Kearny and Pine' (possibly funded by a testimonial of £125 which he had received in Queensland).[28] This proved a risky business: in 1875 he was shot in the back by a discontented bartender, whom he refused to prosecute.[29] Baines was active in the 1877 Kearneyite movement (Workingmen's Party of California), a populist campaign against Chinese immigration. When he published *My life in two hemispheres* in 1889 his views on this subject had not changed:

> There is another rising worthy Irishman, who is deserving of credit and well worthy of public mention in my humble work, namely, David Barry. He is deserving of all praise for his manly stand, in excluding at all times from his cigar factory all Chinese labour, and employing only the white race . . . Few businessmen in San Francisco would sacrifice their own interests as Mr Barry has done when it was within his power to employ cheap Chinese labour . . . He will always meet a hearty support from his fellow citizens on account of his unselfish nature.[30]

The latter pages of the book duly include an advertisement for Barry's 'White Labour Cigars'. 'Poverty is a stranger in California', Baines boasts at another point, 'despite the treaty of introduction at their option of the children of Confucius, loving his nationality but lacking the moral principles'.[31]

---

27 *LTH*, pp 21–5; Amos, pp 188–90, 194. 28 Amos p. 194; *LTH*, p. 52. 29 *Mayo News*, 24 June 1899; *LTH*, pp 41–2. 30 *LTH*, p. 67. Baines does not appear to have been influenced by the more strictly labourist element of the Kearneyite programme, for his book praises numerous Irish-American businessmen, including executives of the railroad, whose political dominance was widely denounced. They were also potential book buyers. 31 *LTH*, p. 97. The Kearneyites demanded revision of the Burlingame Treaty between China and America, which permitted Chinese immigration. See Alexander Saxton, *The indispensable*

During a near-fatal illness in January 1877 Baines married a Miss McCarthy who had nursed him devotedly; he emphasizes that her sister and aunt were Dominican nuns. The couple had two sons, Robert Emmet Baines and Thomas Addis Emmet Baines.[32]

Baines retained links with the IRB; a reference in *Devoy's postbag* suggests Devoy was aware of his presence in California.[33] In 1880 Baines revisited Australia to recover the remains of Patrick Keating, a Fenian military prisoner who had died in Western Australia.[34] He incidentally took the opportunity to visit Michael Dwyer's grave. Baines may have transacted other IRB business on this journey; he mentions that his mission had to be kept secret from the authorities, though he then describes the people and places he visited and reprints testimonials he received in Australia, some mentioning his status as a papal veteran.[35] Baines' presence in tandem with two other Fenian agents was made known to the authorities by an Australian Fenian who initially feared that they were planning a dynamite attack similar to those being carried out in Britain by IRB agents; Baines was almost arrested before the informant discovered and reported to the police the true purpose of his visit.[36] The authorities believed that the planned disinterment was abandoned; Baines claims Keating's remains were secretly dug up and brought to California 'by what means I am not at liberty to state',[37] where Baines tried unsuccessfully to raise funds to bring them back to Ireland for burial in Glasnevin. He stated that he felt responsible for Keating's fate because he had originally recruited him to the IRB, and during the voyage of the *Hougomont* Keating had expressed to him a wish to be buried in Ireland.[38] A San Francisco press report that Baines had gone to Australia to dig up buried treasure for the IRB indicate the colourful image he had acquired.[39]

Shumsky's account of the Kearneyites stresses that late nineteenth-century San Francisco was a place of fluid identity and grandiose self-invention. At one end of the scale were the 'bonanza kings': self-made businessmen, sometimes of Irish descent, who rapidly adopted gaudy imitations of European aristocratic lifestyles and distanced themselves to varying degrees from their origins. Baines praises one of the 'bonanza kings', the former senator James G. Fair, for his generosity to the poor and distressed,[40] but recollects how another 'would not deign to either write a letter himself declining an invitation to act as vice president at an Irish national meeting held in the city of San Francisco in 1886, but directed his secretary to reply, declining

enemy: labour and the anti-Chinese movement in California (Berkeley, 1971). **32** *LTH*, pp 38, 39–43. **33** M. Moynahan to Mortimer Moynahan, in *Devoy's postbag*. **34** *LTH*, pp 85–96. **35** *LTH*, pp 98–105. **36** Amos, pp 259–65. Baines' memoir, unavailable to Amos, conclusively disproves the theory (which Amos mentions) that the whole story of Baines' visit was concocted by the informant as a practical joke against the police. **37** *LTH*, pp 88–9. **38** *LTH*, pp 46–7. Keating was a former private in the 5th Dragoon Guards, whose death sentence (inflicted by court-martial) was commuted to life imprisonment; he and the other military Fenian prisoners were retained when the civilians were released. He died in January 1874 of heart disease, exacerbated by prison labour. See Kenneally, pp 481, 545; and Stevens, p. 126. **39** Amos, p. 273. **40** *LTH*, p. 67.

the invitation in a curt manner'.[41] The other side of this phenomenon was Emperor Norton the First (Joshua Norton), a businessman who reacted to business ruin by retreating into a fantasy world as the self-proclaimed Emperor of America, humoured and indulged by fellow-citizens who saw in him the emblem of their own possible fate.[42]

Baines' last decades were spent in a more economically marginal position than any of the other memoirists. He became a book-pedlar (travelling the state on foot soliciting advance subscriptions for books) which suited his love of rambling. Baines' assertions of his nationalism grew increasingly flamboyant. He vowed never to shave his beard or cut his hair until Ireland was liberated, and became a familiar San Francisco character recognizable by his 'flowing locks, military cape, and soldierly bearing'.[43] Baines remained active at local level in Democrat and Irish politics (the Democrats having reabsorbed the remnants of Kearneyism). In 1883 he was Grand Marshal at a mock funeral honouring Patrick O'Donnell, 'the avenger of every patriotic Irishman in the world in giving his death blow to Carey the informer'. An advertisement for 'W.J. Mallady, Funeral Director and Embalmer', is accompanied by Baines' praise for his 'benevolence and charity' in lending a hearse and six horses for the occasion.[44] *My life in two hemispheres* formed part of this self-assertion: it presented his life in terms of 'what was suffered for love of country', and by leaving the text open through promises of further additions Baines could regard himself as retaining the power to commemorate or damn selected California Irishmen in the eyes of posterity.

Baines was active in the National League in the mid-1880s, and makes admiring references to Bradlaugh and even to Gladstone. At the same time he presents Britain as engaged in a continuing conspiracy against liberty in America as well as Ireland – a view then widespread among the depressed primary producers of western America who attributed the American government's persistent deflationary policies to British influence upon the Eastern élite.[45]

A chapter on 'The Political Tutors of Young Ireland' represents Baines' attempt to reconcile his past loyalties with his subsequent attachment to American republicanism. The 'tutors' in question are the job-hunting Irish politicians of the 1850s who discredited parliamentary action, and the British government, which he presents as not merely supporting but creating revolutionary movements across Europe. His description of this betrays a certain ambivalence. Canning is praised for having seen that there was 'no certain progress for humanity under the baleful conventions of crowned despots' and the revolutionaries are described as 'asserting with fire and sword their inalienable rights to constitutional government'.[46] Elsewhere in the

41 *LTH*, p. 75.   **42** Neil Larry Shumsky, *The evolution of political protest and the Workingmen's Party of California* (Columbus, OH, 1991).   **43** *LTH*, p. 23. The fact that he was 5 feet ten and a half inches in height – unusually tall for the period – must have added to this impression.   **44** *LTH*, p. 105.   **45** Richard Hofstadter, *The age of reform: from Bryan to FDR* (New York, 1955), and *The paranoid style in American politics and other essays* (New York, 1966).   **46** *LTH*, p. 107.

volume he tries to render the defence of the papal states in American terms by declaring that the pope's territories 'were his as legitimately as the quarter section of land which the honest citizen is entitled to in this Republic'.[47] At the same time the British are presented as working through a sinister network of faceless agents who are 'a minister in Vienna . . . a general in Hindostan . . . an admiral in Portugal . . . a Puseyite in Naples . . . a cabinet officer in Rome . . . a super-bible man in Ireland . . . an historian in one country and a pamphleteer in another, a pugilist in a third, a tourist in a fourth'. Palmerston is presented as 'the arch apostle of revolution in central and southern Europe' who

> so worked the Foreign Office as to make it a 'Head Centre' of revolutionary movements . . . Is it to be wondered that Ireland rallied the little strength and pluck that she had left? Can anyone be surprised that she took a lesson from the Right Honourable and extremely versatile Palmerston? That she tried her luck with Phoenix societies and republican clubs?[48]

The contrast between British praise for national self-determination in Italy, and opposition to it in Ireland, had often been commented on by Irish nationalists. Baines even touches on, without fully endorsing, the view widely canvassed in right-wing circles on the Continent and taken up by some prominent Irish priests, that Palmerston[49] was in fact the head of the Illuminati, a super-Masonic society conspiring the general overthrow of government, religion and morality in Europe.[50]

Like other Irish-American polemicists, Baines responds to nativist accusations that the Irish were tools of a Roman plot against American liberties by positing a rival conspiracy theory in which Britain was said to be manipulating Protestant religious sentiment in order to regain control over America.[51] He attributed Grover Cleveland's defeat in the 1888 presidential election to British machinations:

> We can even at this remote day point out the secret, well-developed intrigues of the enemies of America in London now being directed to the United

47 *LTH*, p. 37. 48 *LTH*, pp 108–10. 49 Baines' hesitation is understandable, for Irish clerical exponents of this view frequently invoked the French revolutionary connections of James Stephens and John O'Mahony in order to suggest that they were not merely Palmerston's agents but his employees. 50 George F. Dillon, *The war of Antichrist with Christian civilisation* (Dublin, 1885). A revised version, edited by Denis Fahey with an introduction expounding his own anti-Semitic conspiracy theory, was produced by the Britons Society in 1950 as *Grand Orient Freemasonry unmasked as the secret power behind Communism*. Baines cites 'Dr Cahill, writing in July 1859' who seems to have advanced a similar thesis. The Illuminati have been a staple of conspiracy theorists since the French royalist Abbé Barruel blamed them for the French Revolution in the 1790s. 51 See Michael A. Gordon, *The Orange riots: Irish political violence in New York City, 1870 and 1871* (Ithaca, NY, 1993), pp 47–9, for Irish-American denunciations of the nativist American Protective Association as composed of draft-dodging Canadian Orangemen plotting to subject America to monarchic rule.

States as in the past toward Europe. The revolutionary emissaries of the past are now partly replaced by her wandering representatives known as the Salvation Army [whom Baines as a former saloon-keeper might have personal motives for disliking] . . . It is believed that temperance and salvation is not their objective motive, but rather to advance English interests, for which they are paid by British gold under General Booth, a general, it is presumed, who never yet smelled battle except afar off, and that under his false garb of Christianity . . . Every intelligent reader who reads this chapter on the art of English conspiracy throughout the Continent of Europe can readily see that this line she is now adopting of finding employment for her ex-convicts is a deep scheme to proselytise in her interests in this republic . . . she no longer has any penal settlements abroad and therefore . . . the off-scourings of . . . convict establishments . . . are taken and trained in the name of religion for the Salvation Army of the United States and Canada.[52]

Baines also invokes his former papal service when criticising Leo XIII's rescript condemning the Plan of Campaign. He argues that the fault for this does not lie with the pope but with misinformation from 'some of his prejudiced representatives who visited Ireland[53] who are as ignorant of Ireland as an equivalent foreign visitor might be of Italy':

> It is well known that the hand of British power was behind the conspirators who were instrumental in the destruction of the temporal power of the Pope. In fact she was in full sympathy with Napoleon III, Victor Emmanuel and the Prime Minister of Sardinia, Cavour, who were the arch-conspirators in the destruction of the temporal power in 1859 and 1860.[54] A country that was treacherous to the Pope and a party to the robbery of his dominions should not receive any encouragement from his Holiness now against the struggling of the Irish race for liberty from oppressive laws. The Irish have ever been faithful to the Holy See and came to its rescue when attacked by a combination of royal robbers by furnishing men and money for its defence.

He states that he writes 'under the guidance of two ex-Papal soldiers, who fought at Ancona and were taken prisoners of war at that place by Victor Emanuel's army in September, 1860'.[55]

On 5 April 1899, while paying one of his regular visits to the priests at St Mary's

---

52 *LTH*, pp 110–11. **53** A reference to Monsignor Persico. **54** Napoleon III is included because of his failure to allow his troops stationed in Rome to reinforce the papal garrisons elsewhere in the Papal States during the invasion of 1860. **55** *LTH*, pp 113–4. Baines does not comment on Pius IX's 1870 condemnation of Fenianism, possibly because it did not catch his attention during his imprisonment in Australia. The two ex-Papal soldiers may be Patrick McKeague, best man at his wedding, and Thomas Garvey, who lived at Point Tiburon. See *LTH*, p. 40 (McKeague), and pp 36–7 (Garvey).

College on the Mission road in San Francisco, Baines suffered a stroke; he died on 10 April in St Mary's Hospital, San Francisco. At the time of his death his son Robert Emmet Baines was a US soldier stationed in Cuba; newspapers in Mayo and San Francisco published brief accounts of his career.[56] His account of his own career is too fragmentary to provide a clear picture of how far he was a victim of the upheavals of nineteenth-century Ireland and how much responsibility he bore for his own sufferings and those of others; at times he gives the impression of a Eugene O'Neill character speaking in an idiom derived from *The Nation*. In the end, his self-portrait is a reminder of the ability of romantic nationalism and devotional Catholicism to give a degree of structure and meaning to many turbulent lives.

56 *Mayo News*, 24 June 1899, 5; *San Francisco Chronicle*, 12 April 1899; *San Francisco Examiner*, 12 April 1899.

Mad Irish fiddlers in Paris: music and wandering musicians in Irish Revival writing

MARY BURKE

I'm leaving the land behind me, too; but what's land after all against the music that comes from the far strange places, when the night is on the ground, and the bird in the grass is quiet?[1]

John Millington Synge's time in Germany and France is often quietly discounted, as if 'he had taken a wrong turn and his creative life only began when he returned to Ireland': George Russell told American artist Harold Speakman that Synge 'had done only mediocre things before he learned [Irish]', and a chapter detailing Synge's Aran experience in the biography by David Greene and Edward Stephens suggests that Synge's visit to the Aran Islands in 1898 'must be one of the most remarkable examples on record of how a sudden immersion in a new environment converted a man of ostensibly mediocre talent, a complete failure, in fact, into a writer of genius'.[2] Repudiating W.B. Yeats's downplaying of Synge's time in the French capital, and insisting that the playwright's major creative period can only be properly assessed in relation to the Paris years (Synge resided there sporadically between 1895 and 1902), Mark Mortimer suggests that the budding dramatist's time in the capital is fundamental to any consideration of his artistic development.[3] The Irishman who has immersed himself in bohemian Paris is forever marked by the experience, as Synge intimates in a review of an exhibition at the Municipal Gallery of Modern Art in Dublin:

---

1 Fiddler Conn Hourican's final lines as he leaves his home to return to the road in Pádraic Colum, *The fiddler's house* (Dublin, 1907), p. 61.　2 Katharine Worth, 'Synge', in *The Irish drama of Europe from Yeats to Beckett* (London, 1978), p. 121; Harold Speakman, *Here's Ireland* (New York, 1927), p. 285; David Greene and Edward Stephens, *J.M. Synge 1871–1909* (New York, 1989), p. 79.　3 'In Paris, he read widely and retained what was appropriate to his own artistic and aesthetic growth. In Paris, . . . attending the lectures of d'Arbois de Jubainville on Celtic civilization and languages, he returned to a study of the Irish language and acquired a knowledge of, and a love for, Irish mythology. In Paris, away from . . . shrill voices . . ., he became aware of his Irish identity . . . he saw many great plays and laid the foundations for his work as a dramatist . . . and learned the trade of writing': Mark Mortimer, 'Synge and France', in Joseph McMinn (ed.), *The internationalism of Irish literature and drama* (Gerrards Cross, 1992), pp 92–3.

Perhaps no one but Dublin men who have lived abroad can quite realise the strange thrill it gave me to turn in from Harcourt-street – where I passed by to school long ago – and to find myself among Monets, and Manets and Renoirs, things I connect so directly with the life of Paris.[4]

Synge's journalistic output illuminated the Revival for the French public, and delineated French culture for his Irish readership. Moreover, the dramatist contributed to a continuum of Irish artistic contact with the French capital,[5] and was, in turn, inspired by the contemporary Parisian scene: a lecture on Brittany that Synge attended in 1897 fired his interest in this other 'Celtic fringe', while *Pêcheur d'islande*, an account of Breton sea-faring life, is understood to have influenced *Riders to the sea* and *The Aran Islands*, if only, as Declan Kiberd insinuates, as an example of how *not* to write about island life.[6] Nonetheless, George Moore and Stephen McKenna underestimated Synge's debt to the French capital: McKenna dismissed Synge's ability in the French language to shield him against the accusation of being 'Frenchified' made by immoderate nationalists, whilst Moore presented himself as the only Irishman capable of comprehending French art and literature.[7]

Although much critical attention has been given to Synge's encounters with the tramps of Wicklow, he also studied some of the more intriguing pariahs of Paris. The playwright's fascination with the *rôdeurs de barrière* of the Montrouge district of Paris (the setting of Bram Stoker's morbid 'The Burial of the Rats') had been aroused by reading of their fortune-telling exploits in French studies of occult science.[8] Furthermore, the dramatist's first biographer, the French scholar Maurice Bourgeois, suggests that Revival drama's valorization of the tramp was borrowed from *fin-de-siècle* theatre productions to which Synge was probably exposed. *Le chemineau* ('The

4 Synge, 'Good pictures in Dublin', in Robin Skelton (gen. ed.), *Collected works*, 4 vols (London, 1962–68), vol. 2, p. 391.   **5** Patrick Rafroidi outlines the impact of Thomas Moore, Maturin, Lady Morgan, the Banims and Edgeworth on French Romanticism; Wilde had visited Paris in the decade previous to Synge's visits, and wrote *Salomé* while there; George Moore was part of the Parisian scene; later, Joyce settled in the French capital and wrote *Ulysses*, while Beckett adopted France and its language. Patrick Rafroidi, *L'Irlande et le romantisme: la littérature irlandaise-anglaise de 1789–1850 et sa place dans le mouvement occidental* (Paris, 1972); Mortimer, 'Synge and France', p. 88.   **6** Declan Kiberd, 'Synge, Symons and the Isles of Aran' in *Notes on modern Irish literature*, 1 (1989), 33–4. The dramatist admitted to the influence of French literature in a 1907 draft 'Preface' for the Cuala Press edition of his poems – cited in Jon Stallworthy, 'The poetry of Synge and Yeats', in Maurice Harmon (ed.), *J.M. Synge: centenary papers 1971* (Dublin, 1972), p. 153.   **7** Mortimer, 'Synge and France', p. 87. The dramatist's French biographer, Maurice Bourgeois, felt the need to defend his subject with the assurance that Synge was 'one of the few Irish writers who europeanized Ireland with degaelicizing it': Maurice Bourgeois, *John Millington Synge and the Irish theatre* (London, 1913), p. 63.   **8** Bourgeois, *Synge and the Irish theatre*, pp 26*n*; 44*n*. The standard French dictionary gloss of *rôdeurs de barrière* translates as 'prowlers who attack and rob passers-by'. They appear to have constituted a well-known and much-feared phenomenon in liminal districts of nineteenth-century Paris.

vagabond'), a melodramatic 'Odyssey of the eternal Wanderer'[9] by Jean Richepin (1849–1926), was first produced at the Théâtre de l'Odéon, Paris, on 16 February 1897, and Synge, who lived in the French capital from October 1896 to May 1897, might well have seen the phenomenally successful work;[10] Richepin's play, which thematically resembles both *The shadow of the glen* and *The playboy of the western world*, was one of the most popular and ubiquitous of its era,[11] and Synge's love of melo-dramatic Dublin theatre productions has been well documented. *Le chemineau* opens with the love affair of a village girl and a charming and handsome young tramp working as temporary harvest help. Time passes, and the vagabond returns to the village to claim the son the woman and her husband have raised as their own, thus causing much consternation. All is ultimately resolved, however, and the play ends with the tramp happily setting off, having refused the chance offered by the villagers to settle down. In an echo of the alarm caused by the language deployed in *The playboy of the western world*, Richepin's utilization of a heightened form of naturalistic language in his first book of poems on tramping life led to the author's imprison-ment for its 'immoral' language. All in all, the *Irish independent* review that suggested *Shadow of the glen* was inspired not by the western isles, but by 'the gaiety of Paris', and Arthur Griffith's well-known accusation that it stank of 'the decadent cynicism that passes current in the Latin *Quartier*'[12] are unexpectedly insightful.

The Revival 'tinker' figure partook of an ostensibly subversive trend to which sporadic Paris residents Yeats and Synge were indisputably exposed:

> [T]he terms 'gypsy' and 'bohemian' frequently became interchangeable in nineteenth-century French literature ... In literature, gypsies had been mistakenly called *bohémiens* in France ever since they first arrived in the early fifteenth century. But during the nineteenth century the gypsy began to lend his name to all those artists and other supposed cultural vagabonds who chose to lead a creative life outside the mainstream of bourgeois society, in order to assume an apparent freedom in a precarious, marginal life-style.[13]

Gypsy lore society grandee and American poet, Charles Godfrey Leland, suggested the existence of a 'natural sympathy and intelligence between Bohemians of every grade, all the world over, and I never knew a gypsy who did not understand an artist'.[14] The ubiquitous artistic representation of the *bohémien* in nineteenth-century France, predicated upon a narcissistic containment of the 'Gypsy' as illustrative of

9 Vance Thompson, 'Richepin and the vagrom man', in *French portraits: being appreciations of the writers of young France* (Boston, 1900), p. 145. **10** Bourgeois, *John Millington Synge and the Irish theatre*, p. 150, 150*n*. **11** An English-language adaptation of the play entitled *The Harvester* was staged on Broadway in 1904, and Richepin wrote the libretto for the 1907 staging of an operatic version. **12** Quoted in Greene and Stephens, *J.M. Synge 1871–1909*, p. 159. **13** Marilyn R. Brown, *Gypsies and other Bohemians: the myth of the artist in nineteenth-century France* (Ann Arbor, MI, 1985), p. 2. **14** Charles Godfrey Leland, *The Gypsies* (London, 1882), p. 264.

'cultural vagabondage', undoubtedly inspired the choice of subject matter of Synge's *Tinker's wedding* (1907) and Yeats's *Where there is nothing* (1902). Certainly, immersion in bohemian *fin-de-siècle* Paris appears to have left its mark on contemporaneous Irish letters: the hero of Synge's first play, *When the moon has set* (*c.*1900–01), is a troubled artistic Irish gentleman recently returned from Paris; Gypsies are an element of the undifferentiated bohemian spectacle with which Oscar Wilde's Dorian Gray identifies;[15] while the Irish poet and revolutionary, John Boyle O'Reilly (1844–90), boasts that he'd 'rather fail in Bohemia than win in another land'.[16] Gypsies constituted the most fashionable element of the Great Exhibition held at Paris in June 1878: a Gypsy orchestra was mobbed, while a Russian Gypsy choir sang in the Orangerie to great applause, and the press gave an enormous degree of attention to the '*furor* as regarded *les zigains*'.[17] As early as 1859, Franz Liszt complained that the 'spurious growth called "Paris Bohemia"' had nothing to do with 'real Gypsies', but was merely 'an assemblage of worthless men and women of disorderly life; at which society can only blush'. Lizst, himself the author a study of the Gypsy influence on European music that romanticized his subject, criticizes the unimaginative writer's use of the *bohémien* figure as a *deus ex machina* or effortless dash of colour unembedded in actual history:

> [A]uthors were always ready to discredit the Bohemians with intervening in some wondrous manner in the catastrophes of our wars, in the complexities of our intrigues ... These heroes enjoyed, in their hands, the advantage of being unburdened with any historic luggage, untroubled by any regard for the future.[18]

The composer is particularly scathing of what he perceives to be the postures of suffering and alienation adopted by the Paris artistic *demi-monde*.[19] Nevertheless, the realm of Bohemia was an avidly contested space: John Buchan, on the other hand, argues that the combination of the 'eager, insatiable scholar and the wild, gipsy spirits' constituted 'the true Bohemia'.[20] Overall the modernist bohemian myth was only superficially subversive of the commodified artistic realm and normative values.[21]

---

15 '[He] used to give curious concerts in which mad gipsies tore wild music from little zithers, or grave, yellow-shawled Tunisians plucked at the strained strings of monstrous lutes, while grinning negroes beat monotonously upon copper drums, and ... slim turbaned Indians blew through long pipes of reed or brass and charmed ... great hooded snakes and horrible horned adders': Oscar Wilde, *The picture of Dorian Gray* (Oxford, [1890] 1998), p. 110. **16** John Boyle O'Reilly, 'In Bohemia', in *In Bohemia* (Boston, 1886), pp 14–15, lines 22–3. **17** Leland, *The Gypsies*, pp 74–5. **18** Franz Liszt, *The Gipsy in music / Des Bohémiens et de leur musique en Hongrie*, Edwin Evans, (trans), 2 vols (London, [1859] 1926), vol. 2, pp 214–15. **19** 'The true Bohemian could not be more removed than it is from that of the nihilist': Liszt, ibid., vol. 2, pp 211–13, 221. **20** John Buchan, 'Scholar-Gipsies' in *Macmillan's Magazine*, 70 (July 1894), 213–14. **21** 'The bohemian subject provided the artist, and the artist provided the bourgeois with a needed stimulation. In the marketplace the artist was to the bourgeois what the gypsy was to the artist, and the linked chain of appropriation eventually led to sound art investment': Brown, *Gypsies and other Bohemians*,

Synge first visited the Continent in 1893 to pursue his violin studies, and Bourgeois romanticizes Synge's Continental sojourns as the wanderings of a pica-resque hero: 'He . . . led a free, unconventional life in those days, listening to stories . . ., making friends with servants and poor people, and more than once sleeping out under a hedge or in a farm or a hay-loft'.[22] Similarly, in Yeats's account of his initial meeting with Synge, the tramping playwright is cast as romantic vagrant-artist and 'the Celtic incarnation' of Matthew Arnold's scholar gypsy.[23] Synge performed the *bohémien* in every sense: on a visit to Germany in late 1894, he appeared with his hosts in a 'tableau of a gipsy camp'.[24] In his dress, Synge combined the codes of the shabby Parisian artist and the dandified male Gypsy of literature and touristic Rive Gauche café orchestras,[25] and his physical appearance was interpreted as somehow 'revealing' his innate *bohémien* nature: the Dublin author did not, according to Bourgeois, 'look particularly Irish. There was rather something Scotch and even slightly foreign about him.' A friend went so far as to say 'that in the Wicklow glens you often meet Synge in the person of roadside beggars'. The Synges 'were not as a rule dark', and John's 'swarthy complexion, which a good many people commented on, was just one more feature that set him off from the rest of his people'.[26] Synge seems to have been considered a carnivalesque figure by contemporaries: in Paris, the budding dramatist played the violin 'to friends at night with (as someone who heard him writes) "the wild passion of a gypsy"', while one Aran islander described the playwright as a man who 'used to play the fiddle, and was a great conjurer'.[27] Whether consciously or not, Synge seems to have based his Aran persona – the skilful fiddle playing, the magic tricks, the immersion in outdoor activities – upon the more attractive aspects of the well-established stereotype of the male Gypsy: having damned the early eighteenth-century Scottish Gypsies as robbers and murderers in an article for *Blackwood's Magazine*, Walter Scott and his co-author qualifiy that many Gypsy males 'cultivated music with success; and the favourite fiddler or piper of a district was often to be found in a gypsey town.' Furthermore, they understood 'all out-of-door sports, espe-cially otter-hunting, fishing, or finding game. In winter, . . . the men showed tricks of legerdemain; and these accomplishments often helped away a weary or stormy evening in the circle of the "farmer's ha."'[28]

Synge unequivocally links underclass poverty and suburban creativity in 'The Vagrants of Wicklow': the 'gifted son' of the middle class family, 'usually a writer or

p. 6.   **22** Bourgeois, *Synge and the Irish theatre*, p. 18.   **23** W.B. Yeats, 'Preface to the first edition of *The well of the saints*', in *Essays and introductions* (London, 1961), p. 298.   **24** Edward Stephens, *My uncle John: Edward Stephens's life of J.M. Synge*, ed. Andrew Carpenter (London, 1974), p. 91.   **25** Stephens recalls a random encounter with his uncle at the height of his reputation: 'He was wearing a wide-brimmed hat . . . His cape hung to his knees, and he carried one of his heavy walking sticks. He looked like a figure from a foreign city': Stephens, ibid., p. 176.   **26** Bourgeois, *Synge and the Irish theatre*, p. 66, 66n; Greene and Stephens, *J.M. Synge 1871–1909*, p. 54.   **27** Bourgeois, *Synge and the Irish theatre*, pp 47; 80.   **28** Walter Scott and Thomas Pringle, 'Scottish Gypsies' in *Blackwood's Edinburgh Magazine*, 1 (April 1817), 49.

artist with no sense for speculation', is 'always the poorest', and in the peasant family, 'where the average comfort is just over penury', the gifted son is 'soon a tramp on the roadside'.[29] Honoré de Balzac cynically noted that the bohemian realm included a vast number of unknown but ambitious artists who carefully cultivated the semblance of poverty.[30] While the man *Ulysses* refers to as 'the tramper Synge' made ends meet on a modest allowance from his mother during his Paris sojourns, and died too young to benefit from his professional success, he nevertheless asserted to an early love interest: 'I am a poor man, but I feel that if I live I shall be rich. I feel there is that in me which will be of value to the world.'[31] At the time Bourgeois was writing his biography, he remarks that a rumour had arisen 'which represents [Synge] as suffering the pangs of poverty, sleeping in ditches, and [. . .] earning a livelihood by playing his fiddle to peasants'. Bourgeois notes that this was something the play-wright was never obliged to do, or, if he did, 'it was out of mere æsthetic interest'.[32]

The Revival fashion for depicting tinkers as the antithesis of the expanding Irish bourgeoisie readily maps onto both the *fin-de-siècle* mania for *les gitans* and the *Journal of the Gypsy Lore Society*'s contemporaneous promotion of the exoticized Irish tinker's archaic origins and language. The story line celebrating putative tinker or tramp values was ubiquitous in early Abbey productions: Lady Gregory's *The rising of the moon* (1907) features a ragged ballad singer, while *The travelling man*, her morality play of 1910, portrays Christ in the shape of a tinker; Seumas O'Kelly's *The shuiler's child* (1909) concerns an ill-fated woman of the roads, while Douglas Hyde's *An tincéar agus an tsídheóg* (1902; translated as *The tinker and the sheeog* or *The tinker and the fairy*) celebrates a tinker fiddler. Moreover, in *Modern Irish literature,* Vivian Mercier suggests that Irish peasant values were implicitly rejected in all of Yeats's early output. The increasingly commodified discourse of the bohemian mediated the 'opposition of bohemian vs. bourgeois',[33] or, in the case of the 'the tramper Synge', the abyss between those he moved amongst and their consciousness of his social status. Synge notes that the Aran islanders address him as 'duine uasal', a phrase that ranges in meaning from 'mister' or 'sir' to 'gentleman' or 'aristocrat';[34] the dramatist's 'Tramp' persona (he signed his love-letters thus) may have been an attempt to contain and depoliticize the economic and social chasm between ruling-class artists and the marginalized groups their artistic gaze fell upon, a lacuna exposed by the nationalist rhetoric of the evicted multitudes of Gaelic aristocrats tramping Ireland's byways. *When the moon has set* portrays a crazy woman of the roads named Costello, 'from the

---

29 Synge, 'The vagrants of Wicklow', in *Collected works*, vol. 2, p. 202. **30** 'Bohemia . . . is made up of young men between the ages of twenty and thirty, all of them men of genius in their way; little known as yet, but to be known hereafter, when they are sure to be distinguished': Honoré de Balzac, *Un prince de la Bohême* (1840), quoted in Brown, *Gypsies and other Bohemians*, p. 10. **31** C.H.H. (Cherie Matheson, a.k.a. Mrs Kenneth Houghton), 'John Synge as I knew him' in *Irish Statesman*, 5 July 1924, 534. **32** Bourgeois, *Synge and the Irish theatre*, p. 32. **33** Brown, *Gypsies and other Bohemians*, p. 4. **34** Synge himself provides the pleasing translation 'noble person': Synge, *The Aran Islands*, in *Collected works*, vol. 2, p. 121.

old Castilian family . . . at one time, big wealthy nobles of the cities of Spain'; interestingly, Synge evades class guilt by portraying the play's dispossessed Irish
noblewoman as being of Spanish, rather than 'native' origin.

Rutherford Mayne's *The turn of the road* (1906) might be a dramatization of
Synge's conviction that the gifted son in a family of peasants is soon 'a tramp on the
roadside'. The Ulster Literary Theatre writer's play concerns the struggle of fiddler
Robbie John Granahan, whose musical skill is perceived to be a folly in a farmer's
son.[35] In order to demonstrate to the sensitive and artistic Robbie 'what fiddling
brings a man [to]', his father brings home a drunken fiddler-tramp from the fair. To
Robbie's fascination, the polite and erudite vagabond (who nonchalantly peppers his
conversation with French language phrases) declares that he is the former leader of
'the Blue Bohemian Wind and String Band'. Moreover, Robbie learns that a
German professor of Music, who has witnessed his playing at a *feis*, is urging him to
study the instrument formally; clearly, the fiddle is associated with Bohemia, scholarship, the Continent, beggary and drunkenness, and is perceived by Robbie's
conservative parents to be the antithesis of values required for farming and settlement. Notwithstanding Mayne's play, the reduction of the tramp figure in the drama
of the Ulster Literary Theatre movement in contrast to its valorization by the Dublin
faction indicates that the vagabond motif was pivotal in the construction of the
opposition of the industrial, plain-speaking North and the heritage-laden but impov-
erished South.[36] Gerald MacNamara's *The mist that does be on the bog*, in which a
'tramp' is revealed to be a method-writing middle-class dramatist, 'instinctively
rejected [the] charlatanism' of contemporaneous Abbey productions.[37] Cottage-
owner Michael Quin's fear of cars is expressed in mock-Syngean dialect, and the
situating of such technology within the kind of idealized landscape from which signs
of development were deliberately excluded in Synge's dramatic universe creates the
play's humour.[38]

According to Nicholas Grene, Synge's 'European base' allowed him to evade the
frustration of 'allegiance either to England or Ireland which was the traditional
Anglo-Irish dilemma'.[39] To Synge, potential British impact on his own writing or on
Irish letters in general is diluted within a broad European context or bypassed alto-

35 John Graeme, Robbie's prospective father-in-law, notes: 'It's all very well for quality and
the like to go strumming on instruments, but it's not meant for a sensible farmer':
Rutherford Mayne, *The turn of the road* (Dublin, 1950), p. 40.   **36** See Mark Phelan, *The rise
& fall of the ULT* (M.Phil, Trinity College Dublin, 1998).   **37** David Kennedy, 'The
drama in Ulster', in Sam Hanna Bell et al. (eds), *The arts in Ulster* (London, 1951), p. 55.
38 MICHAEL QUIN: 'Its one thing to hear a motor horn when the sun do be shinin' in
the blue canopy of heaven and the young ewes do be dancin' in the corn – but it's another
thing to hear the toot of a motor horn when the black clouds do be restin' on the top of
the Slieve Girnin and the white mists do be comin' up from the bowels of the sea': Gerald
MacNamara, *The mist that does be on the bog*, in Kathleen Danaher (ed.), *The plays of Gerald
MacNamara* in the *Journal of Irish Literature*, 17:2–3 (1988), 58.   **39** Nicholas Grene, *Synge: a
critical study of the plays* (London, 1975), p. 17; Synge's wide learning 'enabled him to look at
Irish life without the prejudices of the Ascendancy class coming in the way.'

gether; artistic and intellectual influence is seen to flow to and return from the Continent.[40] Although it is predictable that Synge's exposure to the cultural currents of *fin-de-siècle* Paris impinged upon his construct of the vagabond,[41] it should be noted that his islander is equally 'Frenchified': the inhabitants of Aran are bohemian-ized by the erratic Aran climate, which 'seems to create an affinity between the moods of these people and the moods of varying rapture and dismay that are frequent in artists'; even Aran's 'scattered cottages' remind Synge of places he had noticed in France and Bavaria. Moreover, the intuitively urbane islanders are eager to comprehend the French phrases Synge imparts – an interest reciprocated by the French philologists who stay on Aran. The Gallic spirit hovers over every aspect of island life: if the inhabitants' instinctive erudition links them to Paris, then their charmingly primitive superstitions recall the more 'quaint' districts of rural France. The islanders are 'natural' bohemians: the unexpected independence of Aran women measures up to that of the liberated females 'of Paris and New York', and one young woman is amazed by her identification with the Rive Gauche lifestyle.[42] Geoffrey Keating emphasizes Ireland's links to 'the Orient' in the mytho-history-inspired *History of Ireland*, which Synge had avidly read and by which he had been artistically inspired,[43] and the dramatist would have been exposed to somewhat similar theories in his time at the Collège de France.[44] Orientalizing traditions that pre-Gaelic peoples from 'the East' were a long-lasting presence in Ireland also inflect both Synge's belief that 'tinkers' were a 'semi-gipsy' class with 'curiously Mongolian features'[45] and his exoticization of Aran islanders. In a telling replication that explic-

---

40 Synge groups 'Dante and Chaucer and Goethe and Shakespeare' together: Synge, 'Various notes,' in *Collected works*, vol. 2, pp 347–8; Synge stresses the importance of Geoffrey Keating's studies in Bordeaux on his formation as a scholar, while both the Irish and contemporaneous Breton-language theatre revivals are products of the 'Celtic imagination': Synge, 'An Irish historian,' ibid., p. 361; Synge, 'A Celtic theatre,' ibid., p. 393. **41** One Wicklow beggar Synge eulogizes was a well-travelled sailor whose life embodies the antithesis of bourgeois and sedentary values: 'He is not to be pitied. His life has been a pageant not less grand than . . . George Borrow's and like all men of culture he has formed a strong concept of the interest of his own personal aspect . . . The slave and the beggar are wiser than the man who works for recompense . . . Every industrious worker has sold his birthright for a mess of pottage, perhaps served him in chalices of gold': Synge, 'People and places', ibid., p. 196. **42** Synge, *The Aran Islands*, ibid., pp 74, 127, 60, 80, 102, 143, 114. **43** Synge attempted a verse play on Ireland's first inhabitants based on Keating's *History* entitled *Luasnad, Capa and Laine*. **44** Synge readily absorbed d'Arbois de Jubainville's thesis, to judge by his review of a Gregory publication in which he notes that the 'epic of Cuchulain began to take shape in pagan Ireland probably in the same way as the Homeric stories grew up in ancient Greece': Synge, 'An epic of Ulster,' ibid., p. 368. The dramatist elsewhere refers to Cú Chulainn as 'l'Achille de l'Irlande.' Synge, 'La vielle littérature irlandaise,' ibid., p. 353. **45** Synge, 'People and places', ibid., p. 198. Equally, McCormack employs the diction of Orientalism in suggesting that tinkers constituted 'the untouchables of rural Ireland': W.J. McCormack, *Fool of the family: a life of J.M. Synge* (London, 2000), p. 244.

itly links the seemingly shared Oriental origins of tinkers and Aran islanders, Synge had, in an earlier piece, used the exact phrase 'curiously Mongolian features' in describing the Aran women.[46] The nationalist charge of Synge's allusions to the supposed archaic, non-classical ancestry of the islanders derives from the Patriotic antiquarian emphasis on Ireland's circumvention of 'Roman' (that is, English) dominion. The dramatist despised what he perceived to be the England-obsessed parochialism that drove Gaelic League activists,[47] and the 'fraud and hypocrisy' of the League's language policy will only be swept aside, Synge predicts, when Ireland learns 'again that she is part of Europe'. Nevertheless, the incongruities of centuries of religious and linguistic contact problematize Synge's vision of islands blessedly lacking in British and English-language influence, but intuitively in possession of an innate sympathy for all things Gallic. *The Aran Islands* willfully obscures the ambiguities of Aran's long evolution by situating the islanders within a pseudo-historical frame through his allusion to their descent from Fir-bolgs,[48] and by ignoring the fascinating fact, cited in Arthur Symons' near-contemporaneous account, that many inhabitants of Aran were descended from the soldiers of a Cromwellian garrison.[49] Ultimately, the playwright strips the prosaic Galway and Aran of his childhood and family history of its colonial, Protestant, and familial associations: Galway was the location of the estate that allowed Mrs Synge £400 a year,[50] and Aran the site of the generally unsuccessful proselytizing of the dramatist's uncle, the Revd Alexander Synge.

Representations of the metropolitan *flâneur*, the wandering musician, the brigand, the beggar, and the tramp – such an inventory reads like a register of Synge's *dramatis personae* – were encoded within the fluid 'set of meanings the *bohémien* could occupy'.[51] In his youth, Synge cultivated the artistic self-image of a bohemian fiddler, while Hyde's *Tinker and the fairy*, which concerns the dalliance of the musician 'king of the tinkers' with a fairy woman, reinforced the apolitical stereotype of 'innate' tinker musicality. In *Home life in Ireland* (1909), Robert Lynd implies that the fiddle was one of the most 'patriotic' and 'authentic' instruments of the Revival: 'It is good news that in many parts of Ireland the people are taking to the fiddle again, where their fathers were content with the melodeon and its crude noises'.[52] Paradoxically,

---

46 In an embryonic version of *The Aran Islands* entitled 'The last fortress of the Celt': Synge, 'The last fortress of the Celt' (1901), in *A treasury of Irish folklore* (New York, 1983), p. 463. **47** 'Was there ever a sight so piteous as an old and respectable people setting up the ideals of the Fee-Gee because, with their eye's glued on John Bull's navel, they dare not be Europeans for fear the huckster across the street might call them English': Synge, 'Can We Go Back into Our Mother's Womb?', in *Collected works*, vol. 2, p. 400. A satirical play planned by the dramatist suggested that the Ireland of the future would only successfully rid itself of the English language by cutting out the tongues of its population. Synge, *Deafmutes for Ireland*, in *Collected Works*, vol. 3, pp 218–19. **48** During a trip to Dun Aengus, Synge props his book on 'stones touched by the Fir-bolgs': Synge, *The Aran Islands*, in *Collected works*, vol. 2, p. 69. **49** Arthur Symons, 'The Isles of Aran' in *The Savoy* (8 December 1896), 78. **50** Stephens, *My uncle John*, p. 22. **51** Brown, *Gypsies and other Bohemians*, p. 3. **52** Robert Lynd, *Home life in Ireland* (London, 1909), p. 316.

the ubiquitous Revival-era literary motif of the wandering fiddle-playing tinker or stranger is partially predicated upon the historical fact of Irish cultural borrowings from Europe:

> One hundred and fifty to two hundred years ago good fiddles were extremely scarce in many parts of rural Ireland. Introduced into Ireland sometime in the eighteenth century from Britain and the Continent, the violin has remained for many decades an import . . . [and] for many communities the knowledge of playing the fiddle was in the almost exclusive possession of . . . nomadic professionals. [Irish Traveller musicians] most certainly introduced the tin fiddle . . . into the various localities of rural Donegal, and it is quite possible that it was the travelling musicians who popularised the violin when it was first adopted in traditional music.[53]

Predictably, the theme of the uncanny influence or compulsion to wander of the fiddler was popular in plays produced in many Irish theatres during the opening years of the twentieth century.[54]

Although doubtlessly imbricated by the Irish folk valorization of the wandering fiddler, Synge's representation of the ambulant musician simultaneously emerges from a broader formal European musical tradition to which he would have been exposed during his music studies. As conventionally considered, the Romantic period in music collided with the rise of the 'Gypsy' as a ubiquitous trope of chaos and sensuality in European letters, and exemplary Romantic composer Franz Liszt (1811–86) welded both trends in *The Gipsy in music* (1859).[55] Like Synge after him, Liszt sojourned in Paris, where he studied music formally, but later returned to

53 Allen Feldman and Eamonn O'Doherty, *The northern fiddler* (Belfast, 1979), pp 23–4, 38.
54 Aside from Mayne's *The turn of the road*, two other plays utilizing the theme opened near-contemporaneously: E.K. Worthington's *The Burden* and Pádraic Colum's *The fidder's house*, which concerns musician Conn Hourican's desire to return to the road after a five-year stint in a house. The erstwhile itinerant's desire to wander is portrayed as innate and irrepressible. Bourgeois, *Synge and the Irish theatre*, p. 11. Colum, the son of a workhouse master, also self-consciously cultivated a 'tramp' persona. See Colum, 'Vagrant Voices: a self portrait' in the *Journal of Irish Literature*, 2:1 (1973), 64–5. Although conceived somewhat later, T.C. Murray's *The pipe in the fields*, first performed in the Abbey on 3 October 1927, shares the wandering musician theme: farmer's son Peter Keville is enchanted away from the everyday world by a flute sold to him by a vagabond.   **55** *The Gipsy in music* was an 'overgrown preface', whose aim was to elucidate Liszt's *Rhapsodies hongroise*, conceived by the composer as an instrumental 'Bohemian epic': Liszt, *The Gipsy in music*, vol. 1, p. xiii; Evans, ibid., vol. 1, p. xiv. Liszt's construct of the Gypsy musician is undoubtedly imbricated by literary depictions and common stereotypes of Gypsy behaviour, given that his choice of reading profoundly influenced his music. '[An] unusual, as yet unprecedented influence of literature on music and music on literature [was] one of the most distinctive features of the romantic period': I. Belza, 'Romantic literature and music', in I. Sötér and I. Neupokoyeva (eds), É. Róna, (trans), *European Romanticism* (Budapest, 1977), pp 539, 504.

Hungary to immerse himself in Gypsy culture, the source of what he considered '*real music*';[56] in its attempt to articulate the 'soul of the nation', Romantic music appropriated the ethnic, and Liszt integrated Hungarian Gypsy folk music into his widely renowned *Rhapsodies hongroises*.[57] To Liszt, the music of the non-intellectual and child-like Hungarian Gypsy musician expressed genuine emotion and instinctive poetry; in his view Gypsy musical skills were inborn rather than acquired.[58] The 'innate indiscipline' of the Gypsy, so maligned by eighteenth-century commentators, becomes proof of his Romantic credentials in Liszt's estimation; the 'nature' of the Gypsy is reinterpreted to meet the ideological and artistic demands of each setting and era. 'Étude Morbide' (*c.*1899), described by Synge himself as 'a morbid thing about a mad fiddler in Paris', was a veiled autobiography concerning a musician who has a breakdown after a failed concert. The saturation of 'Étude Morbide' with Lisztean ideas indicates the degree to which Liszt's folk musician-as-noble-savage paradigm had permeated artistic discourse.[59] In the unpublished 'Duality of Literature', Synge reveals that he shares Liszt's Romantic concept of the purity and directness of folk melodies, which enfold 'simple' and 'universal' emotions, and 'contain their own signature in a way complex art cannot do'.[60] Synge's immersion in Irish folk traditions and his self-conscious fostering of a Lisztean European artistic sensibility collide in the account of a dream he had on Aran in which he is made frenzied by mysterious music against his will, the result of what he terms 'a psychic memory' attached to the neighbourhood.[61] This incident invokes the folk belief that 'the little people' enticed humans for a brief sojourn to an irresistible realm by their beautiful playing, or could be charmed by skilled human musicians – a peculiarly popular theme in Revival writing; in Hyde's *Tinker and the fairy*, the fiddler 'king of tinkers' agrees, under duress, to kiss a fairy who is cursed to die unless embraced by a mortal; the transformed fairy offers to be his spouse, while in Gregory's

56 Liszt, *The Gipsy in music*, vol. 1, p. xv.   **57** The Romantic era saw an upsurge of interest in Gypsy music and the subject of the Gypsy among European formal composers, the most famous being the opera based on Prosper Mérimée's over-wrought 1845 short story, 'Carmen'.   **58** 'In the very act of passing the bow across the violin-strings a natural inspiration suggested itself [to the Gypsy musician]; and, without any search for them, there came rhythms, cadences, modulations, melodies and tonal discourses': Liszt, *The Gipsy in music*, vol. 1, p. 13.   **59** 'All art that is not conceived by a soul in harmony with some mood of the earth is without value . . . Music is the finest art, for it alone can express directly what is not utterable.' The troubled hero of *Étude Morbide* burns his trite, insincere 'sonnets written in Paris', finding that the only poetry he is only able to read is 'the songs of peasants': Synge, 'Étude morbide,' in *Collected works*, vol. 2, p. 35.   **60** Synge, 'The duality of literature', TCD MS 4382, Trinity College, Dublin.   **61** Synge, *The Aran Islands*, in *Collected works*, vol. 2, pp 99–100.   **62** Gregory, *McDonough's wife*, in Ann Saddlemyer, (ed.), *The collected plays of Lady Gregory* (New York, 1970), vol. 2, p. 116. See See Mary Burke, 'Eighteenth-century European scholarship and nineteenth-century Irish literature: Synge's *Tinker's wedding* and the Orientalizing of "Irish Gypsies"', in Betsy Taylor FitzSimon and James H. Murphy (eds), *The Irish revival reappraised* (Dublin, 2004). In Hyde's *The tinker and the fairy*, the fiddler 'king

McDonough's wife, a preternaturally skilled piper married to a woman rumoured to be 'a tinker's brat' is suspected of having been taught to play by 'the little people'.[62]

An *Irish times* article on young contemporary Aran folksinger Lasairfhíona Ní Chonaola includes the apparently surprising information that the performer 'has a degree from Trinity, a mobile phone and a penchant for designer clothes'.[63] Sympathy towards marginalized population groups is continually revealed in Synge's prose, but his work was instrumental in the constitution of the stereotype of Ireland's non-sedentary and non-mainland peoples as carriers of 'authentic' musicianship and 'primitive', intuitive bohemianism. On an 1857 ethnological expedition to 'the great Firbolg fort of Dun Aengus' on Aran, Sir William Wilde pointed to a prehistoric Fir-Bolg presence on the islands, and implied that the contemporary islanders are descendants of the Fir-Bolg: 'I believe that I now point to the stronghold prepared as the last standing-place of the Firbolg aborigines of Ireland, here to fight their last battle if driven to the western surge.'[64] The Revival linkage of 'tinkers' and pre-Gaelic remnants emerged from the folk belief, collected by Synge, that peripatetic peoples such as tramps and tinkers possessed 'great knowledge of the fairies'.[65] By alluding to the presence on Aran of Fir-Bolg, Synge likewise implies that the islanders are their descendants, since folkloric belief suggested that, once vanquished by the Tuatha Dé Danann, the Fir-Bolg fled to Aran. Later, having been defeated by the Gaels, the Tuatha Dé Danann descended underground and became those afterwards referred to as fairies.[66] The correlation of pre-Celtic population groups and their supposed descendants with fairies implied by Synge allies the islanders with tinkers as a people apart from the majority of 'Gaelic' mainlanders, and reveals the Protestant Synge's identification with the putatively 'non-Gaelic' in a period in which the terms 'Catholic', 'Gael', and 'Irish' were increasingly conflated. His divergent social and religious background, much as he attempts to downplay it within *The Aran Islands*, may be alluded to by a storyteller who refers to a character as 'one of those Protestants who don't believe in any of these things, and do be making fun of us'. Synge comments that a poem he transcribes of an immortal horse present at the

---

of tinkers' agrees, under duress, to kiss a fairy cursed to die unless embraced by a mortal, and the transformed fairy offers to be his spouse; 'Who hears the fairy piper play / Beneath the secret hill, / Though he should wander worlds away / Shall hear that music still': Ruth Duffin, 'The Fairy Piper' in *New Ireland Review*, 26 (Oct. 1906), 95, lines 1–4. In 1911, a fiddler charged with having been drunk and disorderly at Magherafelt petty sessions claimed to have been visited by the 'wee folk' come to hear him play: Court notices in *Irish Independent*, 2 Dec. 1911. Moreover, in Gregory's *McDonough's wife*, a preternaturally skilled piper, married to a woman rumoured to be 'a tinker's brat', is suspected of having been taught to play by the fairies: Gregory, *McDonough's wife*, in *Collected plays of Lady Gregory*, vol. 2, p. 116. **63** See http://homepage.tinet.ie/~seannos/Reviews.html. **64** Sir William Wilde, quoted in Kiberd, 'Synge's Tristes Tropiques: *The Aran Islands*', in Grene (ed.), *Interpreting Synge: essays from the Synge summer school 1991–2000* (Dublin, 2000), p. 83. **65** Synge, 'The vagrants of Wicklow', in *Collected works*, vol. 2, p. 203. **66** Proinsias MacCana, *Celtic mythology* (London, 1970), pp 63–5.

battles of Aughrim and Boyne is 'grotesque . . . doggerel', revealing his discomfort at the poem's naked binary opposition of Catholic and Protestant, Planter and Gael.[67] For Synge, identification with the 'bohemians' of Ireland and Continental Europe is a poignant attempt to transcend exclusionary contemporary nationalist discourses of identity.

67 Synge, *The Aran Islands*, in *Collected works*, vol. 2, pp 180, 171.

European influences and the novels of George Moore: reciprocal artistic impressions[1]

MARY S. PIERSE

The extent of European influence on George Moore (1852–1933) is far from being fully documented and recognized, even three quarters of a century after his death. The effects of a Parisian sojourn on Moore can be seen to have resulted in some rather significant developments in the English novel in the final two decades of the nineteenth century, and to have extended well beyond the literary sphere in causing the inclusion of impressionist paintings in the collection of the Hugh Lane Gallery in Dublin. Many of Moore's debts to French writers have been identified and commented upon; there are other strands in his writing, owing much to French and German parentage, that have proved to be less apparent. This latter group of elements, more subtly woven and encoded into his prose, numbers a variety of interesting contributions linked to French novels, to German music and philosophy, and to French and Italian paintings. From a potentially extensive list of such imaginative derivations and adaptations, some selected examples can illustrate their disparate origins and diverse uses by Moore.

Even in reading just two of Moore's novels of the 1890s, *Esther Waters* (1894) and *Celibates* (1895), the catalogue of European contact points is lengthy: Balzac, Flaubert, Zola, the Goncourts, Mallarmé, Prévost, Péladan and Huysmans are among those on the literary side; Wagner and Palestrina are present, despite their mutual distance in time, place and style of music; Degas, Manet, Monet, Théodore Rousseau and Giovanni Boldini, all visual artists, are encountered in the two texts, as are several other painters, including Raphael, Rembrandt, Dürer and Corot. In addition to writers, painters and musical composers, European thought is represented by the philosophers Schopenhauer and Comte, as well as by Plato and Aristotle. The influences are perceptible in different ways: on occasions, Moore follows some or all of the practice and pattern of the pre-existing model in general subject matter, in specific scenes or characters or their treatment; at other times, the connection is evoked by mere mention of a name or place, or by form; yet again, there may be obvious linkages with an author or visual artist, but the image is no sooner evoked than it is very blatantly discarded by Moore, thus simultaneously signalling his inspiration and his innovation or difference.

1 The author gratefully acknowledges the financial assistance provided for this project by the Irish Research Council for the Humanities and Social Sciences.

While the scale of European reference in Moore's work is considerable, the instances where Moore both embraces and diverges from the original inspiration provide particular interest. The case of *Esther Waters* is illustrative of such selective borrowing and usage. This novel's eponymous central character is a female servant, an occurrence that was novelistically highly unusual for the period; it was certainly not the practice in Victorian literature, where pride of place was given to characters of a higher social standing. The French precedents that are often mentioned in connection with a central servant character are *Germinie Lacerteux* (1864) by the Goncourt brothers, and Flaubert's *Un Coeur Simple* (1877). In their time, both those texts had been remarked upon and attacked for just such an atypical and unacceptable main character. However, it would be erroneous to imagine that Moore's servant girl is similar to those of the earlier French stories, or that Moore would present her in analogous fashion. The manner in which Esther's thoughts and feelings are partially mediated to the reader establishes a marked disparity, almost a chasm, between Moore's servant and those of the Goncourts and Flaubert. Whereas the story of Germinie is told by an obviously educated narrator who assumes the right to recount and interpret the events concerning a socially inferior person, Moore's Esther furnishes much of her own tale and at no stage does the author permit her to be viewed from any superior vantage point. Esther's strength, determination and humanity clearly separate her from the more pathetic servant in Flaubert's story; the survival of Esther and her son distances the Moore novel from the fatally deterministic downward path of Germinie who is drunken and promiscuous. Esther is in a different fictional class. What Moore has taken from those French predecessors is the shock value of featuring a servant as leading character; what is different is the way in which he has radically departed from the nature, the presentation and the novelistic outcomes chosen by them.

At the time of publication of *Esther Waters*, Moore was probably more identified in the public mind with Émile Zola and naturalist fiction, rather than with Edmond de Goncourt or Gustave Flaubert. One might speculate that the reason for the ongoing propensity to associate Moore with the label of naturalism had much to do with an urge to demonize him and his work by linking him to forces deemed to be pollutants of the purity of the English novel and the English mind, and thus a threat to the social fabric. Despite Moore's own denials, the allegations of a Zola connection and a naturalist composition were repeated. The charges were made, regardless of some quite clear evidence that, far from indulging in the extensive and detailed studies that were seen as typical of naturalism, and remote from the naturalist emphasis on decay, fatalism and low life, Moore's new fiction had moved on to different literary shapes. In the case of *Esther Waters*, he expressed surprise that any connection with Zola would be mentioned, claiming that his master was Flaubert and that the final scene with Esther and her grown son was 'pure Flaubert'. Voicing such wonderment could be viewed as disingenuous on Moore's part because, in addition to representing Esther's life, the novel depicts the decline of a county family and a countryside as result of gambling. In addition, it portrays the degeneration associated with excessive drinking, both in the fate of regulars in William's pub, and in the devastation wrought in some families. The similarities to Zola's drinking den in *L'Assommoir* (1876–7), and Moore's departure from the Zola mould, are visible here. Whereas Zola, in the preface to *L'Assommoir*, defined his subject as 'la décheance fatale d'une famille ouvrière' (the fatal decline of a working-class family), Moore strongly disputes that fatalism. Another way in which he has moved away from naturalism is in the sympathy coaxed from readers for Esther's successive misfortunes. Giving or evoking sympathy would not be part of the naturalist method. Obviously Moore had been influenced in the past by the French naturalist group – and this was most apparent in *A mummer's wife* (1885) – but, for Moore, naturalism would no longer be a school with which he would wish to be associated. As a polemicist and a consciously literary artist, naturalism remained a force with which he would engage, if only to highlight its deficiencies, to stress his own difference and to promote alternative literary paths. In this connection, it is interesting to note that when Moore moves, in the course of one year, from the novel about Esther to the short stories of *Celibates*, he chooses for that latter volume a title that is utterly in keeping with the scientific and sociological aims of naturalism; however, the character of that book is far from naturalistic. It veers much more towards the psychological approach, although that is not the only aspect that distances it from Zola and his confrères. This is, of course, typical of the path trodden by Moore in his writing career, always breaking out from the fixed moulds in which literary critics and competitors would like to imprison him.

In commenting on Moore's shift away from naturalism, Joseph Hone, Moore's biographer, places that tendency around the beginning of 1887.[2] Hone credits the influence of Édouard Dujardin and Stéphane Mallarmé. He might well have included Joris-Karl Huysmans or maybe even Ivan Turgenev. The latter, in a discussion with Moore as early as 1876, had commented on the lack of psychology in Zola's novels. Moore's cogitations on the matter were ongoing, and were reflected in his article on Turgenev which first appeared in 1888, and was later reproduced in his *Impressions and Opinions* (1891).[3] Hone remarks, *en passant*, that both Dujardin and Mallarmé were recognised as Symbolists, and that all Symbolists of the time were Wagnerians whereas naturalists were generally indifferent to all music. In the light of that rather sweeping judgement, the allusions to Wagner and to Palestrina in the account of 'John Norton' in *Celibates* deserve comment, but not just for the musical references that could be interpreted as disqualifying that fiction from the naturalist school. References to Wagner and Palestrina are indicative of European influence, insofar as Moore discerns the existence of significant enthusiasms for their music in Paris, and later in London, and determines on their inclusion in the story as a topical note. It is that resolve to set time in the present, rather than the mere mention of

2 Joseph Hone, *The life of George Moore* (London: Victor Gollancz, 1936) p. 143.   3 George Moore, 'Turguéneff' in *Fortnightly Review*, February 1888, 237–51; this piece was reprinted in *Impressions and opinions* (London, 1891).

composers who happen to hail from mainland Europe, that represents a real result of European impact. Moore's direction is a turn away from novels based in the past and written in a dated language; his path is towards what reflects the up-to-date, contemporary fashions and controversies. In this move, Moore had several authors in his sights but he was responding in particular to *Tess of the d'Urbervilles* (1891). In terms of the topical, Wagner was an interesting choice. His music was very much *à la mode* in France of the 1890s. It was also a hot topic: none of the French opera houses would put on Wagnerian works until about 1894 and, when they did, there were riots and protests outside – the events of 1870 were of too raw and too recent memory. Despite that, French composers of the period were very influenced by Wagnerian innovation and Bayreuth was *the* annual destination for the fashionable.

Although the Wagnerian vogue was also gathering steam in England, the references to Wagner and Palestrina in 'John Norton' are more than references to what was chic. Adverting to Wagner has an explanatory and a symbolic role: it can facilitate the readers – if they so choose – in interpreting the character of John by suggesting a selection of possible keys to his mentality. In this book, John is not painted as being interested in women or marriage; indeed, he evinces a certain anxiety concerning the opposite sex. This emerges, intertwined with musical reference, in such opinions as: 'Would you believe it, the lovely music in the cupola, written by Wagner for boys' voices, is now sung by a woman';[4] 'It is as inappropriate to have Palestrina sung by women as it would be to have Brunnhilde and Isolde sung by boys';[5] 'Wagner's music in the cupola is very lovely, but it does not compare with Palestrina'; 'the great duet between Kundry and Parsifal. The moment Kundry calls to Parsifal, "Parsifal . . . Remain!" . . . Wagner inspiration begins, then he is profound, then he says interesting things.'[6] The subtext – provided by allusion to Wagner's Parsifal and Kundry, with its consequent conjuring of visions of romantic crusades and seduction – demands recognition of the total contrast between that picture and John's peculiar and opposite attitudes and inclinations. For the reader of the time, Nietzsche's much-publicized views concerning Wagner's desire to put manliness back into myth and music inject yet a further layer of meaning in relation to John. They constitute another European link and influence.

The presence of Joris-Karl Huysmans and his decadent novel, *À Rebours* (1884), are patently clear in Moore's literary responses in the tale of 'John Norton'. One can find similarity in the descriptions of the bookshelves of Des Esseintes and John, and in the references, in both books, to Schopenhauer; however, once again, while the European influence is considered and spotlighted, it is both modified and rejected. Moore's character of John is not a carbon copy of Des Esseintes: John Norton retires to a bare cell of a room – Des Esseintes constructs a make-believe cell out of luxurious silk; Des Esseintes leads an eventful and dissolute life – John's existence is far from that; Huysman's novel ends with Des Esseintes no longer having 'the consoling

---

4 George Moore, *Celibates* (London, 1895), p. 335. **5** Ibid., pp 335–6. **6** Ibid., pp 336, 338.

beacon-fires of the ancient hope'[7] – while John determines that 'Thornby Place should soon be Thornby Abbey, and in the divine consolation of religion John Norton hoped to find escape from the ignominy of life'.[8] In addition to those related features, there are several other elements that link the two texts and, overall, the evidence of French influence is clear – as is the proof of Moore's deviation from, and/or abandonment of it.

One of George Moore's borrowings or transpositions from Europe, and from France in particular, is his heavily descriptive prose. In certain cases, Moore's descriptions straddle the two roles of description, that of decorative addition, and that of furnishing explanation or symbolism. What is rather unusual about Moore's portrayals is that many of them do not emerge from literary precedent or model; rather they come from the visual arts. This particular feature is relatively common in the story of 'Mildred Lawson' in *Celibates*. Moore was, of course, art critic of *The Speaker* in London from 1891 to 1895 and had published widely on art matters. Moreover, he knew many of the famous painters of the period, including Manet, Monet, Renoir, Degas and Pissarro. He was an early enthusiast for, and a promoter of, their work. A number of examples will serve to illustrate the nature of his transfers from painting to words. One type occurs in the repetition, with slight variation, of depictions of a scene so that they are seen to constitute the equivalent in words of series paintings. Series paintings were a trait of impressionism and Claude Monet's many canvases of haystacks, of trees, of cathedrals, and of water-lilies are well-known. He repeated portraits of the same scene several times, in different lights or from differing angles. In the story 'Mildred Lawson' there is a succession of descriptions bearing an uncanny relationship to Monet's series of poplar paintings. Two of them are 'A formal avenue of trim trees led out of the town of Melun' and 'trees planted in single line and curving like a regiment of soldiers marching country'.[9] This latter image is the prose equivalent of Monet's 1891 picture, *Poplars on the Bank of the Epte River* (fig. 1)

A second and rather different example of European visual impressions on Moore's writing arises in the recurring descriptions of forest and rocks, also in the story of 'Mildred Lawson': 'for the great rocks and the dismantled tree trunk which they had suddenly come upon frightened her, and she could hardly bear with the ghostly appearance the forest took in the stream of glittering light which flowed down from the moon';[10] 'out of the charred spectre of a great oak crows flew and settled among the rocks, in the fissures'; 'isn't that desolate region of blasted oaks and sundered rocks wonderful'.[11] The last image gives the clue to the artistic connection as it clearly identifies Moore's prose with Théodore Rousseau's series of paintings of the area of Barbizon and the forest of Fontainebleau, areas frequented by artists in the nineteenth century. One of these pictures, *Oak Tree in the Rocks*, was moderately renowned as it had been exhibited in the Salon of 1861; apart from that, there was a

---

7 Joris-Karl Huysmans, *Against nature* (London, 1959), p. 220.   **8** *Celibates*, p. 452.   **9** Ibid., p. 130.   **10** Ibid., p. 135.   **11** Ibid., p. 146.

1 Claude Monet, *Poplars on the Bank of the Epte River* (1891).

degree of general familiarity in the art world with Rousseau's typical scenery and subject matter. Moore has directly translated those works to words and he draws attention to those verbal transpositions from the canvases of Monet and Rousseau.

Edgar Degas was another famous artist who painted series of paintings. His ballet dancers are easily recognised, as are his pictures of women washing and drying themselves. A famous 1891 canvas in that latter series, *After the bath, woman drying herself* (fig. 2) hangs in the National Gallery in London and it is the painting that is reflected in 'Mildred Lawson'. Ralph, an artist character in the story, has created a picture of 'A woman who had just left her bath'. The account goes on: 'The picture said something that had not been said before, and Mildred admired its naturalness'.[12] Moore's is a textual account that mirrors the approach, intent and reception of the Degas paintings.

Pierre Auguste Renoir provides a further source for Moore's verbal descriptions. A striking example is of a woman who is recognizable as a model from at least two of Renoir's paintings. One of those pictures, now in the Museum of Fine Arts in Boston, is *Woman with a Parasol and Small Child on a Sunlit Hillside* (1874–76, fig. 3). Mildred is Moore's version and, again, attention is drawn to her attire. She is told that 'you'll never be able to get along in those shoes and that dress – that's no dress for the forest. You've dressed as if for a garden-party'. The sketch of her appearance detailed 'the delight of an expensive white muslin and a black sash which accentuated the smallness of her waist.' It also mentioned 'her little brown shoes and brown stockings and the white sunshade through whose strained silk the red sun showed'.[13] The red sun seen through 'strained silk' immediately identifies the impressionist symbol and practice, as well as the artist, Renoir.

A further example of the influence of European art on Moore's prose is found in the 1892 painting *Fuoco d'Artificio* by an Italian painter, Giovanni Boldini (the canvas is in the Museum Giovanni Boldini, Palazzo Massari, Ferrara). It features a woman, with a minute waist, in a magnificent ball gown – and Moore's depiction does justice to the impression: 'She wore white tulle laid upon white silk. The body was silver fish-scales, and she shimmered like a moonbeam'.[14] Boldini, while not as famous as Monet and Renoir are now, was in Paris at the same time as Moore. His painting has certain similarities with the style of Degas but he was also a society painter and produced many portraits of the rich and beautiful. In providing the verbal rendition of Boldini's society woman and her *haute couture*, Moore simultaneously transposes description from one art to another, and once more registers the contemporary character of his fictional composition.

These illustrations are but a few of the examples which abound in Moore's writing. It is also possible to match various other extracts from *Esther Waters* and *Celibates*, with several paintings from different artists. In addition to direct correlation with specific pictures, the artistic name-dropping is frequent: Millet, Diaz, Puvis de Chavannes and Salvator Rosa are all mentioned. Such references might seem exceptionally appropriate to the story of Mildred Lawson, since Mildred goes to Paris to study art. In the case of Esther, it could be supposed that paintings, and most of all those by impressionist artists, would be far from her world of scullery, workhouse and

12 Ibid., p. 103.   13 Ibid., pp 144, 130.   14 Ibid., p. 175.

2 Edgar Degas, *After the Bath, Woman Drying Herself* (1891).

Soho pub. However, among the visual images that Moore has composed in *Esther Waters* is a scene that mirrors Camille Pissarro's 1888 picture *Apple Picking at Eragny-sur-Epte* (fig. 4). The account of Fred Parson's family and their apple harvesting[15] has just that same calm and idyllic quality that Pissarro's composition captures in paint.

15 George Moore, *Esther Waters* (London, 1894), p. 186.

3 Pierre-Auguste Renoir, *Woman with a Parasol and Small Child on a Sunlit Hillside* (1874–6).

Such pictorialism is but one aspect of Moore's very complex literary impressionism, a mode that, when it is ever acknowledged in his writing, has not been recognised as early as this period. Moore's innovation long predates the more usual identification of such a stylistic feature in the writings of Ford Madox Ford, Virginia Woolf and Katherine Mansfield.[16] The French artistic atmosphere has attached itself to Moore, and in turn, it appears in his prose in a quite novel manner.

Mention of the German philosopher Arthur Schopenhauer is another example of Moore's introduction of contemporary and topical European trends into late-nineteenth-century English fiction. The relationship between Wagner and Schopenhauer was relatively well known to many in England at the time and both

[16] Richard Allen Cave dates Moore's impressionistic style from 1897–8; see *A study of the novels of George Moore* (Gerrard's Cross, 1978), p.168.

names were familiar, even to those who were unsure of, or disinterested in, their beliefs. In *Celibates*, John Norton's internal discourse expresses identifiable Schopenhauerian beliefs: 'Joy is passion, passion is suffering' and 'the wise soon learn that there is nothing to dream of but the end of desire'; however, this is counterposed not just against John's un-Schopenhauerian conviction that 'God is the one ideal', but also against his longing for 'the voices of chanting boys, the cloud of incense, and the Latin hymn afloat on the tumult of the organ'.[17] John's pleasure in stained glass windows is an aesthetic enjoyment that Schopenhauer connects with a state of pure knowing, the polar opposite of the will. Yet John's interest in such windows is more than that of disinterested, joyous contemplation; it encompasses search, acquisition, installation, and pride in that achievement, activities that are remote from pure knowledge.

Schopenhauer's beliefs also appear in *Esther Waters* although the references are more covert. Yet it is impossible to ignore the portrayal of Schopenhauerian compassion and self-renunciation in the person of Mrs Barfield and of the 'will-to-live' force in Esther. In language that is remarkably similar to that in Schopenhauer's *The World as Will and Representation*,[18] Moore shows that Mrs Barfield's peace of mind stems from her perception of other people as part of humankind, and that her concern for their welfare lessens her own suffering: 'that unconscious resignation which, like the twilight, hallows and transforms. In such moments, the humblest hearts are at one with nature, and speak out of the eternal wisdom of things'.[19] This is the Schopenhauerian compassion that penetrates the apparent distinction between the self and others and is a dim perception of the identity of true nature, a making of one's own the suffering and wellbeing of others. In this depiction, Moore would appear to present the philosophy in a favourable light. However, in 'John Norton', Moore's subtext can be interpreted as being quite cynical concerning the intrinsic worth of the Schopenhauerian fashion, its confusions, and the judgment of those who embrace its theories. Moreover, Moore can be seen, in both works, to confront Schopenhauer's theories on literary composition. Schopenhauer was of the opinion that the *da capo* feature in music (one he considered judicious and welcome) should not be transposed to literary or other compositions: he considered that the practice would be intolerable. *Esther Waters* has just such a *da capo* return to the depiction of Esther's initial arrival at Woodview: beginning with 'She stood on the platform watching the receding train', the opening paragraph of the first chapter is repeated at the start of chapter 46 as her life appears to come full-circle. This is not an isolated incident of the technique as, in *Celibates*, Mildred appears on a warm, flower-scented night, and the exact phraseology of the initial chapter is repeated in the final one: 'As she tossed to and fro, the recollections of the day turned in her brain, ticking loudly; and she could see each event as distinctly as the figures on the dial of a great clock'.[20] Here Moore rejects the opinion of one European and embraces a symphonically-

17 *Celibates*, pp 364–5. 18 Trans. E.J.F. Payne (Indian Hills, CO, 1958). 19 *Esther Waters*, p. 369. 20 *Celibates*, pp 1, 308.

4 Camille Pissarro, *Apple Picking at Eragny-sur-Epte* (1888).

related organization of prose that could be traced to the influence of another European, Beethoven.

There is some degree of balance to the tide of European influence where George Moore is concerned. The reverse side of the coin is in Moore's exports to European literature. Robert Niess argues convincingly that Émile Zola purloined from Moore's 1883 novel, *A modern lover*, taking the scenes concerning a conscience-stricken woman posing for a penniless artist and using them in *L'Oeuvre* (1886–7).[21] Adrian Frazier suggests that Guy de Maupassant lifted the plot of that same book, *A Modern Lover*, for his *Bel Ami* (1884). Ironically, it was most often Moore who was accused of plagiarizing *Bel Ami*.[22] James Joyce perceived the modern European quality in *Celibates* when he translated part of that text into Italian – he never

21 Robert J. Niess, *Zola, Cézanne, and Manet: a study of L'Oeuvre* (Ann Arbor, 1968), pp 23–4. 22 Adrian Frazier, *George Moore 1852–1933* (New Haven and London, 2000), p.105.

completed the task. Richard Allen Cave alleges that Joyce used part of Moore's *Vain Fortune* (1891) for 'The Dead'. It could, of course, be said that no matter how European Joyce is, any influence on him by Moore should be considered as intra-Hibernian transfer, rather than as an export by Moore to Europe. Much more clearly a transplant from Moore to Europe, or a prescient creation, is one that derives from *Celibates*: the character of John Norton. Labelled by many (including George Bernard Shaw) as an improbable and unlikely figure, the very features that were seized upon as incredible are those that appear in Huysman's character Durtal. In *En Route* (1895), Durtal retires to a monastery and then, in *L'Oblat* (1903), he becomes a lay member of a religious community. Strangely, this was also the path taken by Huysmans himself; but Moore can hardly be credited with those real-life decisions. The relationship to Huysmans and Durtal is corroborated by the fact that *En Route* was originally entitled *La Bataille Charnelle* (The sensual or carnal battle), just the same internal war that takes place inside John Norton. Durtal, like John, buries himself in study and the past, to evade a present with which he cannot cope. Huysmans was not the only Frenchman who might be seen to have followed Moore: Marcel Prévost's *L'Homme Vierge* is yet another John and Prévost's text was written well over twenty years later. That Prévost should borrow from Moore might be considered fair return since the character of Mildred Lawson in *Celibates* would appear to owe much to Maud du Rouvre, Prévost's leading demi-vierge in his 1894 novel, *Les Demi-Vierges*.[23]

European impressions, whether musical, literary, philosophical or visual, are abundant in Moore's writing. They are put to work by Moore to enrich his prose constructions through intertextuality, and to achieve greater publicity through their topical and sometimes provocative nature. Their presence is not hidden, but rather frequently obvious: it is there to flag Moore's contemporaneity, to mark his superiority to tired Victorian novelists, and to expand possibilities for the English novel. He uses European references to provide additional layers of significance, whether as decorative or informative additions, or as counters to the surface meaning. There are many such instances in *Esther Waters* and *Celibates*; but the examples given here are illustrative of the way various European models are woven into Moore's texts, and how the results emerge in ways and places that are sometimes surprising. There is some balance in the influences and some return of inspiration to mainland European writers; moreover, since European art is so much a part of George Moore, it is fitting that he has also become a permanent part of European art through the sketches and paintings done of him by Edgar Degas and Édouard Manet. Moore would be happy that, through his influence on Edward Martyn, the Hugh Lane Gallery in Dublin possesses a number of French impressionist paintings. He might even be ruefully pleased that his own image is relatively familiar, but less happy that his face is mostly known through a rather unflattering 1879 portrait painted by Édouard Manet. This picture hangs in the Metropolitan Museum of Art in New York and is reproduced in

23 Marcel Prévost, *Les demi-vierges* (Paris, 1894).

their catalogue (and on the cover of Adrian Frazier's recent biography of Moore). Manet said that Moore's face looked like a squashed egg yolk, and that painting is often referred to as *le noyé repeché*, or the drowned man who was fished out again. It was one European impression that Moore did not embrace; it was also one that, despite representations to Manet, he could not change.

Irish men and French food

LUCY McDIARMID

> The body is a model which can stand for any bounded system. Its boundaries
> can represent any boundaries which are threatened or precarious.
>
> (Mary Douglas, *Purity and danger*)[1]

The official police list of all the property found on Roger Casement when he
washed up on Banna Strand contains a number of items that are mentioned in all the
biographies: a ticket from Berlin to Wilhelmshaven, 'envelope containing pieces of
two maps', 'pieces of paper (code)', and so forth – but also one rarely referred to. It
says, 'piece of paper in which sausage was found'.[2] It is not clear whether the police
found the sausage but decided the paper was more important, or whether Casement
had eaten the sausage but saved the piece of paper so as not to leave indications of
his presence. But either way, that sausage, the classic sign of the German spy, offered
evidence of Casement's temporary German enculturation. He had been eating
German food, riding German trains and communicating a bit in the German
language, for a year and a half; and now he was back to Irish food and trains (briefly),
and then English food and trains, as he passed through cultures on his way to the
Tower of London.

The obtrusive foreignness of the German sausage in an Irish context opens up
questions of how food is constructed as native. In 'Food as a Cultural Construction',
Anna Meigs lists some of the 'food rules' of the Hua people of the Eastern Highlands
of Papua New Guinea. One of these is that 'No Hua person may eat food produced,
prepared, or served by a person who is a stranger (that is, a person with whom she
or he does not share *nu* through coresidence or common birth)'.[3] *Nu* is 'the source
of nourishment and growth; it is *the* substance of nurture'. Children 'feed of the *nu*
of their parents,' and the animals people raise 'contain the people's *nu*'.[4]

Although Irish food discourses do not, it seems, have a similar concept, they
manifest, like all aspects of Irish culture, a strong sense of the boundaries between the
friend and the 'stranger', the native and the foreign. Some of the dominant Irish food
discourses focus on the dynamic of intercultural food exchange, especially the notion
of food as a cultural boundary-marker. Eating constitutes a particularly sensitive
register of enculturation because it is so intimate: through digestion, a foreign culture

---

1 *Purity and danger: an analysis of concepts of pollution and taboo* (London: Routledge, 1991), p.
115. 2 Handout distributed at the Royal Irish Academy's Casement Symposium, May
2000. 3 Anna Meigs, 'Food as a cultural construction', in Carole Counihan and Penny Van
Esterik (eds), *Food and culture: a reader* (New York and London, 1997), p. 101. 4 Ibid., pp
98–99.

is immediately – and literally – incorporated into the self. The myth of Persephone exemplifies the way foreign foods – that is, foods in a place to which one is not native – may permanently change the nature of identity. The same dynamic may be found in Irish fairy legends where the person who eats too much fairy food must remain in the OtherWorld. See, for instance, Nuala Ní Dhomhnaill's poem *An Bhatráil* ('The Battering'), in which she rescues her child from the *lios* just in time, after two out of 'three wet-nurses' have 'already suckled him'. In the Paul Muldoon translation, 'had he taken so much as a sip from the third / that's the last I'd have seen of him'.[5]

The great historical example of ingestion as a threat to identity is souperism; but similar threats occur long after the Great Famine. The intimacy and ideological control implicit in feeding determined the passionate and hostile response to the 1913 'Save the Dublin Kiddies' campaign: Archbishop Walsh objected to a socialist plan to feed the strikers' children in England because such feeding would, he purported to believe, make the children English (and Protestant).[6] Sinn Féin objected to the food-ships sent earlier by British trade-unions for the same reason. The way to assert power against a feeder is, of course, to *resist*, as hunger-strikers do, and, on a different level altogether, as did the many people throughout Irish history who refused to toast the English king or queen. It is swallowing the beverage – not just echoing the toast – that has ideological implications.[7]

There is an alternative Irish intercultural food discourse associated with France. It is not defined in terms of guarding the body's boundaries, but of making them permeable; it is not a matter of control and resistance, but of license and liberation; not punishment, but reward and pleasure. Irish eating in France generates a food discourse in which somatic and linguistic; national boundaries give way, voluntarily, to the absorption of a foreign culture. The records of such diverse cosmopolites as Wolfe Tone, Oscar Wilde, and George Moore reveal the way French food is cultur-ally constructed by Irish men as redemptive and compensatory, judged in relation to bad food, or the absence of food, of some other country (usually England or Ireland). French food takes on the qualities of whatever is wanted from France: armies, sex, beauty, pleasure, abundance. It is a food that rescues the Irish eater from some previous unpleasantness; it is revitalizing. Looking at Tone's journals, Wilde's letters and a playful newspaper controversy provoked by Moore, this essay will demonstrate how the consumption of French food is associated with the larger transformation of the writer's culture, and how all three men have participated in and extended the Irish discourse about French food. To study Irish men eating French food is to see

5 Nuala Ní Dhomhnaill, *The Astrakhan cloak* (Loughcrew, Oldcastle, Co. Meath, 1992), pp 24–5. **6** For an analysis of the 'Save the Dublin Kiddies' campaign, see Lucy McDiarmid, *The Irish art of controversy* (Dublin, 2005). **7** Caroline Walker Bynum's analysis of the way medieval women used 'food-related behavior – charity, fasting, eucharistic devotion, and miracles' as a 'way of bypassing ecclesiastical control' is relevant to Irish forms of resistance to food and drink. See Bynum, 'Fast, feast, and flesh: the religious significance of food to Medieval women', in Counihan andVan Esterik (eds), *Food and culture*, p. 148. See also Maud Ellmann, *The hunger artists: starving, writing, and imprisonment* (Cambridge, MA, 1993).

1 James Gillray, *Politeness* (1779). This image offers a catalogue of contrasting stereotypes of England and France. The two figures are framed by a joint of beef and a cluster of frogs, hanging on opposite sides of the wall. The caption reads, 'With Porter, Roast Beef, & Plumb Pudding well cram'd,/Jack English declares that Monsr may be D____d,/The Soup Meagre Frenchman such Language dont suit/So he Grins Indignation & calls him a Brute.'

the small steps by which they may become enculturated in a fantasy place where their wishes are granted.

WOLFE TONE

The revitalizing power of French food is nowhere clearer than in Wolfe Tone's journal entries about the meals he was served immediately after arriving in France in February 1796. The earliest entries list every food or drink he consumes. 'I am ashamed to say so much on the subject of eating', he remarks.[8] As it turns out, he only dwells extensively on food for his first ten days in France. The moment he engages in serious political negotiations, the menus disappear from the text. Food features so prominently at the start because, immediately upon arrival, Tone begins fighting England through its nationalistic food discourses. Every French bite he takes

8 *Life of Theobald Wolfe Tone*, compiled and arranged by William Theobald Wolfe Tone, ed. Thomas Bartlett (Dublin, 1998), p. 463.

becomes part of the larger ideological, political and military struggle. Even before he gets to Paris and meets Lazare Carnot (one of the five members of the French Directory), France has helped him against England by feeding him so excellently.

Tone arrived at Havre de Grace on 2 February, having spent thirty-one days on the voyage from New York. He spent that first night at the Hotel de Paix, and noted: 'Slept in a superb crimson damask bed; great luxury, after being a month without having my clothes off'. Here is the opening of his journal entry for 3 February:

> Rose early; difficult to get breakfast; get it at last; excellent coffee, and very coarse brown bread, but, as it happens, I like brown bread . . . [then he goes out for a walk . . .] . . . went into diverse coffee houses; plenty of coffee, but no papers. *No bread* in two of the coffee houses; but pastry; singular enough! Dinner; and here, as a matter of curiosity, follows our bill of fare, which proves clearly that France is in a starving situation: An excellent soup; a dish of fish, fresh from the harbour; a fore-quarter of delicate small mutton, like the Welsh; a superb turkey, and a pair of ducks roasted; pastry, cheese, and fruit after dinner, with wine *ad libitum*, but still the *pain bis*; provoked with the Frenchmen grumbling at the bread; made a saying: *Vive le pain bis et la liberté!* I forgot the vegetables, which were excellent; very glad to see such unequivocal proofs of famine.[9]

This entry shows Tone's increasing excitement as the food turns into ammunition. The sequence makes it sound as if the consumption of the dinner leads to a new linguistic capacity. Eating it (it is 'excellent', 'delicate', 'superb'), he becomes enculturated and able to speak the language: 'made a saying: *Vive le pain bis et la liberté!*' Tone is flexing his cultural muscles; he says 'made a saying' because he is pleased with himself for putting words together in a foreign language. In the 8 February entry he complains 'that I cannot speak French', and quotes Sir Andrew Aguecheek: 'Oh that I had given that time to the tongues that I have spent in fencing and bear-baiting'. But here he attempts a little phrase: he takes a syntactic structure he understands ('vive' + a noun) and fills in words that are part of his slight French vocabulary.

More importantly, the words he fits into the structure offer a counter-discourse to the 'English culinary nationalism' analyzed in Ben Rogers' *Beef and Liberty*. That contemporary English food discourse linked 'beef' and 'liberty' is the visual argument of James Gillray's famous cartoon of *French Liberty, British Slavery* (1792). The overweight John Bull starts to eat a huge side of beef complaining that his government is overtaxing and 'starving us to death'. That is 'British Slavery' – no slavery at all, of course, when he freely eats such a hunk of meat. The skinny Frenchman, in rags that were once effete courtier-like clothing, with a skeletal face and long cissy hair, chews on scallions and says 'Vat blessing be de Liberte! No more Tax! No more Slavery! How ve live! Ve svim in de Milk and Honey!'[10] But Tone's meal has demonstrated

---

9 Ibid., p. 457.   **10** Ben Rogers, *Beef and liberty* (London, 2000), cover and pp 163–5.

that you do not need a monarch to provide good and plentiful food. Although the Frenchmen complain about the brown bread, Tone enjoys it ('as it happens'), and, with its linkage, his little saying intervenes in and revises the English food discourse. In addition, the Latin phrase for the amount of wine poured – *ad libitum*, at your pleasure, as much as you want – combines with the length of the list, the sense of a great accumulation of foods, and the varieties of excellence, to suggest a wondrous plentitude.

Tone's intervention includes commentary on the production as well as the consumption of food. The profound political and spiritual intensity of that first dinner – the bread of liberty, wine to one's heart's desire, a vision of abundance – reappears in Tone's view of the rural landscape. As he rides from Havre de Grace to Paris on 10–12 February, Tone admires the landscape especially for its cultivation. Between Havre de Grace and Rouen, he notes:

> Every foot of ground seems to me under cultivation, so there will be no starving, please God, this year . . . an orchard to every cottage, besides rows of apple trees, without intermission, by the road side. Why might it not be in *other* countries, whose climate differs but very little from that of *Normandy*? *Think of this!*[11]

Moving southeast from Rouen, he sees 'table land cultivated as before, that is to say, *without one foot of ground wasted*'. He adds, 'I could wish John Bull were here for one half hour, just to look at the fields of wheat that I am passing. It is impossible to conceive higher cultivation: I have seen nothing of a corn country like it in England.'[12] England turns out even to be responsible for the bad and overpriced meals Tone eats in France. When, after spending the night in the small village of Magny, Tone receives a 'most blistering bill for supper' the night before, John Bull is to blame: 'See here it is! For a cold fowl, six eggs and 2 bottles of poor wine – 32 francs, equal to – £1.6s. Damn them!' His linguistic ability deserts him: 'In great indignation, and the more so, because I could not scold in French. Passion is eloquent, but all my figures of speech were lost on the landlord.'[13] The same thing happens at Pontoise, where he has breakfast (the ragout is 'execrable'), and then he figures out why: 'This comes of riding in fine carriages, with blue velvet linings! We are downright *Milords Anglais*, and they certainly make us pay for our titles.'[14] The French expense is blamed on the appearance of English aristocracy; but the richness of the landscape restores his good mood and jolly irony:

> An uninterrupted succession of corn, vines, and orchards, as far as the eye can reach, rich and *riant* beyond description. I see now clearly that John Bull will be able to starve France.[15]

11 *Life of Theobald Wolfe Tone*, p. 460.   12 Ibid., p. 461.   13 Ibid.   14 Ibid., p. 462.   15 Ibid.

A few sentences earlier he used the phrase 'the smiling appearance of the country', but he is clearly trying to practise his French with that *riant*.[16]

Tone's last detailed account of food describes the first meal he eats in Paris, at the Maison Egalité ('formerly the Palais Royale'). He apologizes for harping on 'the subject of eating, but I have been so often bored with the famine in France, that it is, in some degree, necessary to dwell upon it'. Each sip and each bite constitute the prandial dimension of the continuing political argument:

> Our dinner was a soup, roast fowl, fried carp, salads of two kinds, a bottle of Burgundy, coffee after dinner, and a glass of liqueur, with excellent bread – (I forgot, we had cauliflowers in sauce) – and our bill for the whole, wine and all, was 1,500 livres . . . What would I have given to have had P.P. [Thos. Russell] with me! Indeed we would have discussed another bottle of the Burgundy, or by'r lady, some two or three . . . How he would enjoy France, not excepting even her wines! I wish to God our bill of fare was posted on the Royal Exchange, for John Bull's edification. I do not think he would dine much better for the money, even at the London Tavern, especially if he drank such Burgundy as we did. The saloon in which we dined was magnificent, illuminated with patent lamps and looking glasses of immense size . . . every thing wore a complete appearance of opulence and luxury.[17]

It is clear that Tone not only wants to bring France to Ireland, to have orchards and vineyards there in as great abundance as they are in Normandy, but to bring Ireland to France, to have Thomas Russell join him: every time he drinks an excellent wine he longs for Russell. The taste of the meal creates an intercultural configuration: as Tone and his new friend D'Aucourt dine in Paris, they are joined by 'John Bull', who would be edified by seeing how well Tone is eating in Paris, and of course Russell, who would 'discuss' a few more bottles of Burgundy.[18]

16 p. 15. A common eighteenth-century trope, as in Pope's phrase 'laughing Ceres'. **17** *Life of Theobald Wolfe Tone*, p. 462. **18** The way Tone talks about eating when he is in Ireland confirms the distinct Frenchness of this hedonistic discourse. In Ireland Tone mentions drinking quite often, but there is more emphasis on drunkenness than on the quality of the wines. On the night of 1 November 1792, Tone dines with other United Irishmen in Dublin, Hamilton Rowan among them. Referring to himself in the third person, Tone says: 'Very much surprised, on looking down to the table, to see two glasses before him; finds, on looking at Hamilton Rowan, that he has got four eyes; various other phenomena in optics equally curious . . . every thing about him moving in a rapid rotation; perfectly sober, but perceives that every one else is getting very drunk . . . Fine doings! fine doings!' (ibid., p. 168). And then, the next morning, 'Sick as Demogorgon'. In August 1792, at Murphy's Inn in Rathfriland, the landlord 'will give us no accomodation! . . . He has cold beef and lamb chops, and will give us neither, but turns off on his heel' (ibid., p. 143). In October of the same year, he has bad food outside Athlone ('victuals bad; wine poisonous; bed execrable' [ibid., p. 160]) and the next day at breakfast, 'the waiter brings us beefsteaks, fried with a great quantity of onions; nice feeding, but not to my taste'. The next morning, he writes,

OSCAR WILDE

Jack: He seems to have expressed a desire to be buried in Paris.
Chasuble: In Paris! I fear that hardly points to any very serious state of mind
at the last.

(Oscar Wilde, *The Importance of Being Earnest*)

For Oscar Wilde, as for Tone, the value of food in France derives from its function as an ideological counterpart to English food and politics. But it is more than the 'good' term in a binary opposition: the act of consuming it leads to a profound joy and exhilaration, a spiritual experience inseparable from a list of delicacies. The detail and the punctuation ('!!!') in Wilde's description (in a letter to Lord Alfred Douglas) of a party he hosted in France only a month after his release from two years of hard labour show an excitement as great as Tone's. On 23 June 1897 Wilde gave a 'Jubilee Garden Party' at the Hotel de la Plage in Berneval-sur-Mer, five miles from Dieppe. The guests were fifteen 'gamins' from the neighborhood and (according to Ellmann) some 'local worthies'[19] such as the curé, the postman, and the schoolmaster:

> My *fête* was a huge success: fifteen *gamins* were entertained on strawberries and cream, apricots, chocolates, cakes, and *sirop de grenadine*. I had a huge iced cake with *Jubilé de la Reine Victoria* in pink sugar just rosetted with green, and a great wreath of red roses round it all. Every child was asked beforehand to choose his present: they all chose instruments of music!!!
>
> *6 accordions*
> *5 trompettes*
> *4 clairons*
>
> They sang the Marseillaise and other songs, and danced a *ronde*, and also played 'God Save the Queen': they said it was 'God Save the Queen', and I did not like to differ from them. They also all had flags, which I gave them. They were most gay and sweet. I gave the health of *La Reine d'Angleterre*, and they cried '*Vive La Reine d'Angleterre*'!!!! Then I gave '*La France, mere de tous les artistes*', and finally I gave *Le Président de la République*: I thought I had better do so. They cried out with one accord '*Vivent le Président de la République et Monsieur Melmoth*'!!! So I found my name coupled with that of the President. It was an amusing experience as I am hardly more than a month out of gaol.
>
> They stayed from 4:30 to seven o'clock and played games: on leaving I gave them each a basket with a jubilee cake frosted pink and inscribed, and bonbons. They seem to have made a great demonstration in Berneval-le-Grand, and to have gone to the house of the Mayor and cried '*Vive Monsieur*

'Breakfast, more beefsteak and onions;' and that evening, 'Dinner very bad' (ibid., p. 161).
19 Richard Ellmann, *Oscar Wilde* (London, 1988), p. 509.

le Maire! Vive la Reine d'Angleterre! Vive Monsieur Melmoth!' I tremble at my position.[20]

Ellmann says Wilde was 'no doubt pining for his sons', but there was a national as well as a family politics at issue here – an allusion to a recent experience in England.

On 17 May, the day before Wilde left Reading Gaol, he paid the fines of three small children imprisoned for snaring rabbits, thereby freeing them. Wilde wrote to warder Thomas Martin: 'If I can do this by paying the fine, tell the children that they are to be released tomorrow by a friend, and ask them to be happy, and not to tell anyone.'[21] Martin gave a sweet biscuit to one of the children, who was crying; the warder was (therefore) dismissed from his post at the gaol. On 27 May Wilde wrote a long letter to the *Daily Chronicle* about the dismissal, describing at length the 'terror' (Wilde's word) that children feel in gaol. He then writes:

> The second thing from which a child suffers in prison is hunger. The food that is given to it consists of a piece of usually badly-baked prison bread and a tin of water for breakfast at half-past seven. At twelve o'clock it gets dinner, composed of a tin of coarse Indian meal stirabout, and at half- past five it gets a piece of dry bread and a tin of water for its supper . . . [T]he child is, as a rule, incapable of eating the food at all. Anyone who knows anything about children knows how easily a child's digestion is upset by a fit of crying, or trouble and mental distress of any kind . . . In the case of the little child to whom Warder Martin gave the biscuits, the child was crying with hunger on Tuesday morning, and utterly unable to eat the bread and water served to it for its breakfast. Martin went out after the breakfasts had been served, and bought the few sweet biscuits for the child rather than see it starving. It was a beautiful action on his part, and was so recognised by the child, who, utterly unconscious of the regulation of the Prison Board, told one of the senior warders how kind this junior warder had been to him. The result was, of course, a report and a dismissal.[22]

The Jubilee party was given only twenty-six days after this letter was written, and it seems clear that the French setting, the French food, and even the French language participated in the same intercultural discourse present in Tone's journals. The pleasures of the Jubilee party were redemptive and compensatory. French food offered qualities that had been lacking in England: abundance, beauty, sweetness, and tolerance. Wilde could do in France what he – and what the warder – could not do in England.

Although we know from James Murphy's *Abject loyalty* that the Irish people liked Queen Victoria more than was officially acknowledged among nationalists at the end

20 *The complete letters of Oscar Wilde*, ed. Merlin Holland and Rupert Hart-Davis (New York, 2000), pp 906–7. **21** Ibid., p. 831. **22** Ibid., p. 850.

of the nineteenth century, it looks nevertheless as if there is a disconnect here.²³ It is one thing to give a party in France and feed children chocolates and cakes, straw-berries and cream, as Wilde could not have done anywhere in England, let alone in Reading Gaol; but why celebrate the queen whose laws sent him to Reading Gaol? Why praise la Reine d'Angleterre as he is celebrating his liberation from Angleterre's gaol and narrow-minded society?

To answer that question, consider the way Wilde described Victoria the day after the party, when he was asked if he had ever met her. He 'replied that he had, and described with admiration her appearance ("a ruby mounted in jet"), her walk, and her regal behavior'.²⁴ This ruby mounted in jet is not a symbol of the state, not the queen of Reading Gaol, but (with her jewels, rich colours, and theatricality) an aesthetic queen, a 'nineties queen, a queen of camp. She is a queen fit for a cake of pink sugar and red roses, a Titania, a fairy queen of decorations, sweets, flags, straw-berries and cream. The glory of the party, for Wilde, was not the taste of the food, which he never mentions, but its richness, its elegance, its visual display, and the pleasure of distributing toys and sweets to so many children. The party was a magic world constructed by its festive materials. The monarch's title in French – *la Reine d'Angleterre* – exoticizes her a bit, and incorporates her into the delights possible for Wilde only in France. It is interesting that he invokes France as a gendered nation, emphasizing its maternal nature: *mère de tous les artistes*. Victoria takes on some of that maternal quality too, when she is toasted in French. Wilde's moments of French joy, expressed through the toasts, are reminiscent of the joy in Tone's '*vive le pain bis et la liberté*': in both cases, the man newly arrived in France seems to have found there his heart's desire.

When the children immediately link his name with the President's, he is galli-cized, reborn in French, not only because he is *M. Melmoth*, but because he has become acceptable – indeed more than acceptable: a superior public personage, worthy of association with the head of state. In their post-prandial excitement the children kept on calling out in joy – '*Vive Monsieur le Maire! Vive la Reine d'Angleterre. Vive Monsieur Melmoth!*' Because the occasion of the fête was a national one, and because officials like the curé and schoolmaster were present, the party participated to some extent in the public sphere. The linking of names in the toast joined the private and pseudonymous M. Melmoth with the English monarchy and with French national and local politics. What sphere, then, did the party occupy? A theatrical array of beautiful materials transformed the little garden that could only hold six (but that day held fifteen) into a magic space where the reasonably clear categories 'public' and 'private' did not apply. In a kind of festive hilarity, cultures were mixed and identities obscured: Wilde's proper name and nationality were neither known nor mentioned, England became *Angleterre*, all speech was in French, the former prisoner was host to civic dignitaries and ritually linked with two heads of

23 James H. Murphy, *Abject loyalty: nationalism and monarchy in Ireland during the reign of Queen Victoria* (Washington, DC, 2001). 24 Ellmann, pp 509–10.

state, and only dessert was eaten. As Wilde says, it was 'an amusing experience' for someone barely a month out of gaol, a redemptive, compensatory one, and also, of course, a fantasy created and sustained by French pastry and fruit. It was as great a joy as Tone got from his first French dinner.

GEORGE MOORE

> He dragged the policeman into the dining-room and said, 'Is there a law in this country to compel me to eat this abominable omelette?'
>
> (Moore, as quoted by Yeats in *Dramatis personae, 1896–1902*)

The culinary revolution that Wolfe Tone might have wanted to bring to Ireland, had things gone differently, was attempted on a smaller scale by George Moore, who tried to introduce a single fish, once tasted in France, to Irish cuisine. In his revenge on Moore for *Hail and Farewell*, Yeats claims that in spite of Moore's 'French, his knowledge of painting', and general air of sophistication, 'nature had denied to him the final touch: he had a coarse palate';[25] that deficiency was unknown to Moore himself. On 4 February 1910, the *Irish Times* published a letter from Moore telling the story of his introduction to this fish in Henri's restaurant in Paris in '1894 or 1895'. The *maitre d'* told him that the fish was called *le bar*, and fourteen years later, so he says, he at last learned that the wonderful fish he had eaten in Henri's was a grey mullet. He wrote to the paper in order to create a demand for the fish, so that Dublin fishmongers would carry it, and also to elevate taste generally:

> Grey mullet will be appreciated here, I feel sure of that, for notwithstanding all efforts to suppress civilisation in Dublin there are many amongst us who will find it at least as delectable as turbot. Others of finer taste will discover in it a still rarer delicacy.[26]

The mullet becomes part of the French-inspired cultural revolution that Moore had been trying to bring to Ireland for years, especially in the form of French painting and French attitudes to sex, morality, and religion. A year after the mullet letter, having done his damage, Moore left Dublin for London, so the campaign to introduce this final mark of sophistication to Ireland was either a parting shot or a parody of all the other shots. The entire correspondence amounted to almost 8,000 words printed in the *Irish Times* between the 4th and 15th of the month.

The general tendency of the correspondence is to de-exoticize and *gaelicize* the fish that Moore had *gallicized*. Moore had placed Paris in the centre of the universe, and Dublin on the remote periphery, a sad place where the grey mullet is not marketed. In the many letters that respond to Moore's, his geopolitics is reversed: Ireland takes centre-stage, and France falls almost altogether out of view, as the corre-

25 W.B. Yeats, *Dramatis personae, 1896–1902: the autobiography of W. B. Yeats* (New York, 1965), p. 297.   **26** George Moore, Letter, *Irish Times*, 4 February 1910.

spondents say precisely where on the *Irish* coast the fish may be caught. The letter columns of the *Irish Times* fill with mullet-lore, to such a great extent that each letter competes with previous letters in its display of knowledge. The accumulation of expertise, all of it quite detailed, constitutes an implicit rejection of Moore's distinction between French sophistication and Irish ignorance.[27]

Moore's letter is written in the dry, witty, man-of-the-world voice of *Hail and Farewell*, which he was perfecting at the time. The tone itself becomes inseparable from the grey mullet and from the cosmopolitanism associated – by Moore – with European cuisine and culture. The excessive length of the letter, its leisurely, detailed and digressive style, clearly derive from the kind of person who has the time to write lengthy letters to the newspaper about the gustatory aspects of fish. Money is no object to him: the availability of the fish is more important than its price. Moreover, all the people invoked and quoted in the letter have no other object in life but to satisfy the desires of George Moore.

The opening vignette – and the letter is a series of vignettes – presents a wealthy, passive, gentlemanly consumer waiting to be fed:

> It must have been in 1894 or 1895 that the *maitre d'hotel* in Henri's restaurant wheeled a dumb waiter to where I was sitting, and lifting a cover showed me a large fish, some four or five pounds in weight, and in shape resembling a salmon. It had just come from the pot, and a slight vapour curled amid the white napkins. When he cut it I noticed that its flesh was white, and, not recognising the fish, I asked its name, and he said *le bar*. I had never heard the words before, and asked him how this was, and he told me that the fish was coming into fashion. But he could not tell me what *le bar* was called in England, nor could the cook who had been to England, nor any of the waiters. For the next few days I consulted my friends and the dictionaries, without being able to discover the English words for *le bar*.[28]

All the physical activity belongs to others here: the *maitre d'* wheels and lifts, whereas Moore just sits. The image of the vapour curling 'amid the white napkins' suggests the hedonistic leisure of the customer. Then, implicitly, the *maitre d'* walks off stage to consult the cooks and waiters about the fish's English name. Moore consults his friends (who are not designated by job titles, like the others in the story) and his dictionaries – notice the plural. This is a man with access to many books. Still unable to discover the *provenance* of the fish, he advised his friends 'to seek it out when they went to Paris' (all of his friends are rich travellers also). Moore finally learns the name from a 'genial Jew' in London,

> a man who can give information upon all subjects. He can tell one where the last pair of embroidered braces worn by the last king of Poland are lying, how

27 The 'grey mullet' controversy continued in the *Irish Times* on 5, 7, 8, 9, 10, 11, and 12 February 1910. **28** Moore, Letter, 5.

much you will have to pay for an egg of the great auk, and what statues are likely to be discovered in the buried cities of Turkestan.[29]

This one-man search engine is clearly used to being questioned by people as idle and eccentric as Moore. Asked about *le bar*, he explains that grey mullet is 'a most excellent fish' and 'coming again into fashion in Parisian restaurants'. Moore's extensive staff – his fishmonger Mr McCabe, and McCabe's London correspondent Mr William E. Chitty – both oblige with more mulletana, which Moore includes in his letter. They appear to agree with one another that the fish is caught off the coasts of Devon and Cornwall but is not widely available in London or Dublin. Moore lets his readers know that these represent a small part of his total correspondence on the grey mullet. Mr Chitty (could he be an invention of Moore's?) ends his letter by remarking, 'I have no doubt a discussion in the Irish papers re this intensely interesting matter would arouse a wide world sensation'. Moore says he does not want a sensation, just a large popular demand for the fish, so it will appear on the market in Dublin. He finishes with a recipe for boiled grey mullet with *sauce hollandaise*.

The letters that pour in to the paper in response to this eccentric hedonism echo Moore's tone to some extent: they are dry and almost academic in their presentation of mullet-lore; but they repatriate the grey mullet (in Ireland). The very echo of Moore's tone in missives contradicting what he says makes knowledge of the mullet a touchstone of cultural sophistication. People write in with fancy names ('Ichthyophagist' et al.) and drop terms like the Latin *mugil capito*, the Irish *muleid, murleat,* or *lanach,* the French *mulet* or *umbrine*, the Italian *corvo*, and the Greek *labrax*. Many others write in saying that the fish Moore was served at Henri's restaurant was not a grey mullet but some other kind of fish: white salmon, bass, umbria, pike and barbel are among the suggestions (the Larousse confirms the claim of many correspondents that *le bar* is bass).[30] They also recommend the French *langouste* (crayfish) and offer recipes for all sorts of fish. The formality of a letter signed 'Ichthyophagist' responds to the tone even as it reverses the geopolitics. The response begins, 'The letter of Mr George Moore relative to the "grey mullet" deserves public encomium, as it displays his patriotic desire to render popular one of the most delicate of our Irish food fishes'.

According to the collective wisdom of the letters, the grey mullet can be caught on the coasts of Louth, Derry, Donegal, Sligo, Galway, Mayo, Kerry, Cork, and Waterford. Several people claim to have seen it caught in the Liffey. Quite a number point out that the grey mullet feeds on 'the garbage of the foreshore', and that whatever taste it has derives from whatever it has consumed. Some correspondents who have seen it eat garbage say they will never eat it. Others explain how best to catch the grey mullet. 'Epicurus' recommends a series of nets joined and stretched across the mouth of an inlet. Mr Barron of Waterford recommends 'hairy bait on a small hook'. '*Pecheur d'Irlande*' (the French style of this Irish identity shows how sophisti-

29 Ibid.   **30** The Larousse also offers the translation 'sea-dace'.

cated Irish fishers can be) says he saw a small boy catch one by hand. 'Piscator' recommends that they be caught by the Royal Irish Constabulary 'with tackle, which, in the hands of an ordinary angler, would be entirely useless'. Mr Henry of Sligo claims to have *shot* a grey mullet on the shore. Mr Hackett of Ventry catches them 'a very few yards from my house'. The cumulative effect of the letters is a privileging of the local against the cosmopolitan and the Continental. The letters collectively construct a native discourse of angling masculinity around the grey mullet, cancelling out the effete French scene of consumption in Moore's original letter.[31] The boundaries of the island are reasserted.

EATERS & FEEDERS

To return to Casement and his sausage paper: when Casement walked inland from Banna Strand, he walked into an Irish food discourse different from the intercultural ones discussed in this essay. Contrary to popular opinion in the rest of Ireland, Casement was not 'betrayed' by the people of Kerry. According to North Kerry folklore, he spent most of his thirty hours there eating and drinking. The poor man 'must be starved with hunger', they thought, and he was given tea, steak, more tea, eggs, and milk, and was grateful to the people who took him in and fed him.[32] This higher abundance, especially in the domestic site, is typical of the tradition of Irish hospitality – 'higher' because the hospitality often seems to be impractical or in violation of some law. So St Brigit gives butter, bacon, or milk to poor dogs, or poor people, or druids, because 'everything she put her hand to used to increase', and she breastfed Christ.[33] So 'vast quantities of meat and drink' were served at wakes, 'whiskey, white wheaten loaves and tobacco' even when the hierarchy forbade 'such odious, pernicious, and detestable practices'.[34] So Mrs Kearney of Tralee, wife of Constable Kearney at the Tralee barracks, where Casement was imprisoned, cooked a steak for the prisoner even though it was Good Friday.

Folklore and myth have long shown the way national, cultural, and spiritual matters may be involved in the eating and feeding practices of one or two people: foreign languages pass through the body as foreign foods do. As Ireland now in large-scale, official ways opens up to Europe in treaties and currency, or closes itself off to other nationalities in new legislation and definitions of citizenship, it remains valuable to study the small-scale and unofficial ways in which single individuals became routes of exchange, conduits between the native and the foreign.

---

31 I am grateful to Mary S. Pierse for letting me know of Moore's poem (in French) about 'le bar'. See John Eglinton (ed.), *Letters from George Moore to Ed. Dujardin 1886–1922* (New York, 1929), pp 105–6. The poem was written in 1920. **32** See Lucy McDiarmid, 'Secular relics: Casement's boat, Casement's dish,' in *Textual Practice*, 16:2 (2002), 285. **33** Lady Gregory, 'Brigit, the Mary of the Gael,' in *The Blessed Trinity of Ireland* (Gerrards Cross, 1985), p. 9. **34** Patricia Lysaght, 'Hospitality at wakes and funerals in Ireland from the seventeenth to the nineteenth century: some evidence from the written record', in *Folkore*, 114 (2003), 408, 410.

Alicia Le Fanu's *Don Juan de las Sierras, or, El Empecinado* (1823): appropriations of Spain in Irish romanticism[1]

ASIER ALTUNA-GARCÍA DE SALAZAR

Within the European background of the nineteenth century, the use of Spain, Spanish history and Spanish literature by some Anglo-Irish authors as a pivotal element for their construction of the Anglo-Irish discourse of the Romantic period, has received cursory critical attention. Indeed, although a myriad of Anglo-Irish writers had recourse to the history, tradition, religion and even landscape of a contemporary nineteenth-century Spain, many of these poets, novelists and play-wrights have been considered non-canonical and minor in importance by literary criticism on the grounds of their lack of aesthetic quality and their political, social and religious partisan biases. Even if this pre-assumption is conceded, this is rapidly counterbalanced by the nuanced 'will to be heard'[2] of a considerable bulk of Anglo-Irish writing with Spanish referents. This essay focuses on Miss Alicia Le Fanu's multiple appropriations of Spain in *Don Juan de las Sierras, or, El Empecinado: a romance* (1823). Through her choice of this nineteenth-century European 'anecdote',[3] Spain and Spanish referents, Le Fanu also tackles contemporary issues in Ireland, thus estab-lishing a seminal dialogue within a specific 'signifying system' (Ireland in the nineteenth century). Thus her superficially 'Spanish' novel is able to interrogate equally 'Irish' issues, such as race, secret societies, patriotism, religion, the forging of heroes, intermarriage and the eventual construction of Anglo-Irish tradition and identity.

Alicia Le Fanu (1791–1844, or later)[4] is one of the few Anglo-Irish female writers of Irish Romanticism who turns to contemporary Spain for inspiration.[5] Although,

1 I owe great thanks to the Department for Education Eusko Jaurlaritza-Gobierno Vasco for postdoctoral fellowship support that made this research and writing possible. I am also grateful to my colleagues, especially Prof. Tadhg Foley, at the Centre for Irish Studies, NUI Galway, whose reading group discussions on this paper provided valuable suggestions.
2 Stephen Greenblatt, *Shakespearean negotiations* (Oxford, 1988), p. 1. 3 For Joel Fineman, anecdote is a determinant factor in the practice of historiography. See Joel Fineman, 'The History of the Anecdote', in H. Aram Veeser (ed.), *The new historicism* (London, 1989), p. 50. 4 In Hogan's *Dictionary of Irish literature* we find the most precise reference to Alicia Le Fanu's biographical data to date. See Robert Hogan (ed. in chief), *Dictionary of Irish literature: revised and expanded edition*, 2 vols (London, 1996), pp 693–4. 5 In *Lady Morgan's memoirs* we are told that she also collaborated in writing a musical operetta, 'The Whim of the Moment', with a Spanish theme. The scene of the operetta, now lost, was set in Spain and

little is known about the writer's life, Le Fanu belonged to an important Anglo-Irish family which influenced both the English and Irish literary panoramas during the eighteenth and nineteenth centuries.[6] A friend of Thomas Moore,[7] Alicia Le Fanu was author of longer poems and romantic novels of minor importance.[8] *Don Juan de las Sierras, or, El Empecinado*, in its three volumes, is the only one of her novels to deal with contemporary Spanish history, making special reference to the Peninsular War (1808–14), or the War of Independence as it was known within the Spanish context. Le Fanu depicts El Empecinado's figure, a well-known, hardy folk 'guerrillero', who became a great support to the troops of the Anglo-Irish Duke of Wellington, Arthur Wellesley, in the Peninsula.[9] The figure of the Spanish El Empecinado was well known both in Britain and Ireland, as numerous entries in *The Times* attest;[10] but from the very start Le Fanu warns the reader of her national imagining and her construction of Spanish history, when she states in the preface that 'the management of the story is entirely [her] own, [so] it is necessary to caution the young reader

involved 'Spanish ladies and Irish lovers'. The operetta was produced in Dublin in 1807 'before a crowded audience'. *Lady Morgan's memoirs: autobiography, diaries and correspondence*, 2 vols (London, 1863), vol. 2, p. 316. **6** Alicia Le Fanu was Richard Brinsley Sheridan's niece. Both her mother (Elizabeth Le Fanu) and her aunt were authors; the latter, Alicia Le Fanu, had 'a leading place in literary society in Dublin and particularly in private theatricals which were then much in vogue': T.P. Le Fanu, *Memoir of the Le Fanu family* (Manchester, 1924), p. 51. **7** Thomas Moore maintained correspondence with the Le Fanus and there are many instances in which, as early as 1818, he shows a special interest in getting Alicia Le Fanu's works published in London by Longmans, most probably as a personal favour as Le Fanu had collected and copied materials for Moore [who was preparing a book on Sheridan; *Memoirs of the life of Richard Brinsley Sheridan* in 2 volumes, published in 1825]: Thomas Moore to Mrs Le Fanu [Miss Alicia Le Fanu's mother], 16 September 1818. Moore even offers to read manuscripts of her novels, most probably *Leolin abbey*, before submitting them to the Longmans: Thomas Moore to Miss Alicia Le Fanu, 21 December 1818. Most of Le Fanu's major works were published before 1826 and Moore continued to encourage her work: Thomas Moore to Alicia Le Fanu, 5 January 1828; also on 3 April 1829. See Wilfred S. Dowden, *The letters of Thomas Moore*, 2 vols (Oxford, 1964). **8** *The flowers of the sylphid queen* (1809), *Rosara's chains, or the choice of a life* (1812), *Strathallen* (1816), *Helen Monteagle* (1818), *Leolin abbey* (1819), *Tales of a tourist* (1823), *Memoirs of the life and writings of Mrs Frances Sheridan* (1824), *Henry the fourth of France* (1826). Ibid., pp 76–7. **9** 'Spain was to be saved, in fact, not by grape-shot, greybeards and grandees, but by hardy guerrillas and the sudden flash of the knife. These peasants spontaneously organized themselves into small, do-or-die bands, at least one to each province headed by folk heroes: Juan Martin Diaz 'El Empecinado', the dweller-by-the-stream in the Guadalajara mountains; Julian Sanchez, the farmer in Old Castile whose family had been murdered by the abhorred French dragoons; El Marquisito in the Asturias, El Medico; the Minas, Elder and Younger'. See Elizabeth Longford, *Wellington: the years of the sword* (London: Weidenfeld & Nicolson, 1969), vol. 1, p. 211. **10** The most significant are: *The Times*, 30 March 1811: 15 July 1812: 16 May 1823: 17 August 1824: 9 September 1825. These note El Empecinado's prowess against injustice, mainly French, and present proclamations issued by El Empecinado aimed at obtaining a Constitution, religious freedom and liberty.

against identifying, in every thing, the "Empecinado" of romance, with the Empecinado of history'.[11]

In this vein, Le Fanu's treatment of this contemporary historical event intermingles Spanish legend and history, ballad and literary quotation, social differences and political biases, although Le Fanu's political statements and her vision of Anglo-Irish society underlie the main progression of the novel. Katie Trumpener's analysis of another of Alicia Le Fanu's novels published that very same year, *Tales of a tourist* (1823), induce her to class Le Fanu within that group of Irish novelists whose works became 'a prime genre for the dissemination of nationalist ideas'. For Trumpener, *Tales of a tourist*, which introduces the character of an antiquary named O'Carolan in close reference to the famous eighteenth-century Irish poet and harper Turlough Carolan (1670–1738), exemplified a 'coherent revival' in the literature of nationalism because 'it commemorate[d] and celebrate[d] its [Ireland's] own history'.[12] The case of Le Fanu's novel *Don Juan de las Sierras, or, El Empecinado* offers, however, a few intriguing ambivalences. Indeed, if Le Fanu's romances partake of a trend to spread 'nationalist ideas', what is the reason for the exclusion of Le Fanu's novel with contemporary Spanish referent from the Irish literary canon? Is it actually a 'literary work regarded as too minor to deserve sustained interest and hence marginalized or excluded entirely from the canon'.[13]

Le Fanu's novel follows the life of an orphan boy adopted by the noble Spanish family of Almarez in the Andalusian 'Sierra de Ronda', an enclave renowned for its picturesque 'guerrillas' and banditti. She highlights the dichotomy between the patriot peasants and the landowning 'Big House' of Almarez, whose situation resembles the predicament of the Anglo-Irish ascendancy in Ireland. From the start of the romance, Le Fanu opposes the model being proposed by Irish cultural nationalism which closely linked national claims to racial and physical traits, when she recalls how a gipsy woman, a 'serrana', delivered the hero-figure of the romance, Don Juan de Las Sierras, to Donna Rosaura de Almarez. In her revealing approach towards the inhabitants of the enclave of the 'Serrania de Ronda', Le Fanu attributes to this hardy people features which did not divert from any prejudiced profile of the Irish peasant of the time. Le Fanu thus objects to this exchange of national for racial characteristics when she mentions traits of race and complexion. Accordingly, the gipsy woman,[14] a peasant, wild and sunburnt (Irish) – even a tinge of 'nigrescence' can be

11 Alicia Le Fanu, *Don Juan de las Sierras, or, el Empecinado* (1823), pp i–ii. Further references to this novel appear in parentheses. 12 Katie Trumpener, *Bardic nationalism. The romantic novel and the British empire* (Princeton, 1997), pp 13–14. Trumpener compares Sydney Owenson's *O'Donnel: a national tale* (1814) with Le Fanu's *Tales of a tourist* (1823) in their use of characters with names which recall past historical revivalists (for example, Sylvester O'Halloran, Charlotte Brooke and Carolan). 13 Stephen Greenblatt and Catherine Gallagher (eds), *Practicing the new historicism* (Chicago, 2000), p. 9. 14 Even if the figure of the gipsy presents different connotations in Ireland at the time of Le Fanu's composition, we could be tempted to compare the Spanish gipsies with representations of 'the tinker' in Ireland. Jane Helleiner has published a detailed study on the subject and laments the lack of

seen here – contrasts with the figure of the boy: fair-skinned, exquisite and beautiful, the future hero (Anglo-Irish):

> this was a female, of patagonian size, and ferocious countenance, habited in a peasant's dress, of coarse, but shewy materials. Her harsh features, black, and sunburnt complexion, and wild, yet picturesque habiliments, of red and light blue cloth, announced her at once for one of that lawless and hardy race which inhabited the mountains near the Castle of Almarez, know by the name of the Serrania de Ronda. She held, or rather grasped, the hand of a boy, three years old, of such exquisite infantine beauty, that, realizing the description of the poet, he might be said, indeed, to look, 'by his dusky guide, like Morning brought by Night.' (I, 16)

Le Fanu's use of the stereotyped Spanish Serrano not only 'satisfies the mid-nineteenth-century demand for details of the lives or foreign of alien races',[15] but also sets a clear example of the implementation of the figure of the 'Other' in Anglo-Irish discourse. Thomas Crofton Croker's contemporary work *Researches in the south of Ireland* (1824), although written in a 'light unusually clear for his period, and . . . diligently, lovingly and, almost invariably, truthfully of them [his fellow countrymen]',[16] also establishes this Irish racial distinction, adding tinges of a likely former Spanish colonization, when he compares the manners and customs of the country peoples, the mountaineers, of Cork and Kerry. Both Le Fanu's and Croker's works had London publishers and were first destined to an English reading reception, which enabled the deployment of the figure of the Irish 'Other' before the English and – most importantly – Anglo-Irish readership:

> Both the fanciful eye of the antiquary and the more sober one of the agricultural tourist have observed the Spanish contour of feature in the peasantry of Kerry, and, indeed, it is impossible not to be struck with the resemblance; but the discussion of the colonization of remote ages does not fall within the object of this chapter, which is rather an attempt to detail such customs amongst the Irish peasantry as will appear most striking to the English reader, and to illustrate them with any occasional anecdotes they may suggest. The difference of costume and personal appearance in the lower orders of different

attention paid to Irish travellers in the nineteenth-century: Jane Helleiner, *Irish travellers: racism and the politics of culture* (Toronto, 2000), pp 32–3. El Empecinado's actual story differs in the fact that most guerrilleros were neither travellers nor gypsies, which reinforces the idea that Le Fanu's use of the gypsy community aims at offering a clear distinction in terms of race between the Gaelic Irish and the Anglo-Irish.   **15** William Carleton, *Traits & stories of the Irish peasantry*, 2 vols (Gerrards Cross, 1990), vol. 1, p. 10.   **16** Kevin Danaher in the introduction to Thomas Crofton Croker, *Researches in the south of Ireland: illustrative of the scenery, architectural remains and the manners and superstitions of the peasantry with an appendix containing a private narrative of the rebellion of 1798* (Dublin, [1824] 1981), p. viii.

districts can scarcely fail of being remarked, and the inhabitants of one barony are easily distinguished, by their peculiar dress, from those of another. On the border of the counties of Cork and Limerick, the women are generally short and plump figures; the men well-proportioned, tall and rather handsome. In some of the southern parts of Cork and Kerry the very reverse is the case; and, in the latter county, the race of small and hardy mountaineers, with light hair, grey eyes and florid complexion, added to a circular form of counte-nance, are strangely contrasted with the tall, spare persons of the Spanish race, if I may so term them, with sallow visage, dark, sunken eye, and jet-black hair, falling loosely over their shoulders; wearing the great-coat in the fashion of a mantle, fastened by one button under the chin, and its sleeves hanging down unoccupied by the arms.[17]

This biased argument, which boosts the superiority of the Anglo-Irish as a way of explaining their appropriateness within the Irish discourse, is reinforced when Donna Rosaura's maid, Dame Margarita, travels to the Serrania in order to seek information about the orphan boy, Don Juan. The terrified maid beholds a scene in which Le Fanu's seemingly Carletonian portrayal of the distinct traditions of the Serranos cements a clearly debasing approach to these contemporary Spanish moun-taineers, and in turn the Irish:

> I thought all the inhabitants of the Serrania a parcel of poor, low, miserable wretches, that lived on the flesh of their goats and kids. No such things, I promise you! Such drinking and feasting! The women all dressed as fine as Indian queens, . . . Observing these ladies made a ring, and surrounded two women who stood in the centre of it, I prepared myself to see some dance of their country, executed after their barbarous fashion; for you may suppose I did not expect to see in the Serrania a fandango or a saraband, much less a bolero. . . I arranged my veil to walk and see the holiday sports. But such sports! Would you believe it, the masculine wretches were challenging each other at wrestling! (I, 48)

Le Fanu's approach to this 'peculiar people', this 'other', expresses a deep fear of the gypsies not 'remaining "nature" but entering "history"' through an extended belief that the gypsies, and in turn the Irish where the 'only remaining site of cultural autonomy'.[18] She thus radically opposes the model proposed by Irish cultural nation-

---

17 Croker, *Researches in the south of Ireland*, p. 221. **18** Although she makes no mention of Le Fanu's work, Katie Trumpener traces the representation of the gypsies in literature in a seminal article, in which she explains how the development of the gypsy-figure varied from the exoticized, the villain, the beggar, the primitive, and the superstitious to a final cultural and racial essentialism at the end of nineteenth-century English literature: Katie Trumpener, 'The time of the gypsies: a "people without history" in the narratives of the west', in Kwame Anthony Appiah and Henry Louis Gates (eds), *Identities* (Chicago, 1995), pp 338–79.

alism in her exemplification of what is to be feared if the gypsies (in her schema, the Irish) come to rule and impose their culture on the Anglo-Irish.

In her novel, Le Fanu also envisages in the contemporary Spanish 'guerrillas' movement – to some extent similar to the rural uprisings of secret societies in Ireland – an idea of the Irish peasantry directly connected to their traditional community and the soil, which according to Seamus Deane 'belongs to a nationalist and communal conception of Ireland as a cultural reality',[19] which Le Fanu clearly tends to attack. For the historian Edward Blaquiere (a contemporary of Le Fanu's) the Spanish guerrillas movement in the Serrania de Ronda represented the only possible outcome for these Spanish peasants, who 'goaded to madness by their tyrants civil, religious, and political, as well as encouraged by the weakness of the government, fled to the mountains of Spain and formed themselves into "guerrilleros", or banditti, spreading terror in every direction'.[20] Edward Blaquiere's historical analysis of the Spanish contemporary situation, with which Le Fanu may have been acquainted, and which went through various editions at the time, seems to beg comparison with the situation in Ireland.[21] The figure of what have been termed secret societies[22] in Ireland – Whiteboys, Rightboys, Ribbonmen, Oakboys, and Rockites – termed the 'banditti' of the time by R.F. Foster,[23] had become a regular revolutionary socio-political characteristic in peasant Ireland from the 1760s onwards. However, the climax of all these popular movements was reached in the first half of the nineteenth century mainly because just after the Napoleonic wars, European and Irish agriculture experienced congested holdings and depressed prices.[24] Besides, these secret societies sought to redress the limited grievances which their communities felt had

19 Seamus Deane, *Strange country: modernity and nationhood in Irish writing since 1790* (Oxford, 1997), p. 10. **20** Edward Blaquiere, *An historical review of the Spanish revolution, including some account of religion, manners, and literature, in Spain; illustrated with a map* (London, 1822), p. 165. **21** Fanu's approach to these Spanish, and in turn Irish, mountaineers differs from Croker's portrait of the Irish mountaineers. For Croker, in a clear attack against absenteeism, if the Irish mountaineers are turbulent and disaffected the cause can be found not in their 'personal dislike to the British monarch, or political objections to the British constitution that have induced the Irish cottagers to appear in arms against both; but the want of superiors to encourage their labours, and to whom they might with confidence look up for support and protection': T Crofton Croker, *Researches in the south of Ireland*, p. 14. **22** For T. Desmond Williams the term secret societies denotes 'organised groups which have pursued political, ideological or economic objectives by secret means and very often through violent action. Secret societies are not private societies, though they may have kept their affairs very private indeed': T. Desmond Williams (ed.), *Secret societies in Ireland* (Dublin, 1973), p. 1. **23** R.F. Foster, *Modern Ireland 1600–1972* (London, 1989), p. 292. **24** The case of the chronology of Ribbon revolts reflects this fact. 'Grain prices fell 30 per cent after the bumper harvest of 1813, having been exceptionally high during the previous four years. The winter of 1813 proved unusually severe, and grain prices fell a further 15 per cent in 1814–15. Farmers were unable to pay a rent . . . the immediate cause of unrest of 1821–23 was the attempt . . . to evict tenants who had fallen into arrears or were unprepared to agree to the terms of new leases': Joseph Lee, 'The Ribbonmen', in Williams (ed.), *Secret societies in Ireland*, pp 26–35.

been inflicted by the Anglo-Irish ascendancy in particular. Le Fanu was well acquainted with the literature about these societies which circulated widely in Ireland. On 30 March, 1822 the Chief Justice Bushe, in his address to the grand jury of Kilkenny, observed how the 'newspapers present but a FAINT AND FEEBLE PICTURE . . . of the atrocities' committed by the peasantry:

> The peasantry had actually taken possession of the county – the gentry were obliged to seek protection against the most atrocious violence, by converting their own houses into garrisons – society, no longer secure from the encroachment of outrage, was completely disorganized – the daily repetition of crimes the most revolting; plunder, burnings, murder, the frequent infliction of torture, gave a character of peculiar horror to the crimes of the infatuated peasantry.[25]

For Catherine Maignant, however, the figure of the secret societies in Ireland, which were seen as no more than a 'healthy exercise and, as such, viewed in rather a favourable light'.[26]

In Le Fanu's romance the 'Big House' of Almarez vividly represents the cleavage between the Spanish nobility and the mountaineers of Ronda, as they do not partake of the prevalent social contract in Spain. This distinction is augmented by their Catholic fervour, which is not in consonance with the House of Almarez – a situation which, curiously enough, would have been Catholic in the Spanish context as well. Most certainly Le Fanu's intention resided in the exposition of the prevalent religious conflict; thus, the Irish peasants like the Spanish serranos are blinded by their religion and find no point of identification with their Anglo-Irish masters. At the centre of Le Fanu's depiction of the Spanish guerrillas lies a separation of peasants and gentry 'by strong social and religious barriers';[27] thus mirroring the situation in nineteenth-century Ireland, which Le Fanu constantly contrasts in her construction of the Anglo-Irish discourse via her imagining of contemporary Spain. But, behind this facile assumption, Le Fanu's fiction denounces the widespread belief that the Irish Catholic church was not denying the right to rebel and was, most securely, according to Le Fanu, even assisting and espousing revolt.[28]

---

25 *Historical notices of the several rebellions, disturbances, and illegal associations in Ireland, from the earliest period to the year 1822; and a view of the actual state of the country, and of the events generating, or connected with, its past disturbances, and present discontented and demoralized situation; with suggestions for the restoration and maintenance of tranquility, and for promoting the national prosperity and happiness* (Dublin, 1822), p. 57. **26** Catherine Maignant, 'Rural Ireland in the nineteenth century and the advent of the modern world', in Jacqueline Genet (ed.), *Rural Ireland, real Ireland?* (Gerrards Cross, 1996), p. 21. **27** Gearóid Ó Tuathaigh, *Ireland before the famine 1798–1848* (Dublin, 1990), p. 147. **28** S.J. Connolly's seminal study, *Priests and people in pre-famine Ireland, 1780–1845* (Dublin, [1982] 2001), establishes the opposite view. Priests had the task of supervising these societies and there are reports of assaults and killings of priests at the time of Le Fanu's writing. S.J. Connolly, *Priests and people*, pp 208–44.

In the autumn of 1822, in Dublin, W.C. Plunket, acting as attorney general, led the prosecution of a group of Ribbonmen. Although Plunket favoured Catholic Emancipation for some members of the Catholic establishment, he had 'pushed the evidence too far'.[29] Thomas McGrath produced a letter from Daniel Murray (coadjutor archbishop of Dublin), to James Warren Doyle, bishop of Kildare and Leighlin, in which Murray denounced Plunket's statement that 'there exist[ed] among Catholics (of the lowest description to be sure) a conspiracy for murdering all the Protestants of the Kingdom'.[30] Donald A. Kerr has recently traced this connection between secret societies and the Catholic church in Ireland during the nineteenth century and provides familiar contemporary examples, which must have been known to Le Fanu. Doyle consistently denounced the violence of secret societies, especially Ribbonmen, but also wrote and published many vindications of the religious and social rights of Catholics, to the extent he asserted that if a rebellion were to take place, this would not be opposed by any member of the Catholic priesthood in Ireland.[31] For Le Fanu, this intricate link between the Catholic creed and the secret societies in contemporary Spain mirrored a widespread fear by the Anglo-Irish at the time. This communion between faith and guerrilla factions constituted a major attack on the social order she was trying to defend. In the novel the power of the priest over his community of 'guerrilleros' is complete:

> Lawless as they were, and insensible to the force of moral ties, this wild people were not deaf to the voice of religion – religion! *that* power which speaks to the rudest mind, and can only be rejected by an artificially corrupted – not by a naturally feeling people! It formed the only bond of society they acknowledged; and feuds and quarrels, otherwise implacable, and never to be quenched but in the blood of the offender, were suspended at once by the appearance of the holy sacrament among them, and the voice of the priest accomplished what chiefs and alcaydes would have striven to effect in vain. (I, 29)

The young Don Juan's education is undertaken by both the duke and the countess of Almarez, though they have different points of view with regard to nationality, heritage and tradition. The recourse to native heroes as bearers of nationhood

---

29 Thomas McGrath, *Politics, interdenominational relations and education in the public ministry of Bishop James Doyle of Kildare and Leighlin, 1786–1834* (Dublin, 1999), p. 15. **30** Murray to Doyle, 12 December 1822, Kildare and Leighlin Diocesan Archives, quoted in S.J. Connolly, *Priests and People*, pp 15–16. **31** J.W. Doyle's most significant letters, which are contemporary with Le Fanu's work, include *A vindication of the religious and civil principles of the Irish Catholics* (Dublin, 1823) and *Letter to Robertson esq. M.P. on a union of the Catholics and Protestant churches* (Dublin, 1824). Cited in Donal A. Kerr, 'Priests, pikes and patriots: the Irish catholic church and political violence from the Whiteboys to the Fenians', in Stewart J Brown and David W. Miller (eds), *Piety and power in Ireland 1760–1960: essays in honour of Emmet Larkin* (Belfast, 2000), pp 16–42.

and tradition is central to Le Fanu's novel: Don Juan d'Almarez (epitome of that nobility seeking prestige and refuge in a different tradition, as their key to their permanence in power in the land), reminds the orphan boy of French heroes, as being the bearers of legend and tradition. Conversely, his sister, Donna Rosaura presently reveals her preference for 'native' Spanish heroes:

> 'The names of Gaston de Foix, the Chevalier Bayard, Du Gueschin, Lahire, Dunois, awaken my heart (as the readers of Froissart say) like the sound of a trumpet.' 'And must you look so far for heroes?' interrupted Donna Rosaura in her silver voice – 'have *we* not our great captains too? – our Pelayo – our Cid – our Gonsalvo of Cordova?' (I, 69)

The recalling of past heroes as repositories of nationality constitutes a key element of romantic nationalism. Le Fanu's turn to Spanish traditional heroes partakes of an 'explicit homage to an earlier literary nationalism ... because the literature of nationalism is concerned, again and again, with the renewal of past glories and traditions'.[32] But Le Fanu's romance recognizes the ambivalent reality which sprang from the Union of 1801 and the role the ascendancy played afterwards: those who overtly favoured England, and those who defended an Irish cultural nationalism; Le Fanu clearly prefered the former. On one occasion in the novel Don Juan wanders in the 'Serrania' to find a place of refuge and solace when suddenly some pieces of paper fall at his feet:

> They consisted of English verses; but, since her alliance with Spain, Don Juan had made the language of that country his study; and the conformity of the sentiments to his own perhaps aided his comprehension of the following effusion: . . . (I, 84)

This unforeseen discovery consists of a poem, written by a Spanish patriot, praising English help in the Peninsular War. The poem recalls the ominous presence of Joseph Napoleon, the French emperor's brother, as King of Spain and prefers the sense of continuity and tradition, the Burkean organicism, envisaged by Le Fanu and defended by the Anglo-Irish. England comes to Spain's rescue as a defender of the old order against the widely feared Napoleonic revolutionary tyranny:

The Spanish Patriots

> While round Iberia lowers the storms of fate,
>   While threating myriads swarm upon her coast,
> Say shall she bend beneath oppression's weight,
>   And sooth a bloody tyrant's haughty boast?
> Shall the mock king the pomp imperial grace,
>   Shall crouching nobles his accession greet,

---

32 Trumpener, *Bardic nationalism*, p. 13.

Say, shall his pride a pure, an ancient race
   Trample to dust and tread beneath his feet?
Oh no! the patriots disdain
To wear a despot's galling chain.
The land of loyalty and love
Its pristine valour pants to prove –
The land that distant worlds subdu'd
Shall feel her ancient pride renew'd –
Shall teach the tyrant's heart to fear
The hour of his destruction near.
And when, to bless the conquer'd plain,
Returning Peace shall smile again,
When Nature's joyous mien shall own
The scourge of Heaven, fierce war is gone,
The fair, the pious, and the brave,
Shall bless the hand held out to save;
To generous Albion, Virtue's friend,
The proud Castilian learns to bend,
To her, who first destruction hurl'd
Against the tyrant of the world. (I, 85–6)

Le Fanu has a calculated aim in reproducing these lines. The Duke Don Juan d'Almarez favoured the French influence because it helped him remain in prominence and power in Spain – a close allusion to the Anglo-Irish Ascendancy's situation in Ireland, and their defence of the order after the union with Great Britain in 1801, which kept them in power – although weakened legislatively – in Ireland. The countess and the young Don Juan, on the other hand, preferred Spanish heroes and the defence of Spanish nationality, which had also been aided by England during the Peninsular War. In her translation of contemporary Spain into an Anglo-Irish discourse was Le Fanu implying that Ireland's ancestry and nationhood were best defended by England's cooperation? All in all, Le Fanu presents this to the reader as two sides of the same coin. She attacks revolutionary Jacobinism (and hence, the attendant imperial penetration by Napoleon in Spain) which turned Spain into a colony of the Napoleonic empire. But she also firmly advocates the defence of the union, epitomised by the help of 'generous Albion', between Spanish and British forces in Spain, a clear glimpse of the necessity of the social, political, religious and cultural union between England and Ireland, which reduced the achievements of the Grattan era. Le Fanu's idea of empire and colony applies to the first example but not to the issue of Irish and British relations, as Ireland was not technically defined as a colony after the Union. As Katie Trumpener contends, Le Fanu's conception of romantic nationalism is clearly 'subject to uneven political and formal development',[33] which may account for the lack of critical attention which Le Fanu's writings have received.

33 Ibid., p. 14.

De las Sierras returns to the 'Sierra' to help the Spanish cause with the people of the mountains. His patriotism gradually increases when he meets his former friend and forlorn hero Juan Gonsalez. The identification of land and hero signals an anxious trend to form a link with a former tradition as a means of initiating a conquest for the future:

> My country became my idol, my parent, my all; and in the character of patriot I strove to forget that I could neither call myself son or brother to any one existing. Judge then . . . the feeling with which I viewed the unprincipled invaders, who advanced to make a desert of our beautiful land. That moment I vowed to them a hatred that should never be extinguished, as long as the print of a foreign footstep should profane the soil of Spain. (I, 188)

The spirit of religious re-conquest of a 'profaned' soil permeates through Gonsalez's words in a 'commitment to a traditional notion of custom, and of solidarity: "the cause", which did not need to be defined'.[34] From that moment on Juan Gonsalez and Juan de las Sierras act together as leaders in the Serrania de Ronda. The union epitomised in the cooperation of Juan Gonsalez and Juan de las Sierras is legitimized through the ultimate anchor of both the Irish and Anglo-Irish, in the novel Juan Gonsalez and Juan de las Sierras respectively. Le Fanu was once more legitimizing her own idea of Irish romantic nationalism through her belief in the reality which emerged after the Union between Ireland and England. However, the characters' friendship turns into suspicion when Juan de las Sierras starts to understand the real identity of Gonsalez, an assassin of the Serrania de Ronda, and unlike the actual Empecinado of history, who will stop at nothing to save his country. In Le Fanu's effort to express her repulsion at all disturbances and risings, Juan Gonsalez's words recall Robert Emmet's famous speech from the dock of 20 September 1803:[35]

> No! – salvation to Spain, and hatred – eternal, inextinguishable hatred to her enemies, shall be my latest words in life, and when I fall, I wish no other epitaph. (II, 115)

---

34 Foster, *Modern Ireland, 1600–1972*, p. 293. **35** 'Let no man write my epitaph; for as no man who knows my motives dare now vindicate them, let not prejudice or ignorance asperse them. Let them and me rest in obscurity and peace; and my tomb remain uninscribed and my memory in oblivion until other times and other men can do justice to my character. When my country takes her place among the nations of the earth, then, and not till then, let my epitaph be written. I have done.' Emmet's dock speech was printed in *Dublin Evening Post* (20 & 22 Sept. 1803); copied by *The Times* and in the *Morning Post* (27 Sept. 1803); an unadorned version printed by William Ridgeway, a lawyer for the defence and a printer in his own right, was published shortly after, being reprinted by him with accounts of other trials of August, September, and October 1803; a similar version printed in *Walker's Hibernian Magazine* (Sept. 1803). From www.PGIL-EIRData.org.

Las Sierras believes that if Juan Gonsalez continues with his despicable behaviour his fame all over Spain as 'El Liberador' – Le Fanu's brief hint at the figure and achievements of Daniel O'Connell[36] – will be exchanged for that of '*El Empecinado*'.

Las Sierras's love life is also intertwined with his patriotic deeds. He has fallen in love with Juan Gonsalez's sister Constantina; this relationship changes when he meets Louisa, the supposedly murdered daughter of the duke of d'Almarez. On his return to the House of Almarez Don Juan de las Sierras discovers that Louisa and her father, the duke, too much a man of blood against the patriotic cause, have been taken prisoners by the serranos, who decide to make the duke of d'Almarez swear he will unite his daughter, Louisa, to the patriot General Las Sierras. In the meantime Las Sierras receives a revealing letter:

> The hour of grace is nearly past – that of a terrible reckoning is at hand. False to your love, you associate openly with your country's bitterest enemies, and, to crown the whole, espouse the daughter of her deadliest foe. Repent in time. Think you, because the heart of Constantina shrunk in vengeance, that while her sworn protector lived, her wrongs could sleep? The blow that annihilates you will fall like lightning, but it will not be less sure. *If you dare to conclude that unhallowed union, know, to a certainty, we meet again.* Trust not in friends or influence – *your* name is great, but *mine* is all-powerful in Andalusia. At a breath I can summon a thousand voices to condemn you. Nor trust to former friendship, Las Sierras – you thought you knew me, but *you knew me not all. More* might have marred the plans that required you should be *wholly mine.* Acting under a thousand forms, but still actuated by the same principle, read here and tremble, while you learn that HE whom you knew under the name of Juan Gonsalez, is the avenger whose fiat never went forth in vain, *Juan el Empecinado* (III, 127)

El Empecinado explains – in religious terms – the impossibility of a union with the foes of his country. For Le Fanu, when this statement slides over into an the Anglo-Irish discourse, it emerges as the voice of the native Irish who saw in the 1801 Union of Ireland with Great Britain the end of their aspirations for freedom. A marital union between Las Sierras, already a Serrano, and the daughter of Don Juan Almarez, a representative of Spanish cooperation with France, would have encapsulated Le Fanu's desire to unite both 'irreconcilable enmities' in Ireland and her opposition to the theories of racial purity. In fact, Le Fanu proposes Las Sierras as the prototype of

---

36 Contemporary events in the life of O'Connell at the time include the publication of *Address to the Catholics of Ireland* (Dublin, 1821), in which he called for action for Repeal of the Union and the foundation in 1823 – the same year in which Le Fanu's *Don Juan de las sierras; or, el Empecinado* was published – of the Catholic Association. Around this date the launch of mass meetings was commenced and evinced the movement of Catholics in Ireland towards legal, religious and social emancipation, which was most probably feared by Alicia Le Fanu, as the reference shows, and in turn by the Anglo-Irish at large.

the new Irish, rather than the new Anglo-Irish after the Union. Le Fanu is against a non-inclusive Irish nationalism 'which abhors multi-ethnic states'.[37] In this light, Le Fanu was addressing a common fear among the Anglo-Irish ascendancy at the time. During the 1820s (a decade which saw the commencement of the so-called religious Second or New Reformation) there also existed a well-known prophecy which predicted that Protestantism would be wiped out in 1825. These predictions of Signor Pastorini were a great cause of disturbance, and such political prophecies were found in many broadside ballads of that period.[38] This prophecy found ample support within the Irish rural community and 'became widespread in Ireland in the 1820s, where excerpts were circulated in broadsheet form, feeding into the Rockite disturbances'.[39]

Le Fanu's novel seems to differ in this respect from much used solution of intermarriage, such as those deployed by Maria Edgeworth[40] and Lady Morgan. For Robert Tracy, novelistic versions of Anglo-Irish/Irish (or English/Irish) marriages assumse that this 'happy coalescence of apparently mutual and irreconcilable enmities makes an attractive literary and political solution'.[41] Edgeworth and Morgan encompassed in their novels the 'legal right of the Anglo-Irish with the traditional right of the Irish'. In the impossibility of Las Sierras's marriage to Louisa (an instance of intermarriage as he is already an ideal Serrano against the French) Le Fanu not only diverges from Edgeworth's and Morgan's literary solution,[42] but denounces, as

---

37 Joep Leerssen, *Remembrance and imagination: patterns in the historical and literary representation of Ireland in the nineteenth century* (Cork, 1996), p. 22. **38** For example, this 'garland' was printed in Limerick in 1821: 'Now the year 21 is drawing by degrees,/ In the year 22 the Locusts will weep,/ But in the year 23 we'll begin to reap./ Good people take courage, don't perish in fright,/ For notes will be of nothing in the year 25;/ As I am O'Healy, we'll daily drink beer.' Reprinted in Georges-Denis Zimmermann, *Songs of Irish rebellion: political street ballads and rebel songs 1780–1900* (Dublin, 1967), p. 30. **39** Charles Walmesley, titular bishop of Rama and fellow of the Royal Society (1722–1797) had written a book in 1771 under the pseudonym 'Signor Pastorini', entitled *The general history of the Christian church, from her birth to her final triumphant state in heaven, chiefly deduced from the Apocalypse of St John the Apostle* (reprinted in Dublin in 1790). This book contained a prediction that Protestantism would be wiped out in 1825. See Leerssen, *Remembrance and imagination*, p. 252. **40** For Kevin Whelan, this is evidence of Edgeworth's 'bistadialism' in Ireland; that is, the Protestant Irish were at the same level of 'civilization' as their British counterparts while the native Irish remained in an earlier feudalism. In *Ennui* (1809), *The Absentee* (1812) and *Ormond* (1817), Edgeworth reach a 'desired balance' which is 'symbolised by the national marriage which concludes all three novels'. Kevin Whelan, 'Foreword' to Sydney Owenson, Lady Morgan, *The wild Irish girl: a national tale*, ed. Claire Connolly and Stephen Copley [London: Pickering & Chatto, 2000], p. xiv. **41** Robert Tracy, *The unappeasable host: studies in Irish identities*, (Dublin, 1998), p. 30. **42** Claire Connolly warns about these 'somehow transparent or self-evident' literary devices used by Edgeworth and Lady Morgan to finalise the social and political issues in Ireland as the Union of Great Britain and Ireland had been 'rapidly succeeded by Robert Emmet's rebellion in 1803, and so by 1806 [in the case of Lady Morgan's *The wild Irish girl*] had already proved far from harmonious'. Claire Connolly, 'Introduction' to Lady Morgan, *The wild Irish girl*, Claire

she has done before with the example of the woman of the Serrania de Ronda, 'the exclusivism of nineteenth-century sectarian claims [which] has its secular form also, in the emergence of a romantic nationalism [Catholic in Le Fanu's case] which veered in some instances towards theories of racial purity'.[43] At the end of the novel, in a fictional manoeuvre, Le Fanu trammels the two main characters' lives in such a way that the reader will forgive Las Sierras, a representative of the Spanish nobility but also a truly patriotic Spaniard in favour of the 'cause', and put all the blame on El Empecinado. Las Sierras had been captured by Gonsalez's men and sentenced to death because he was a traitor, as he did not accede to El Empecinado's wishes concerning Don Juan's marriage to Constantina, El Empecinado's sister. Donna Rosaura, the Countess d'Almarez, on knowing the sentence on Las Sierras runs to save his life. Donna Rosaura appears at the camp and tells Juan Gonsalez, El Empecinado, to revoke Las Sierras's death sentence. He says he cannot do it because he is a traitor to the Spanish cause; but presently she declares that Las Sierras and El Empecinado are brothers. El Empecinado's character is eventually stained with his own kin's blood.

Le Fanu's translation of the Spanish El Empecinado's life and times into an Anglo-Irish discourse thus succinctly summarises the key political issues of her Spanish/Irish novel. First, she rejects cultural nationalism's reduction of peasant culture, or gypsy culture, through a debasing use of the 'other' figure and racial terms of 'nigrescence'. Second, as a dramatic aspect of the history of Ireland, Le Fanu addresses the issue of the secret societies, which 'featured widely in Irish fiction: . . . notable literary treatments include Thomas Moore, *Memoirs of Captain Rock* (1834); William Carleton, "Wildgoose Lodge" (1833); and Mrs S.C. Hall, *The Whiteboys* (1845)'.[44] Le Fanu, however, contextualises the problem of rural riots in Ireland in order to address the critical plight of the Anglo-Irish Ascendancy. She *re*-establishes the economic origin of these societies and places them in the context of the loss of power which the Ascendancy was experiencing. Third, she tackles the religious predicament of both communities in the new reality after the Union of 1801. Fourth, she despises a possible 'social concept of heroism'[45] through the representation of her two heroes, El Empecinado and Don Juan de las Sierras. Las Sierras follows the patriotic (and even adopts nationalist) tendencies of Irishness because he is the epitome of the new reality Le Fanu wants to represent, a new Anglo-Irish individual who defends the vision of Ireland from a unionist perspective. His brother, El Empecinado, stands for a rural Ireland attached to the soil, a 'guerrillero' who epitomizes an old nationalist Ireland, which rejects a possible union between both identities on the island. El Empecinado encapsulates the opposite side of the hero,

Connolly & Stephen Copley (eds), p. xxvi. In the case of Le Fanu's romance, the chronology of Irish history expands and offers many other examples of disruptive harmony. **43** W.J. McCormack, *From Burke to Beckett: Ascendancy, tradition and betrayal in literary history* (Cork, 1994), p. 79. **44** Robert Welch (ed.), *The Oxford companion to Irish literature* (Oxford, 1996), p. 512. **45** Sean O'Faolain, *The vanishing hero: studies in novelists of the twenties* (Freeport, 1971), p. xiii.

that of the villain. Le Fanu's conundrum is solved with a close look at the title of her romance. Her choice is neither ambivalent nor equivocal: *Don Juan de las Sierras, or, el Empecinado*. Le Fanu clearly sides with the former.

In the final analysis, Le Fanu's romance *Don Juan de las Sierras* adopts and *re*-fashions conventionalities of what has been traditionally considered romantic nationalism. She endows both heroes with a love for the soil and race that could have enabled her, to a certain extent, to enter a canon of romantic nationalism in Ireland,. However, she also portrays the tragic end of the Anglo-Irish Ascendancy, in Las Sierra's death, and, what is worse, she criminalizes his brother, El Empecinado, extending this 'Biblical' contest between the two brothers to the two sides of Ireland; that is, the Irish and the Anglo-Irish.[46] Fanu envisages the end of the Anglo-Irish Ascendancy in the death of the romantic hero, Las Sierras; but she also blames nationalist Ireland, portrayed in the serranos, the secret societies, the patriots and El Empecinado – an Irish nationalist hero – for this traumatic end of the Anglo-Irish Ascendancy. A general sense of betrayal[47] and guilt is extended to a nationalist Ireland in Le Fanu's novel through her appropriation and recourse to contemporary Spain. It is therefore not coincidental that Le Fanu and her writings, inclduing *Don Juan de las Sierras, or, el Empecinado: a romance*, are excluded from the Irish canon, since, as Trumpener suggests, her 'noncanonization is of historical and political interest'.[48]

46 For Bishop James Doyle, the Ribbonmen had a love of Catholicism and hatred of Orangeism. But he insisted that the Orangemen were 'our brethren in Christ': see James Doyle, *Pastoral*, Nov. 1822, pp 11–12, cited in Thomas McGrath, *Religious renewal and reform in the pastoral ministry of Bishop James Doyle of Kildare and Leighlin, 1786–1834* (Dublin, 1999), pp 192–3. Miss Alicia Le Fanu fiercely attacks these pastorals in her fiction as she does not believe in the promises and efforts of the Catholic Church in Ireland at the time. **47** Examples of the opposite nature can be found in W.J. McCormack, *From Burke to Beckett*. **48** Trumpener, *Bardic nationalism*, p. 131.

Index

Page numbers of illustrations are given in italics.